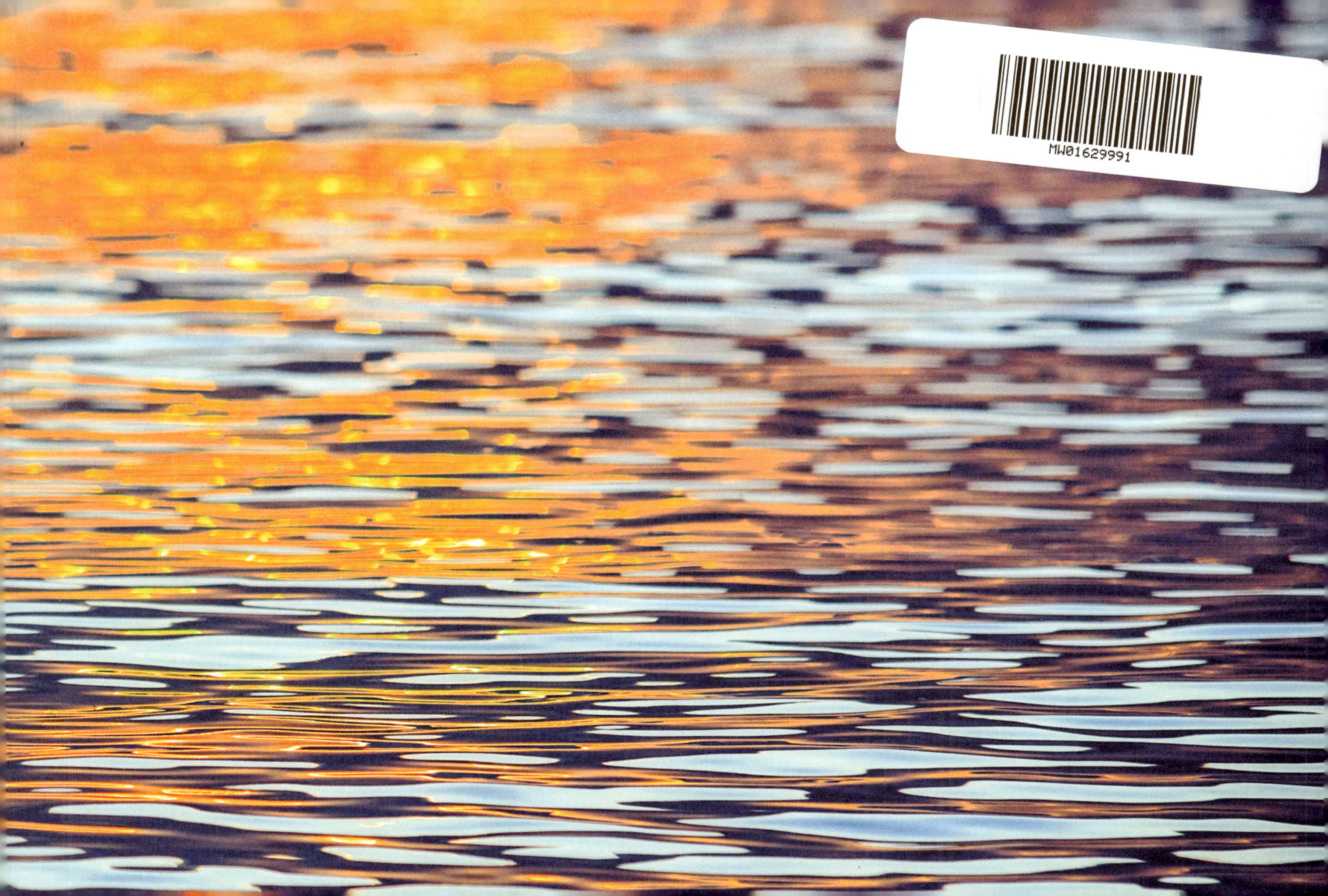

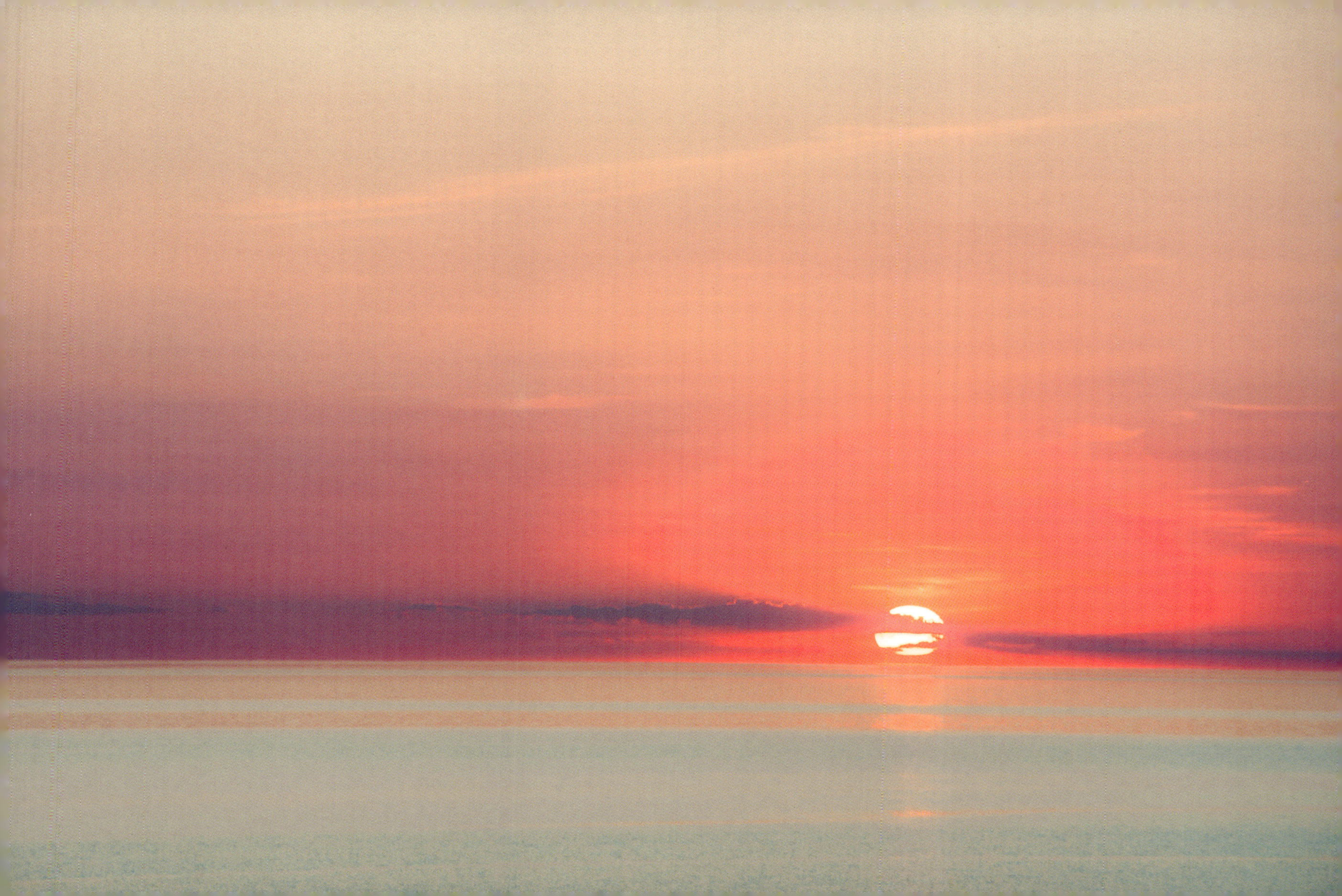

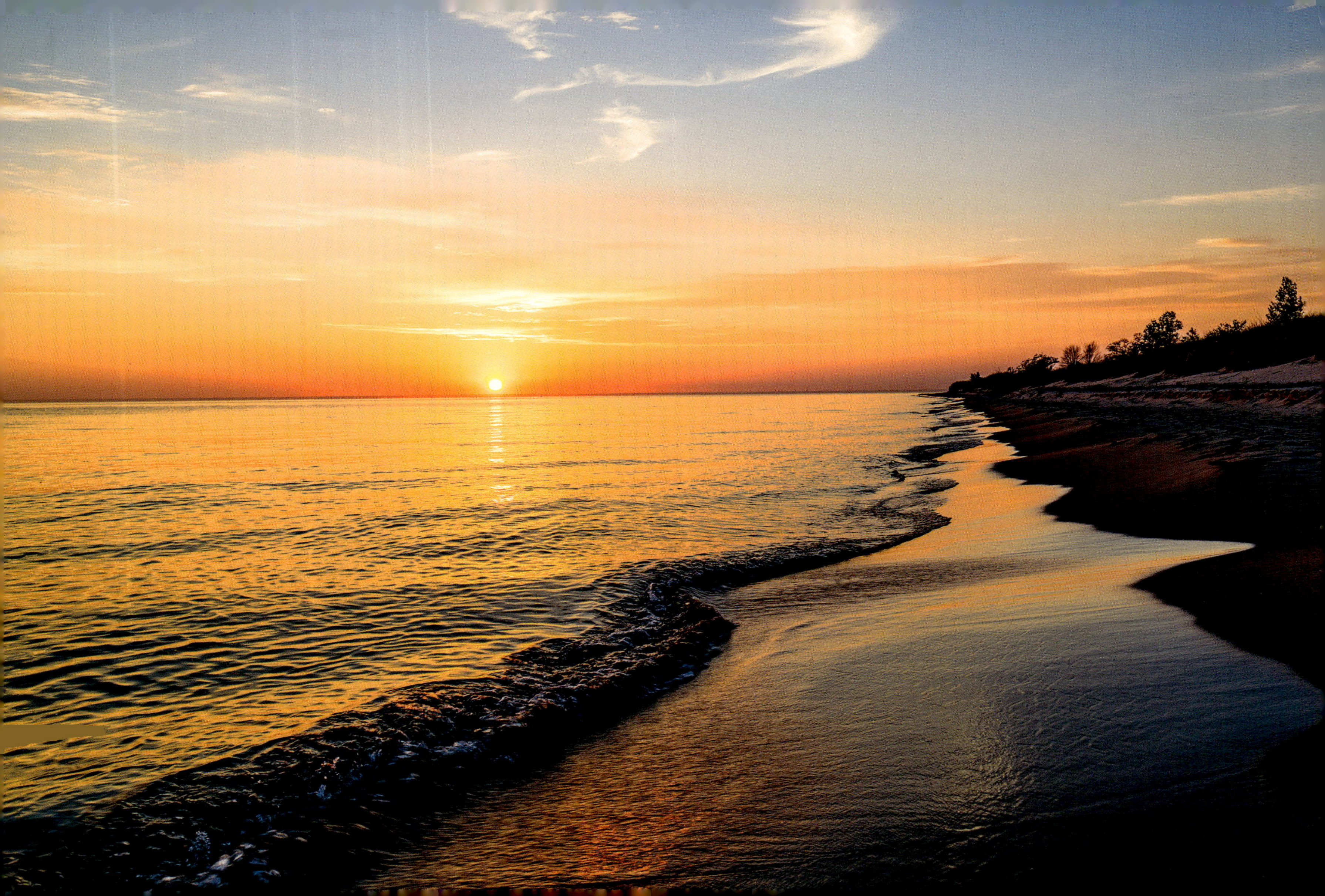

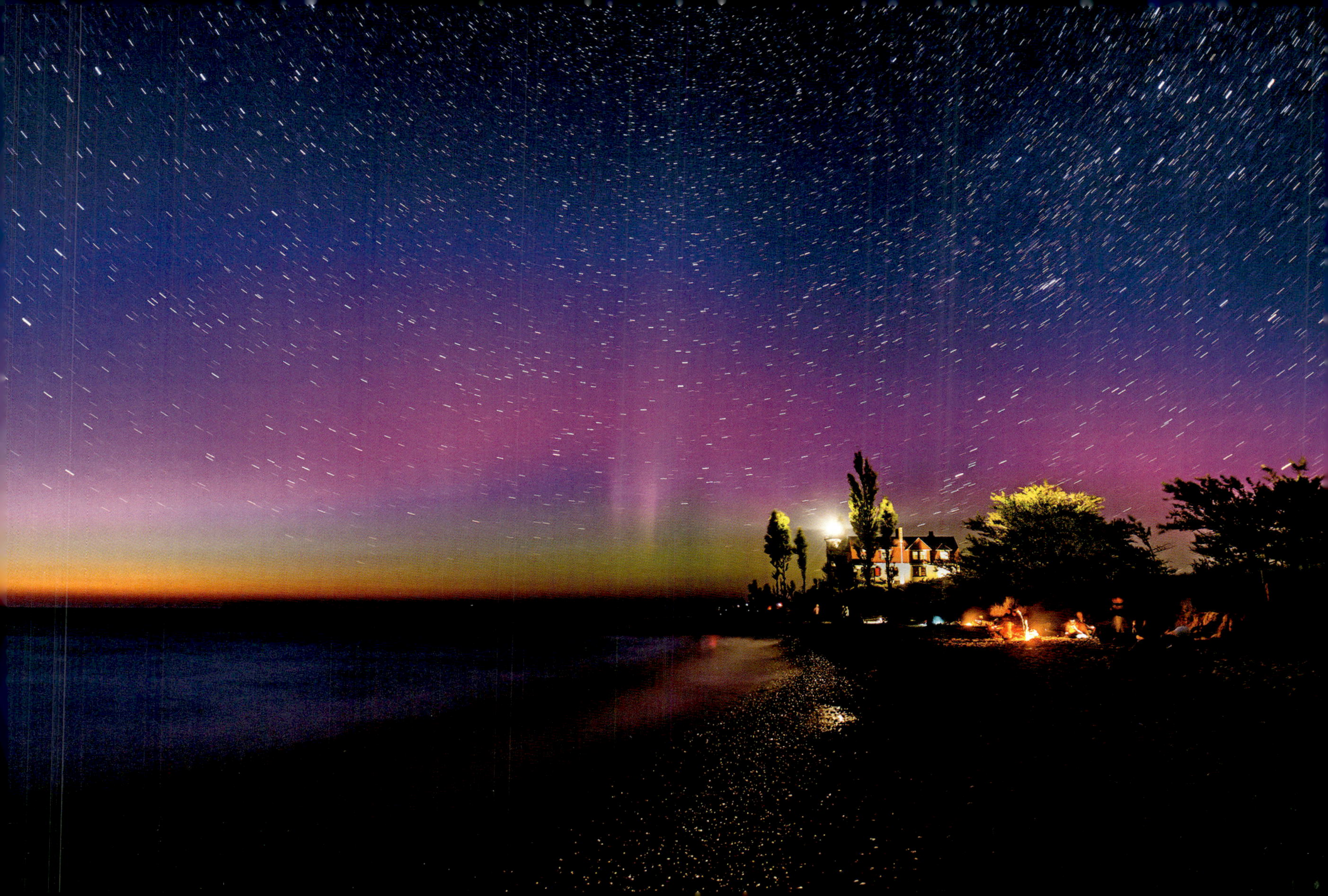

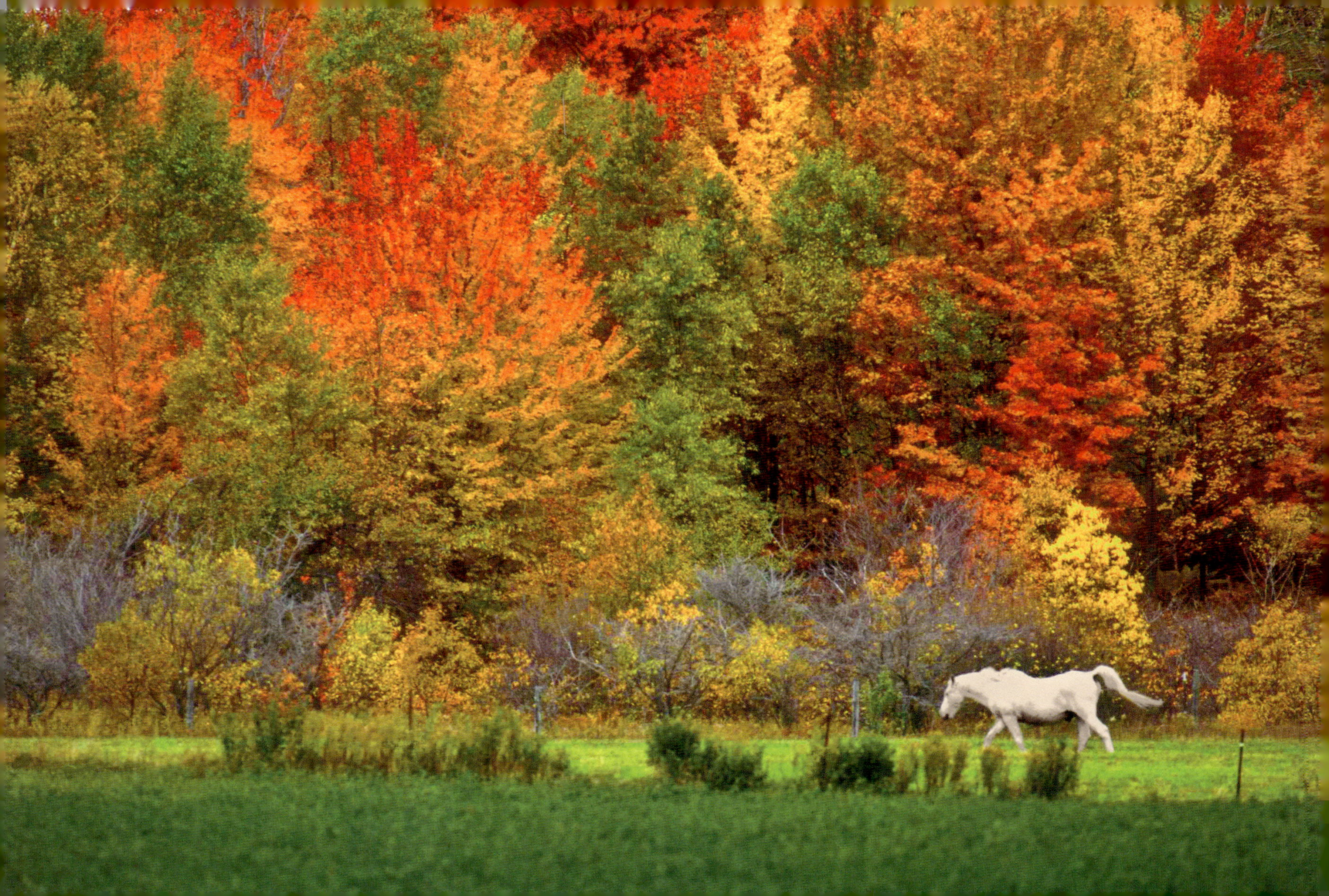

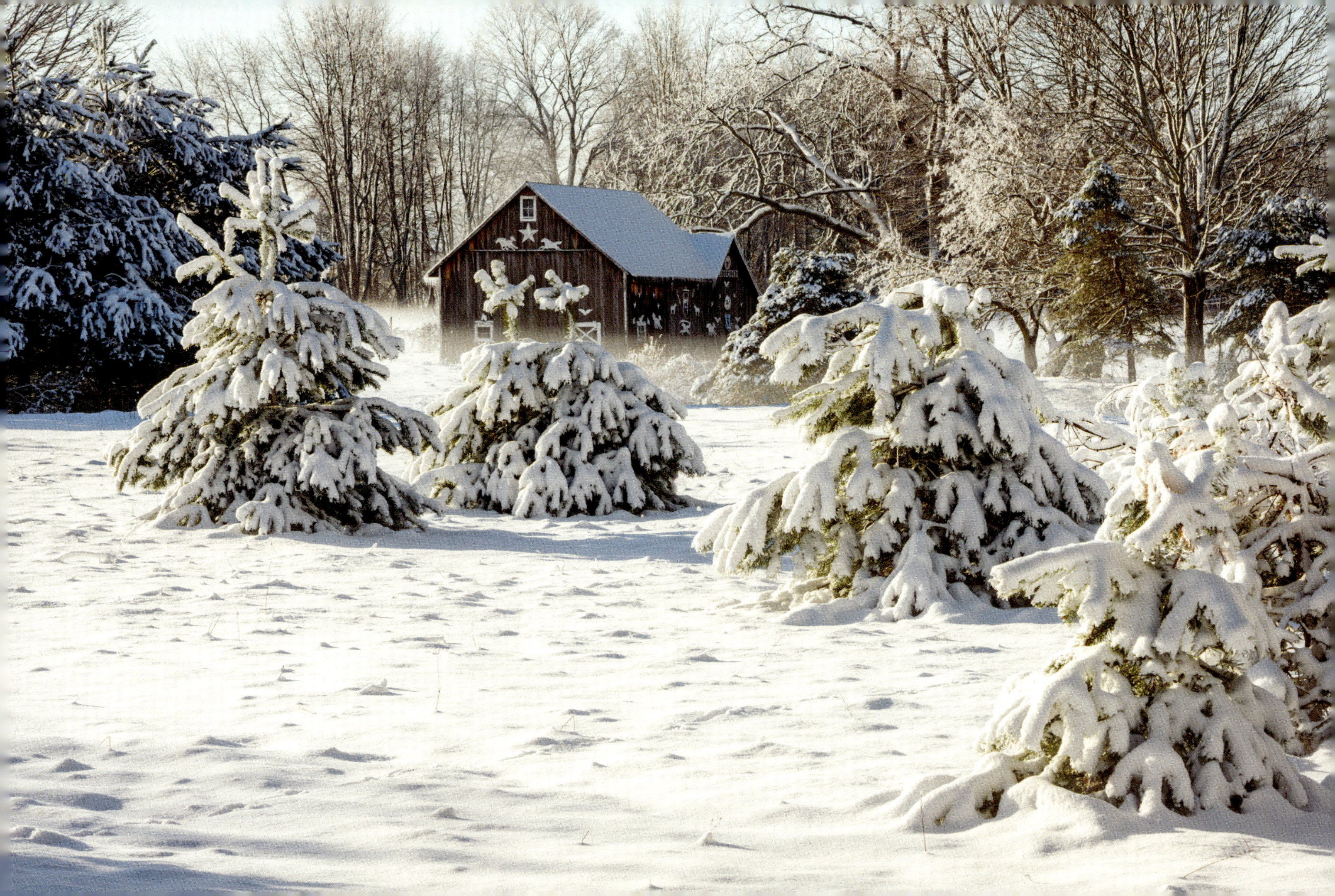

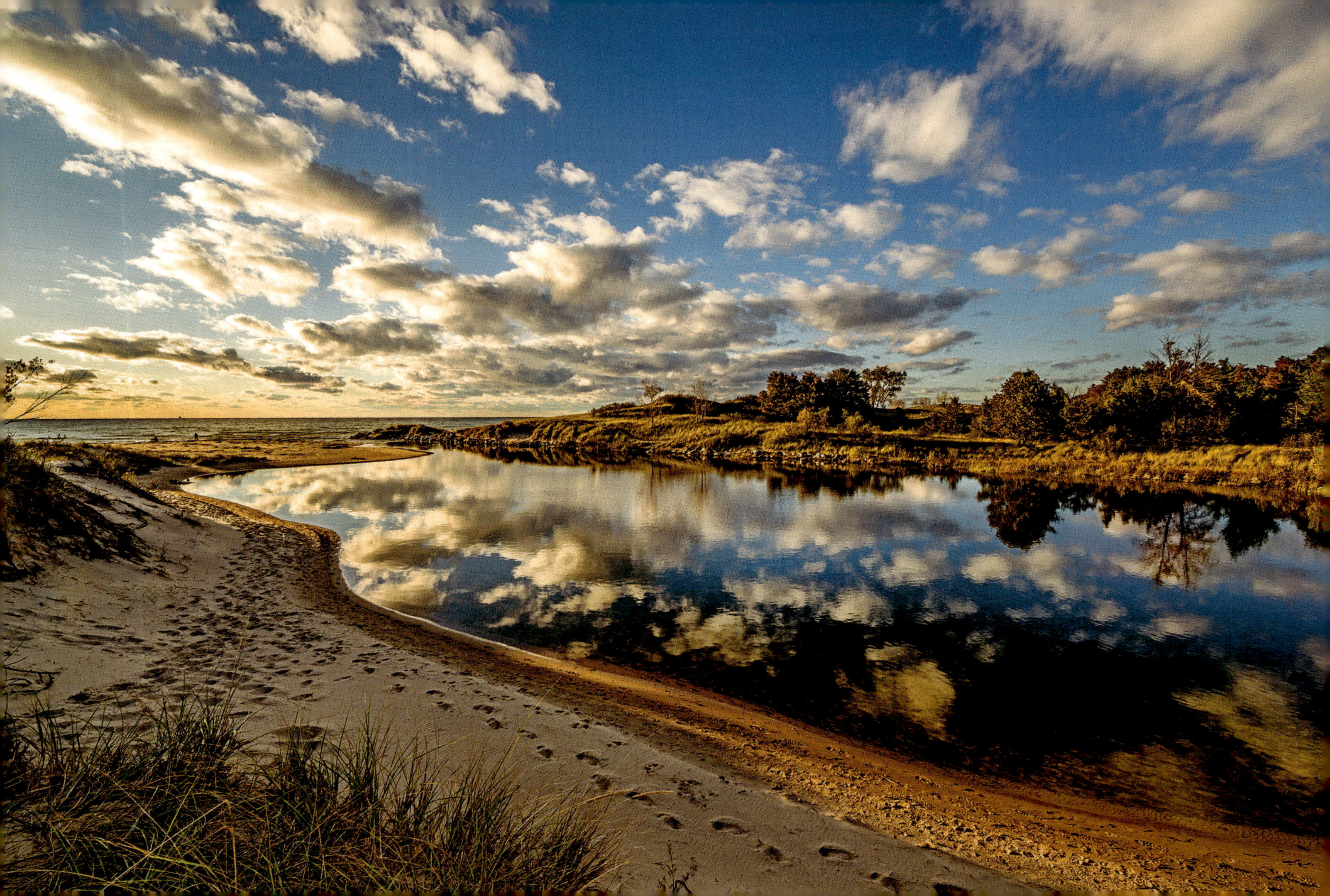

WONDEROUS WEST SHORE

by Todd and Brad Reed
and West Shore Bank

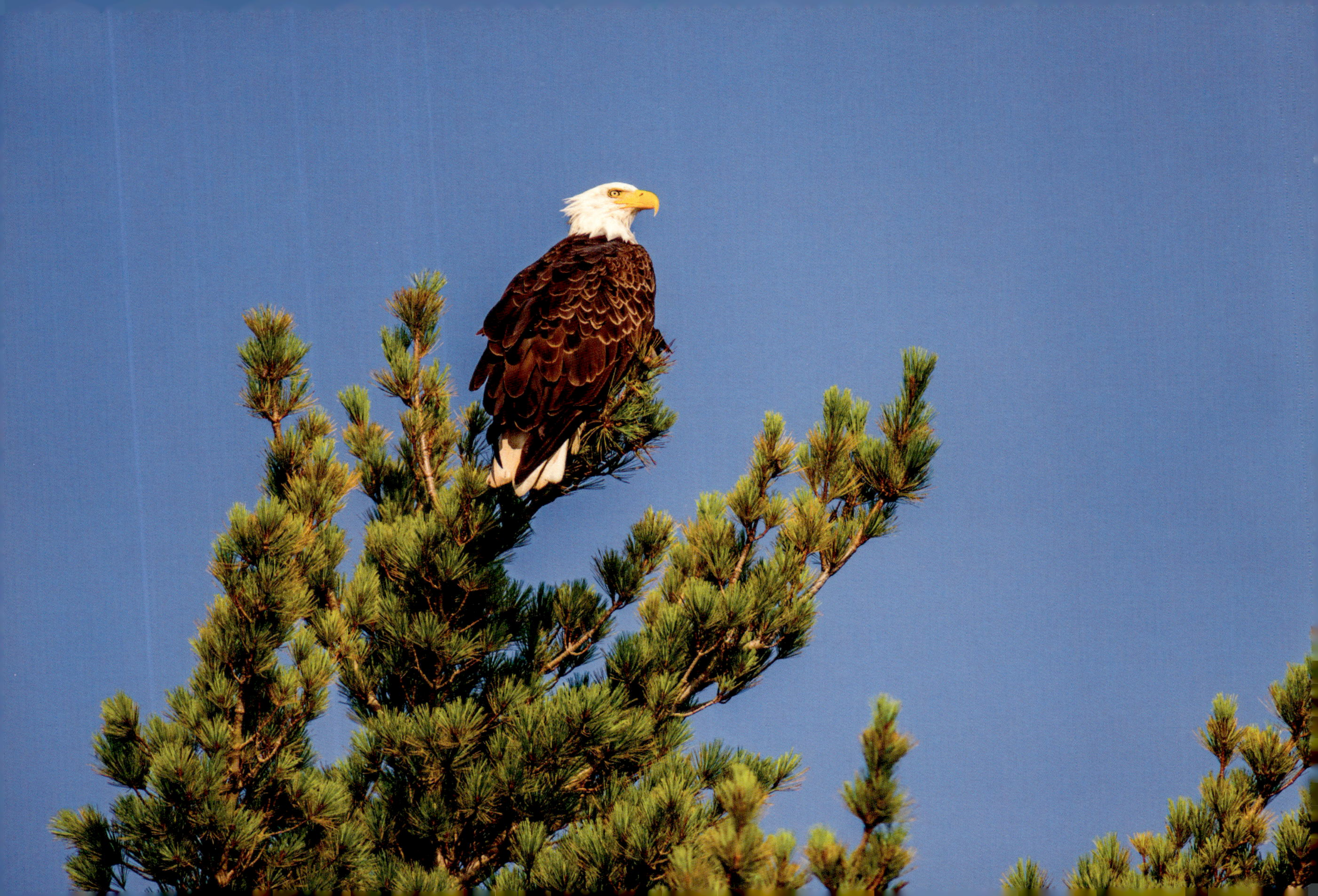

Dedicated to all those who work
to protect and preserve Michigan's beauty.

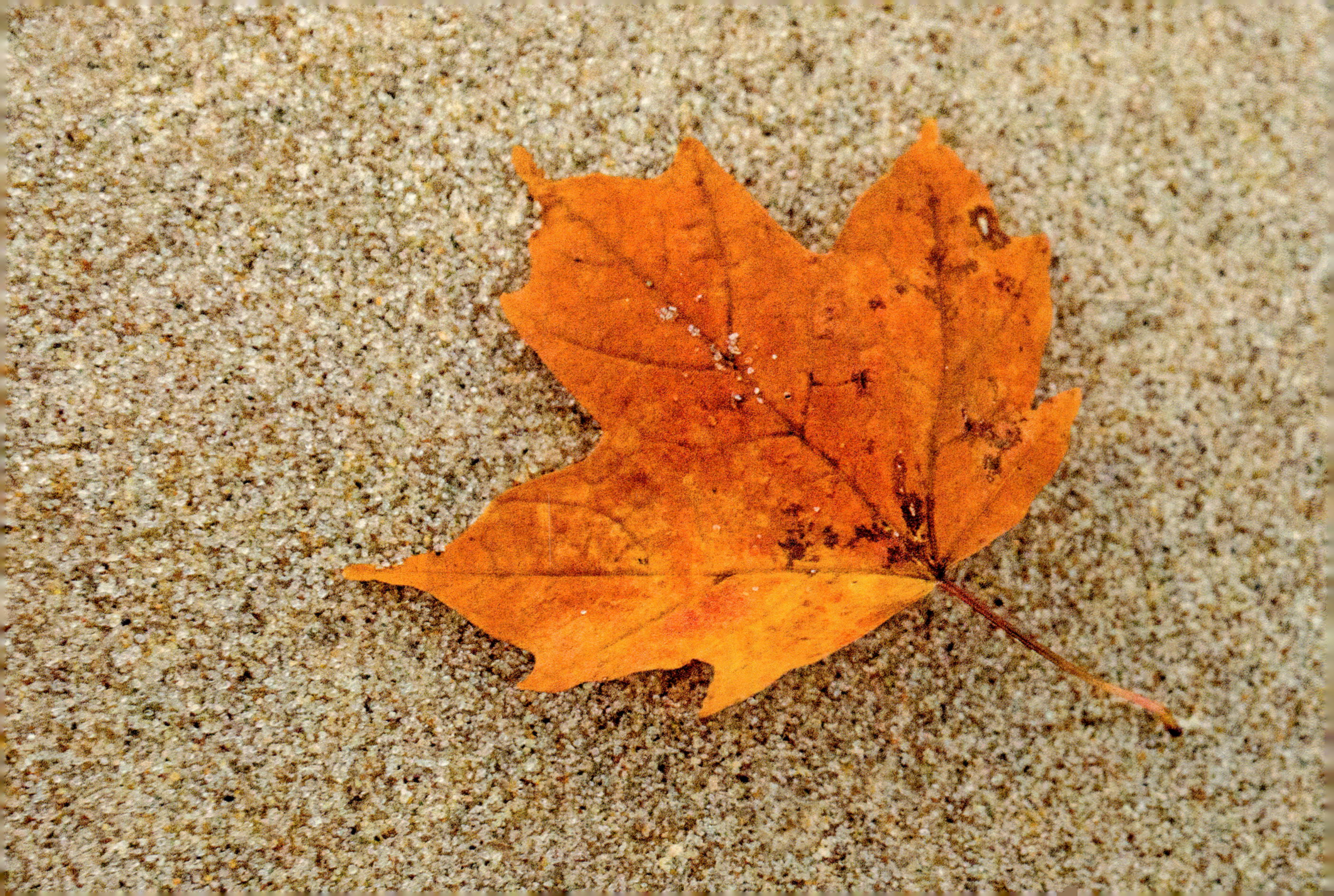

Table of Contents

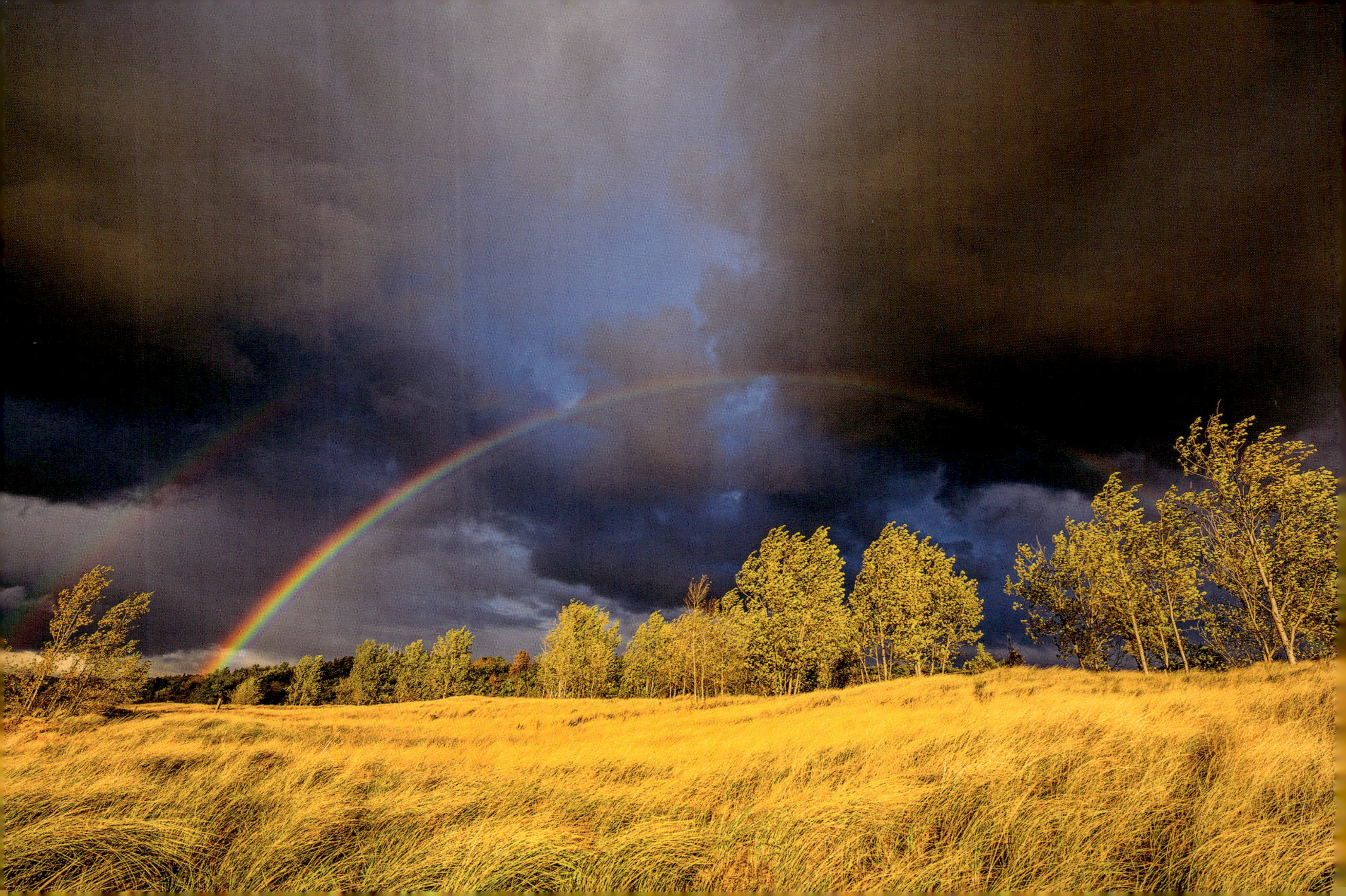

Foreword

As a community bank, West Shore Bank is focused each day on how to do what's best for the people we serve. Day after day, our employees are driven by our mission to make a difference for the people and businesses along Michigan's west shore–engaged and involved in giving back to our communities. And we love every minute of it because we love our home.

At West Shore Bank, we don't see people as being "just customers." They're family, friends, and neighbors. Hardworking people. Friendly faces. Bold thinkers and entrepreneurs. Folks rooted in tradition and pride.

Not only are the people great–the shoreline scenery captivates our attention as well. From well-known scenic landmarks to gems located off the beaten path, Todd and Brad Reed have a stunning talent for capturing the beauty and marvel of the west shore. Every image is a photographic masterpiece and a visual tribute to this place we call home. Breathtaking sunsets, the stark beauty of a fresh winter snowfall, our captivating lakeshore. Every page lets you discover just a bit more of this wonder that we are fortunate enough to experience every day. With each photograph our gratitude for the beauty of the west shore grows stronger. This is home.

It is our hope that through this collection of images, more people are able to take in the wonder of our scenic west shore. From Muskegon to Ludington to Traverse City – there is a world of beauty inside these pages just waiting to be discovered. West Shore Bank is honored to partner with Todd & Brad Reed Photography in showcasing our home. There's just no place like it!

Raymond A. Biggs

Raymond A. Biggs, President & CEO
West Shore Bank

Our Focus

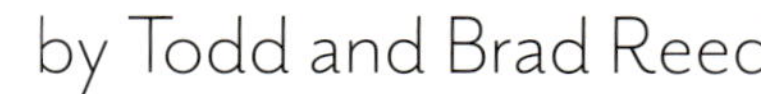
by Todd and Brad Reed

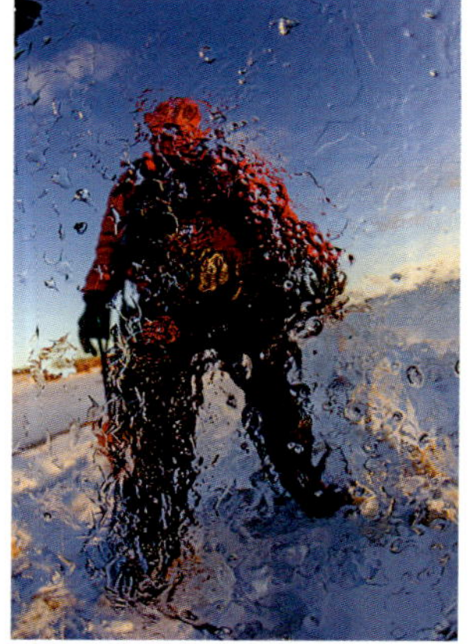

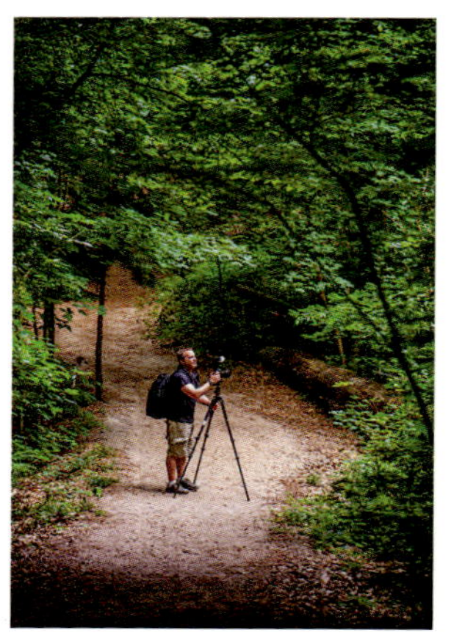

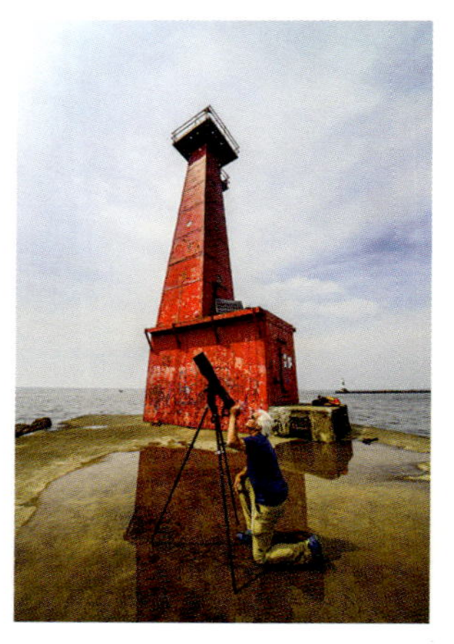

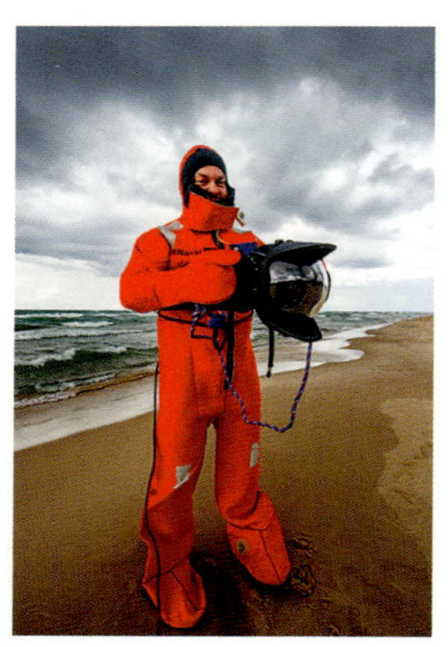

We have spent our entire adult lives looking at Michigan through a camera viewfinder. The beauty we have seen only makes us yearn to see more of the Michigan outdoors.

For our previous two books, we focused on all of Michigan. We discovered beauty wherever we turned, and the experience was as thrilling for us as the award-winning results.

Life is full of timing. After searching far and wide throughout Michigan for magic moments to photograph, we longed to come home. We needed to get more intimate again with our own backyard—the Lake Michigan shoreline and connecting waterways and lands within a couple hours' drive of our splendid lakeshore hometown, Ludington.

For more than two years we traversed the west shore of Michigan from Grand Traverse Light at the tip of the Leelanau Peninsula to Big Red Lighthouse at Holland in search of the visual wonder of the Michigan outdoors in our West Michigan backyard.

We also immersed ourselves in the abundant beauty of woodlands and countryside, inland lakes and rivers of Old Mission Peninsula, and the counties of Grand Traverse, Leelanau, Benzie, Manistee, Mason,

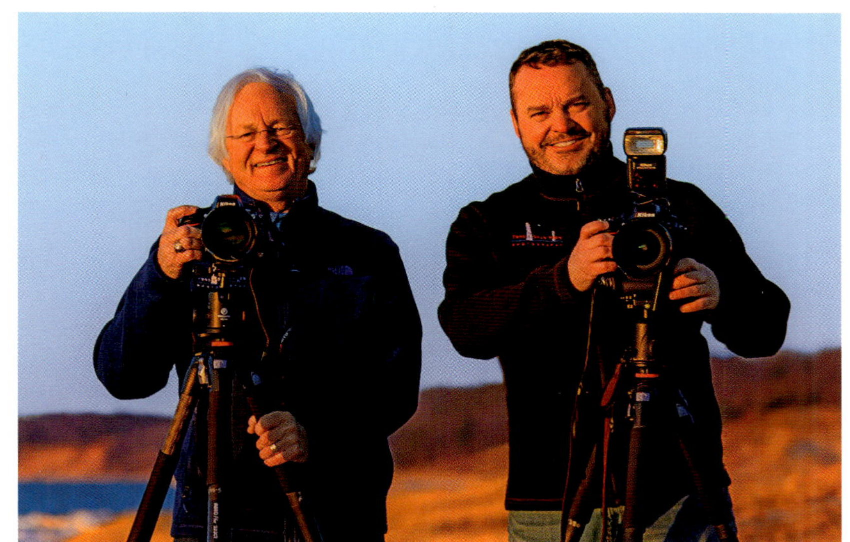

Oceana, Muskegon, Kent and Ottawa. We relentlessly pursued the magic of Michigan's four seasons.

What a ride! This book is a celebration of the beauty we found. We pared the images down to those that we found most wonderous and representative of this splendid region.

We had to leave a lot of the beauty we discovered and photographed on the editing table for space reasons. The images that appear here are intended to increase appreciation for this amazing region as a whole more so than for any particular location.

The title of this book was born from the visual wonder we experienced in countless locations while photographing this project. Having grown up in Ludington and having spent most of our lives here, we already knew we live in one of the most beautiful areas in the United States of America. Our travels during this project made that far more apparent to us.

We hope you experience the wonder of our region of the west shore as you turn these pages. We are most grateful to West Shore Bank for helping us make it possible to undertake this mission to showcase and celebrate the beauty of this area of Michigan's west shore. We share our love of home with all of you in these pages.

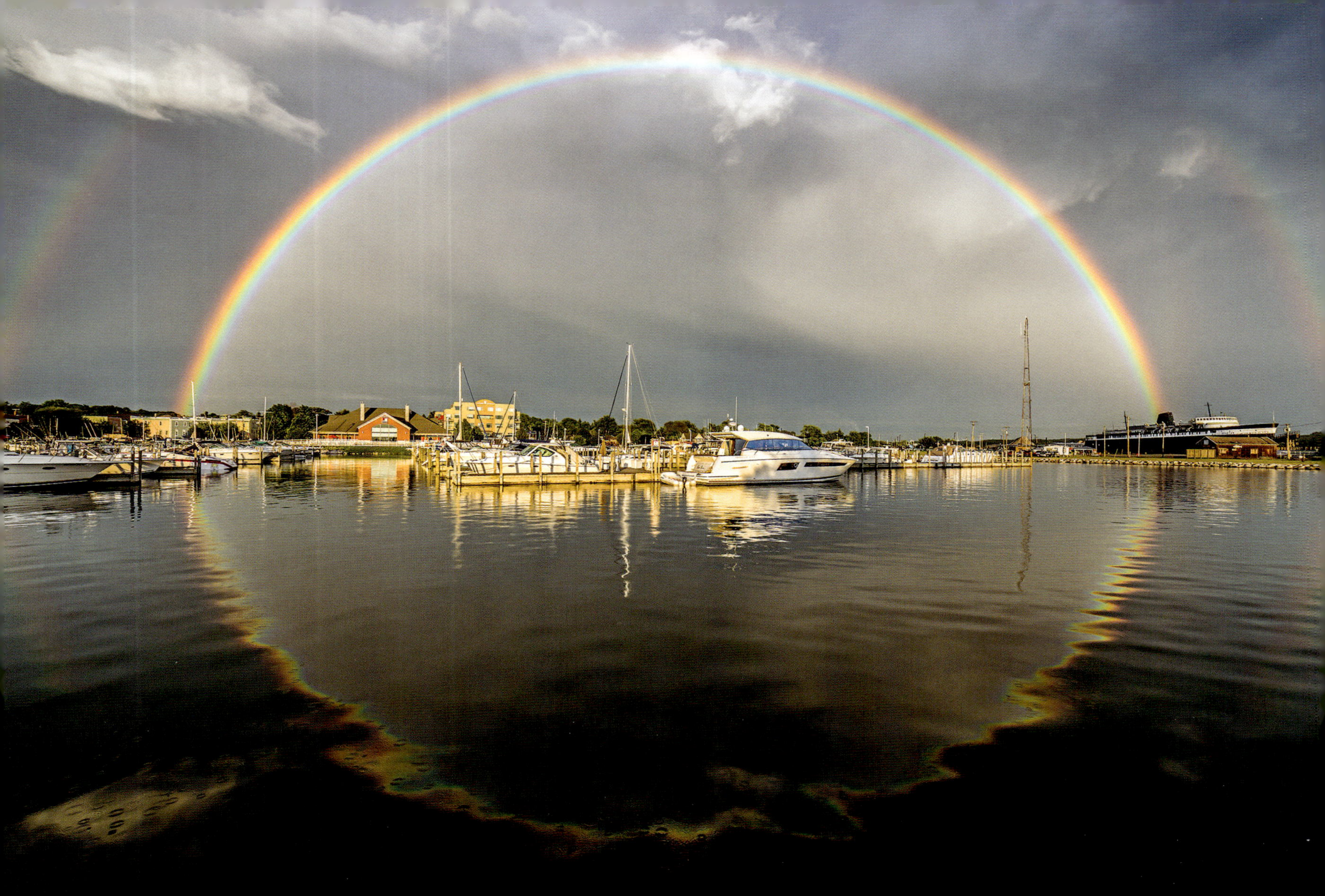

SEEING THE WEST SHORE

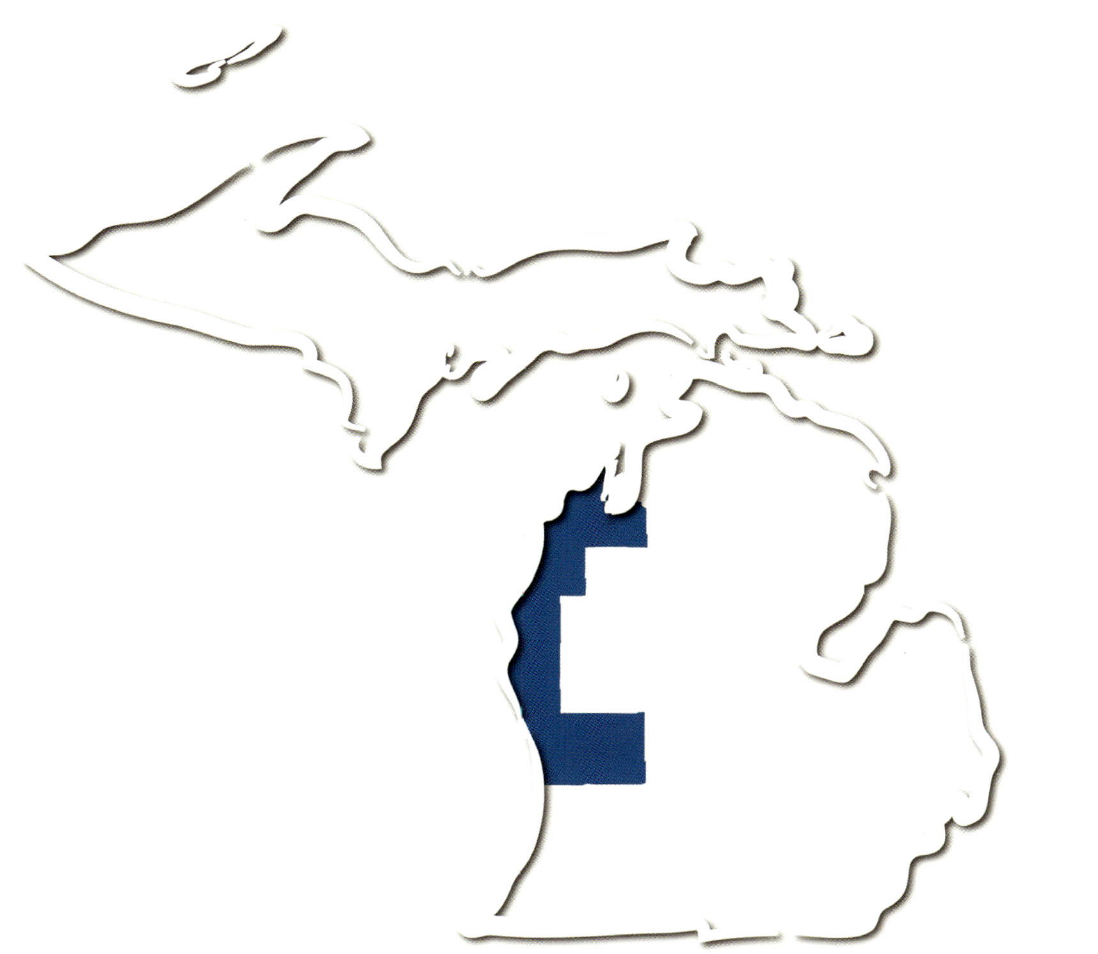

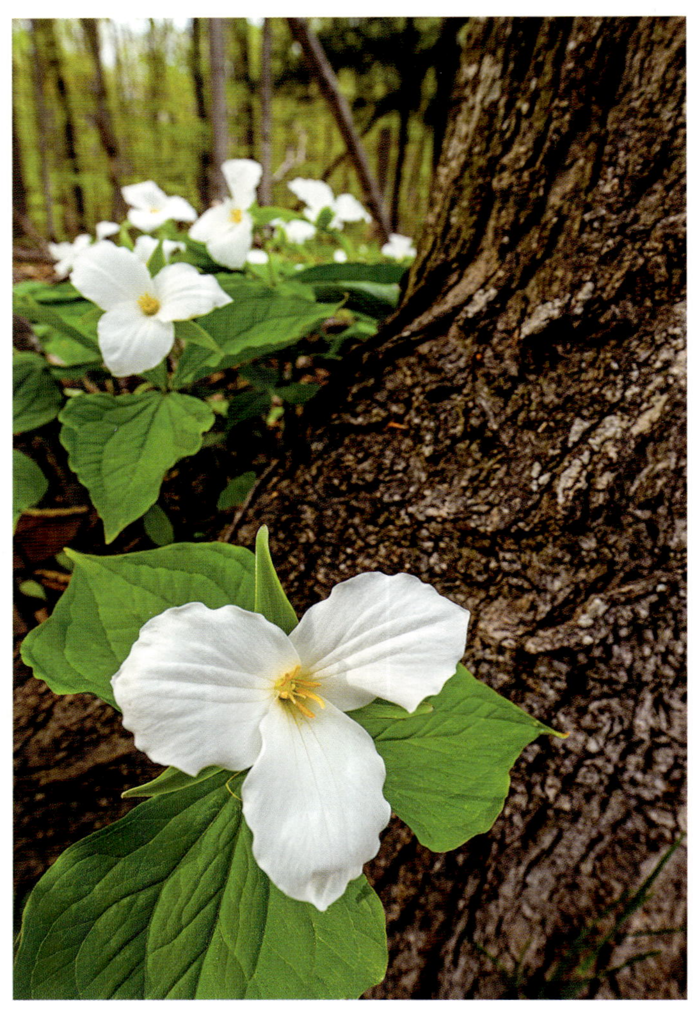

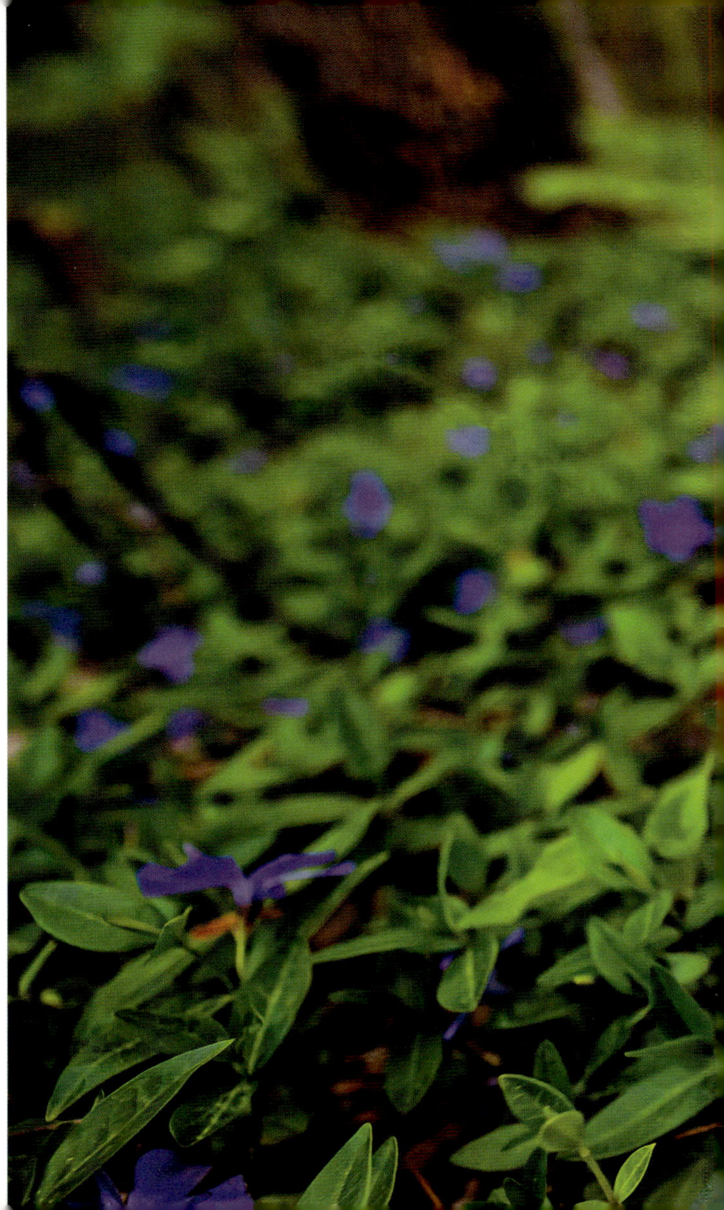

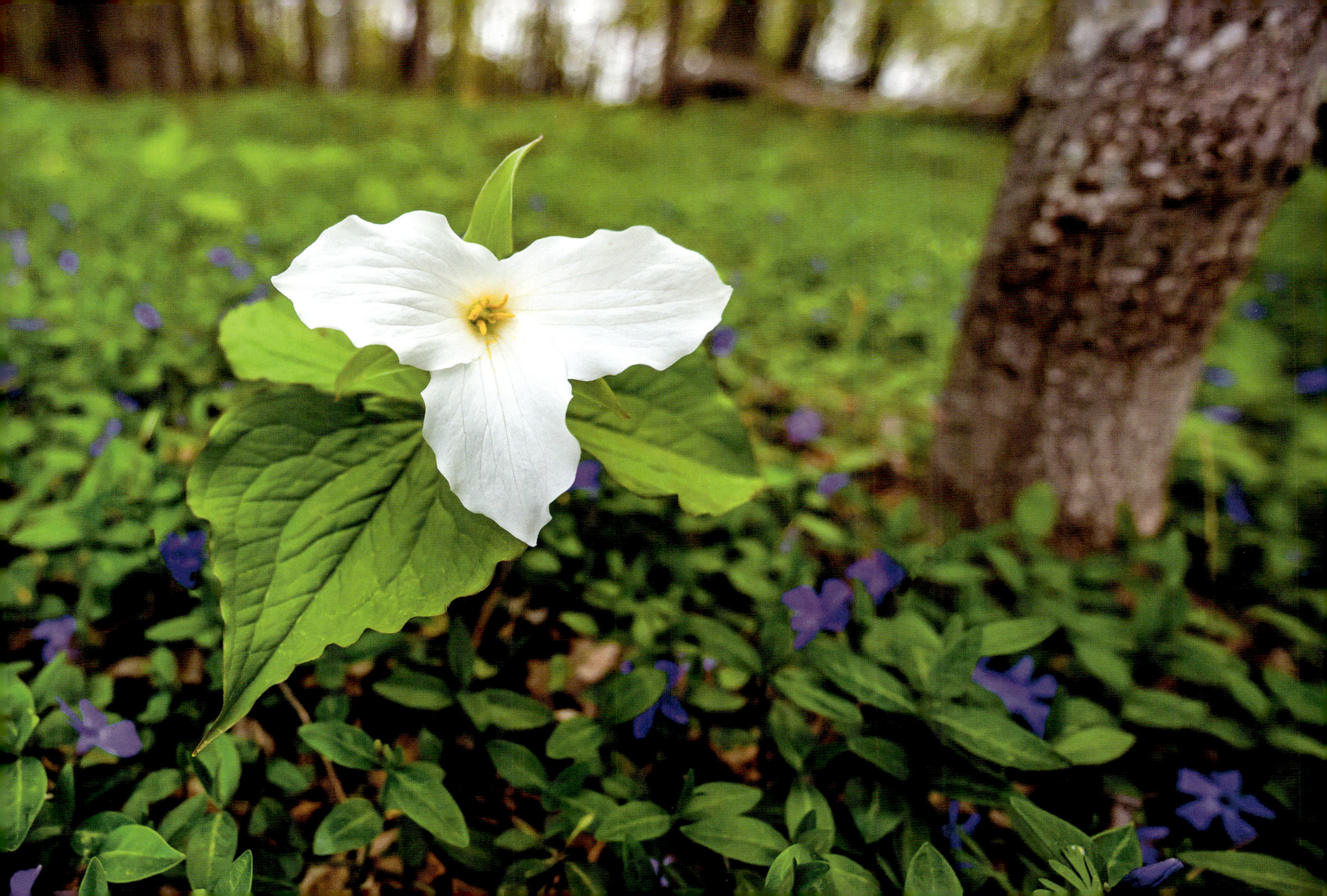

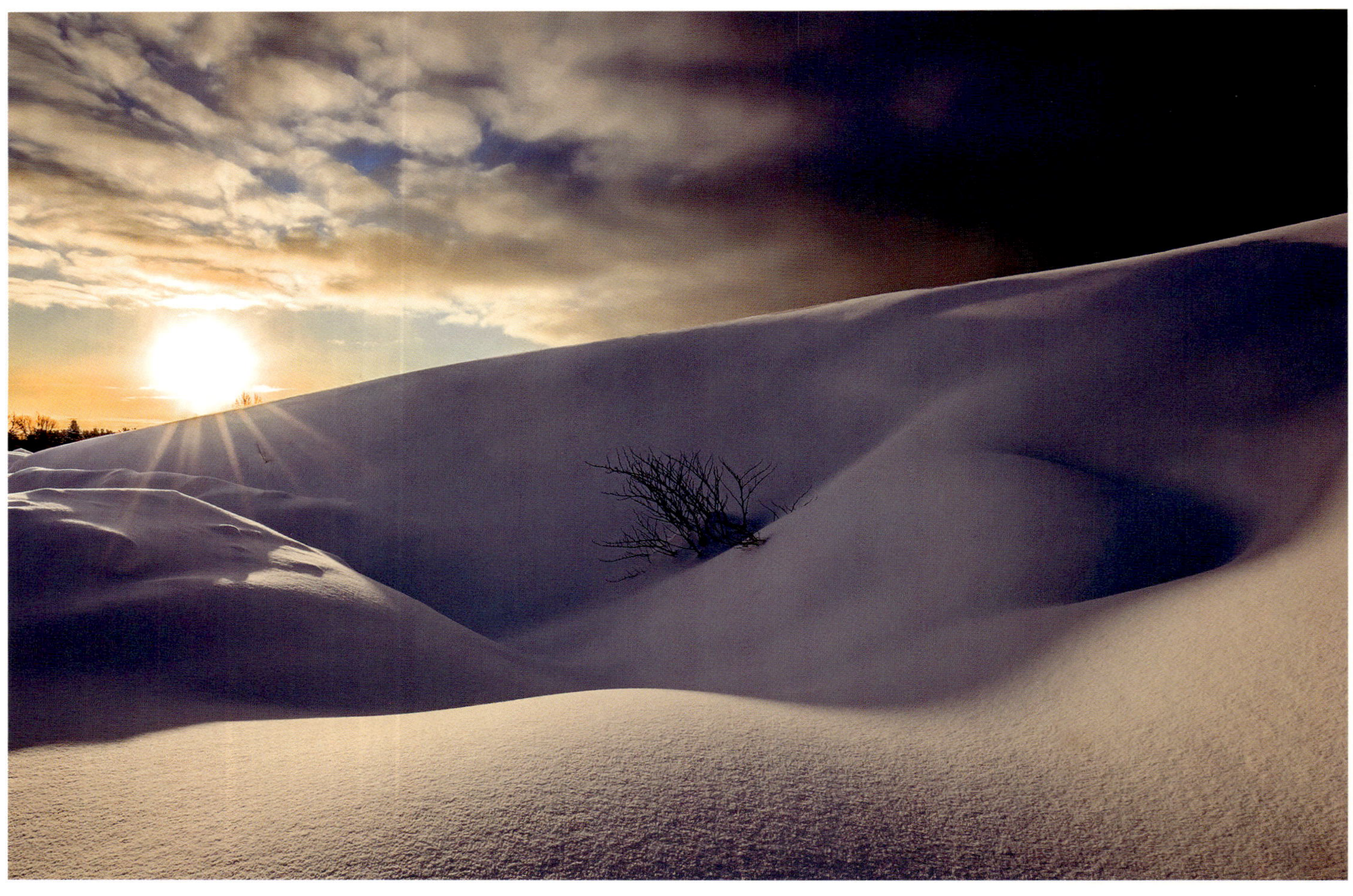

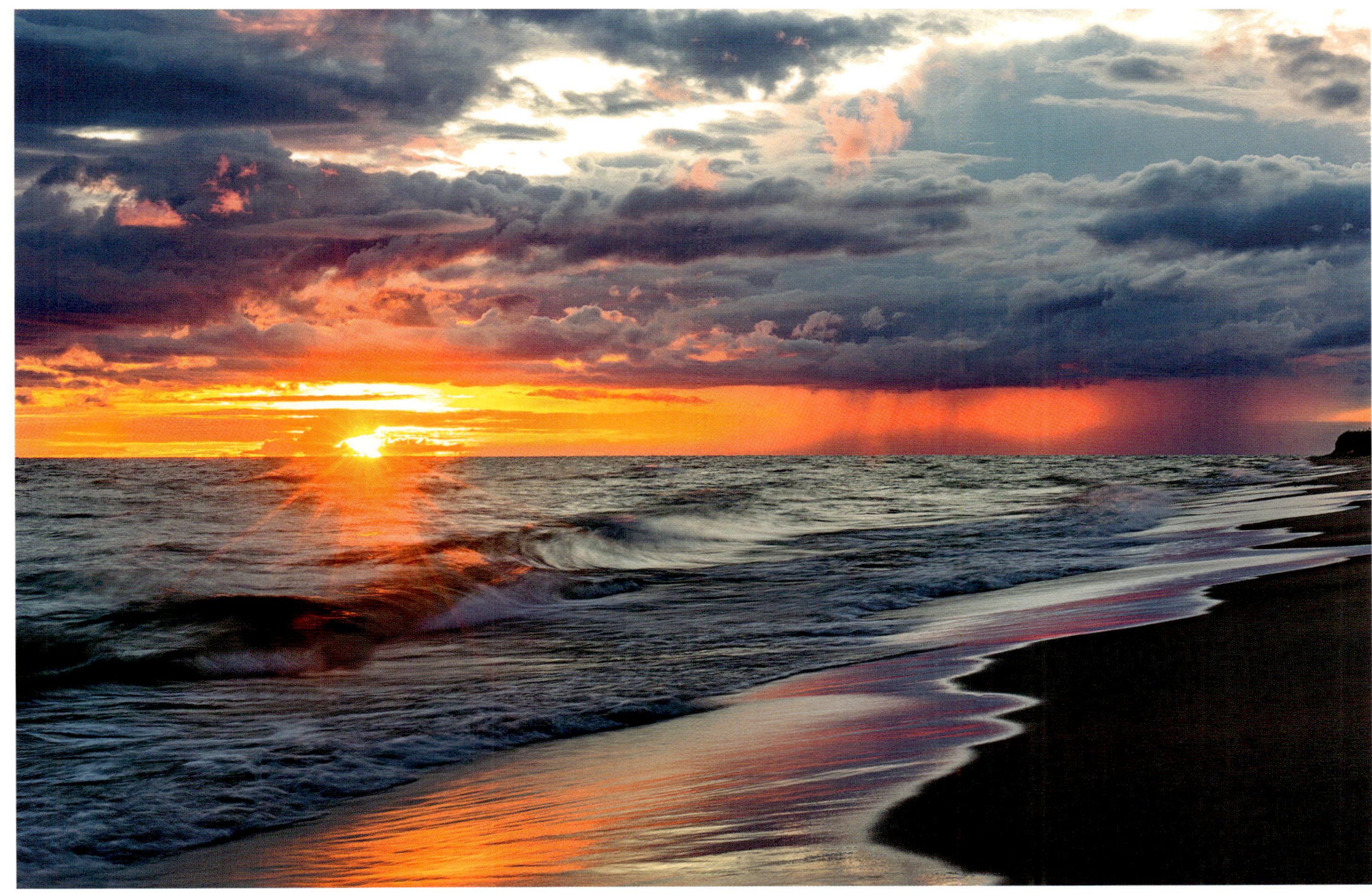

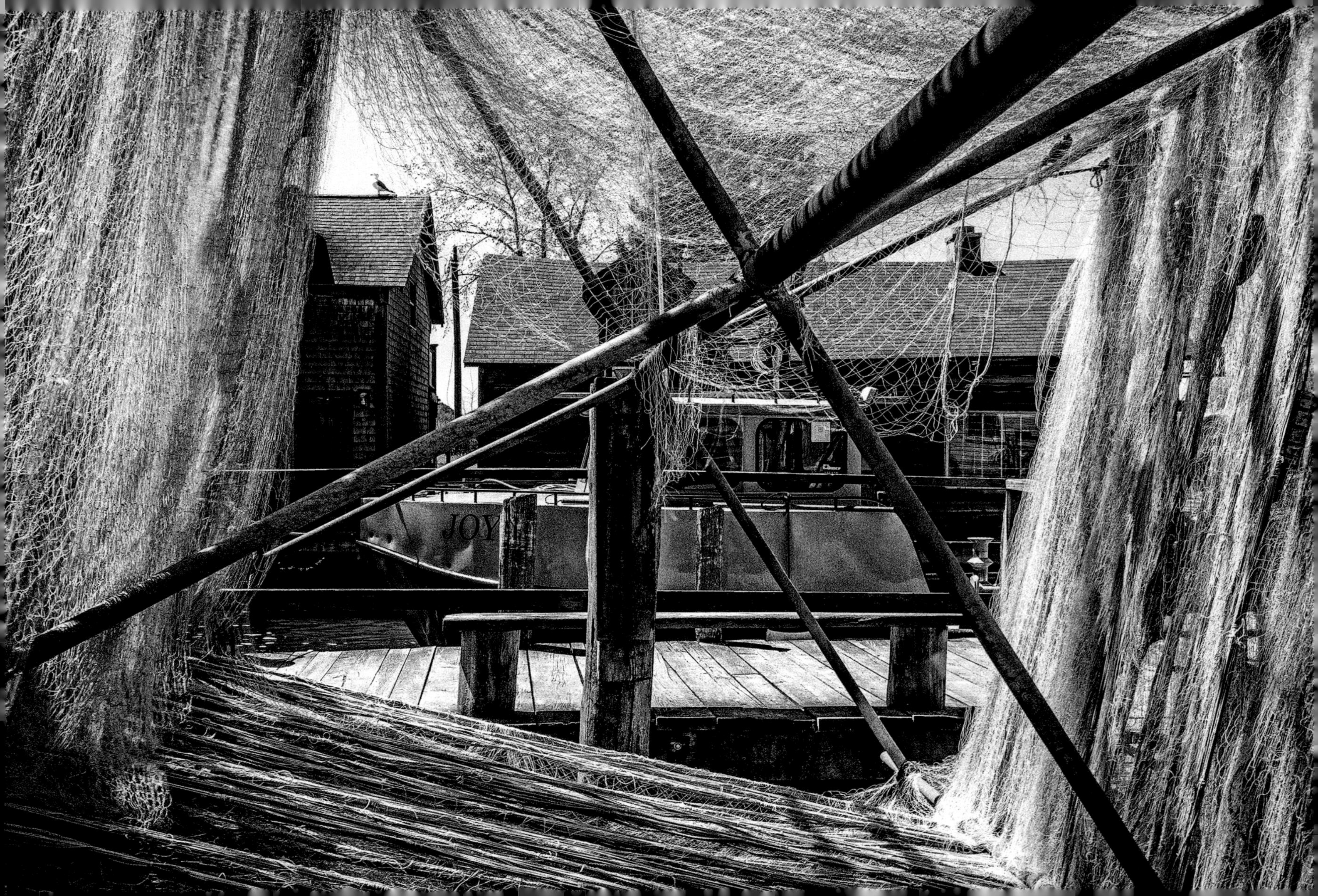
JOY

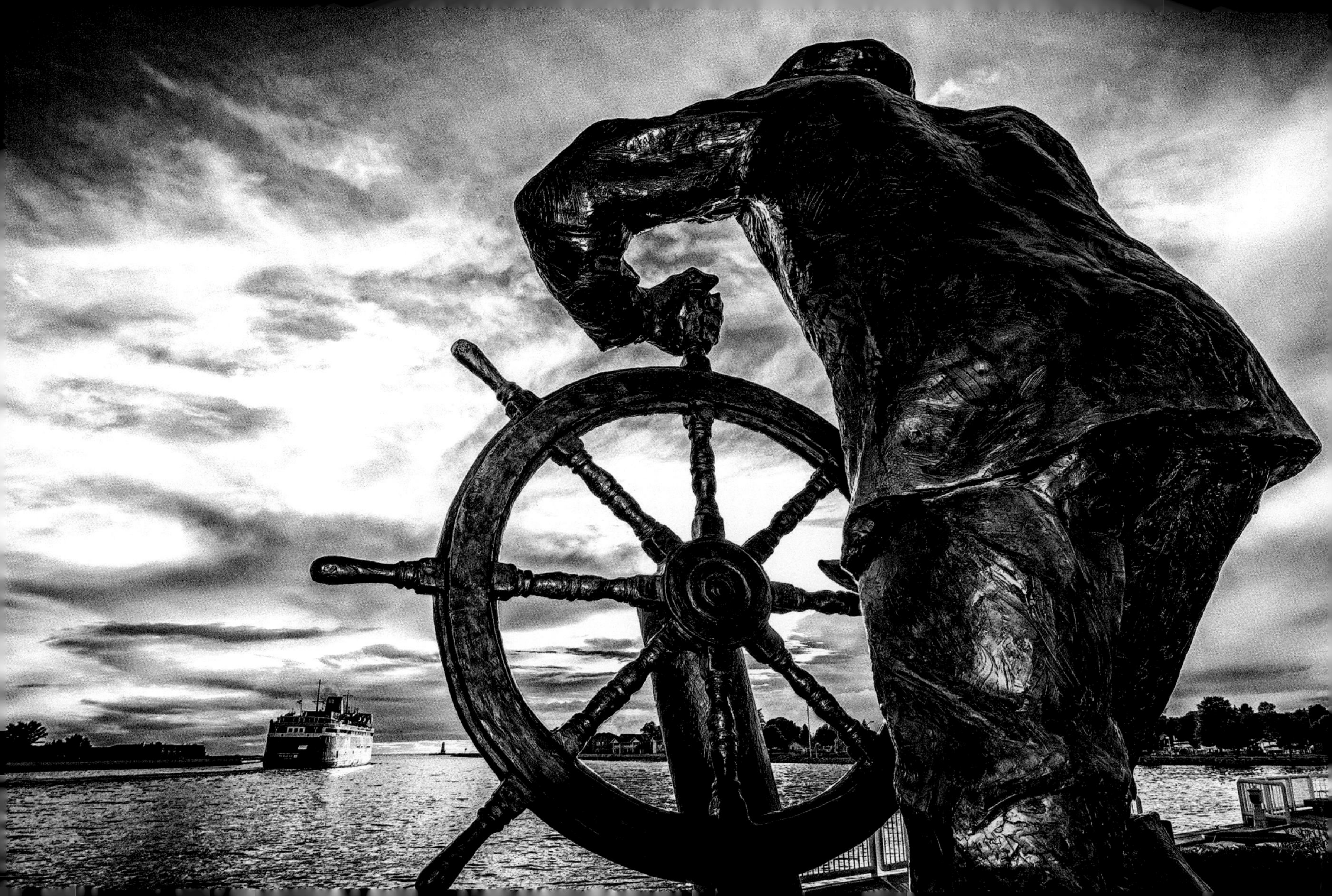

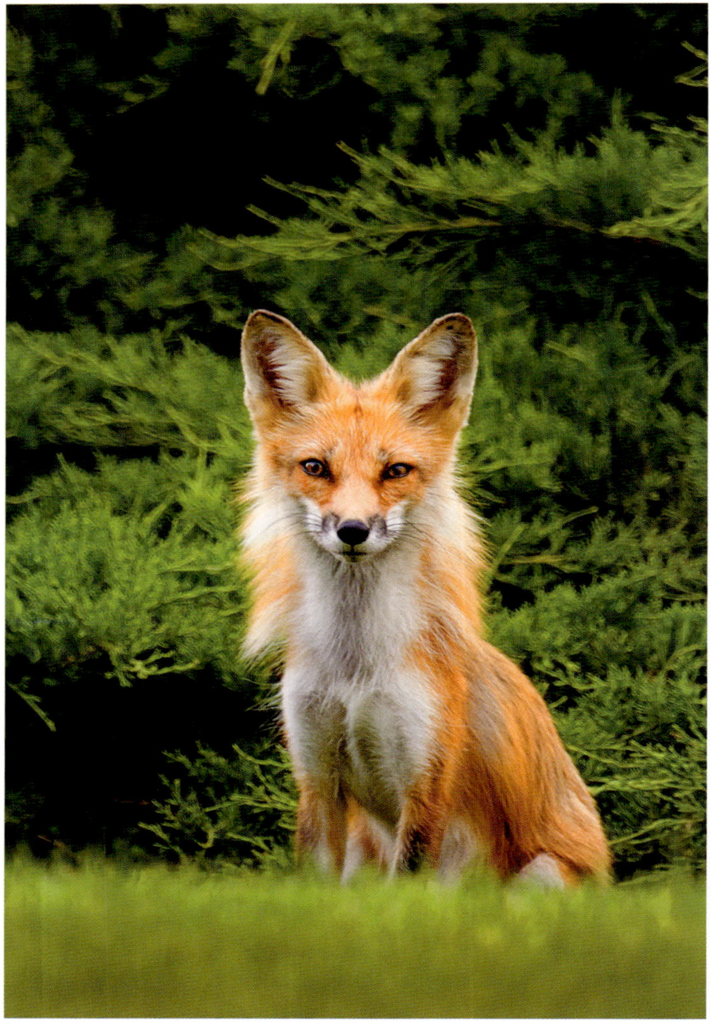

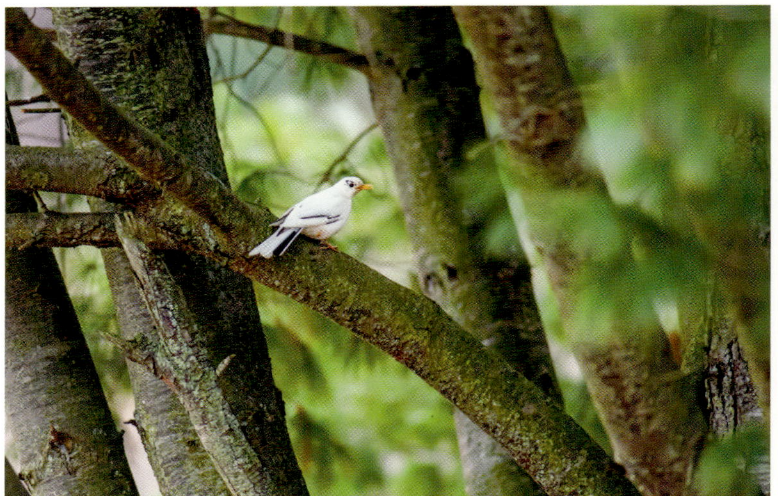

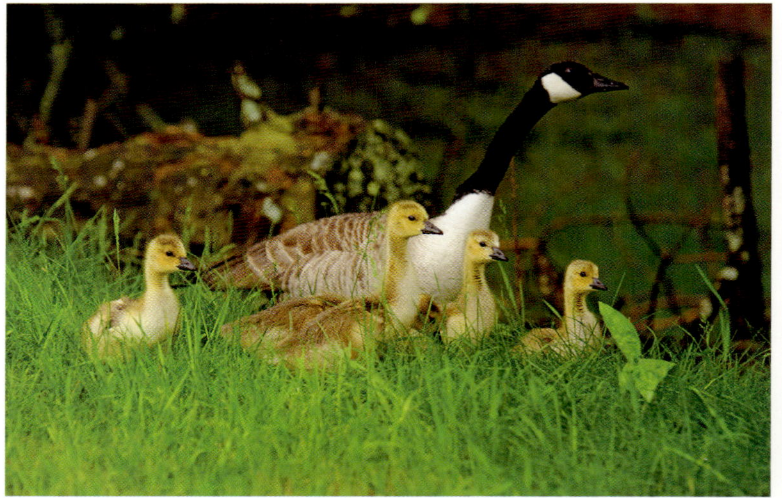

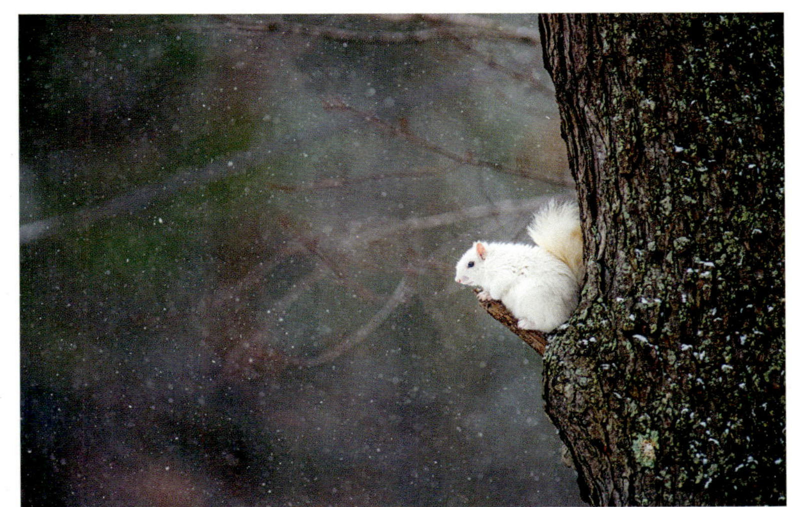

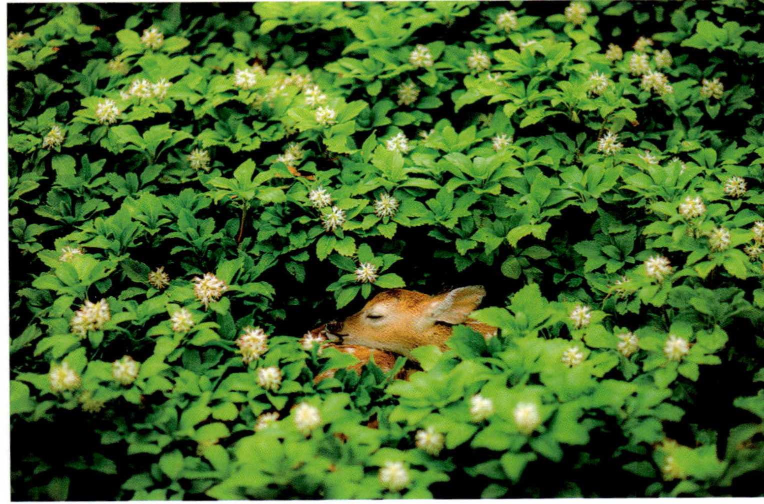

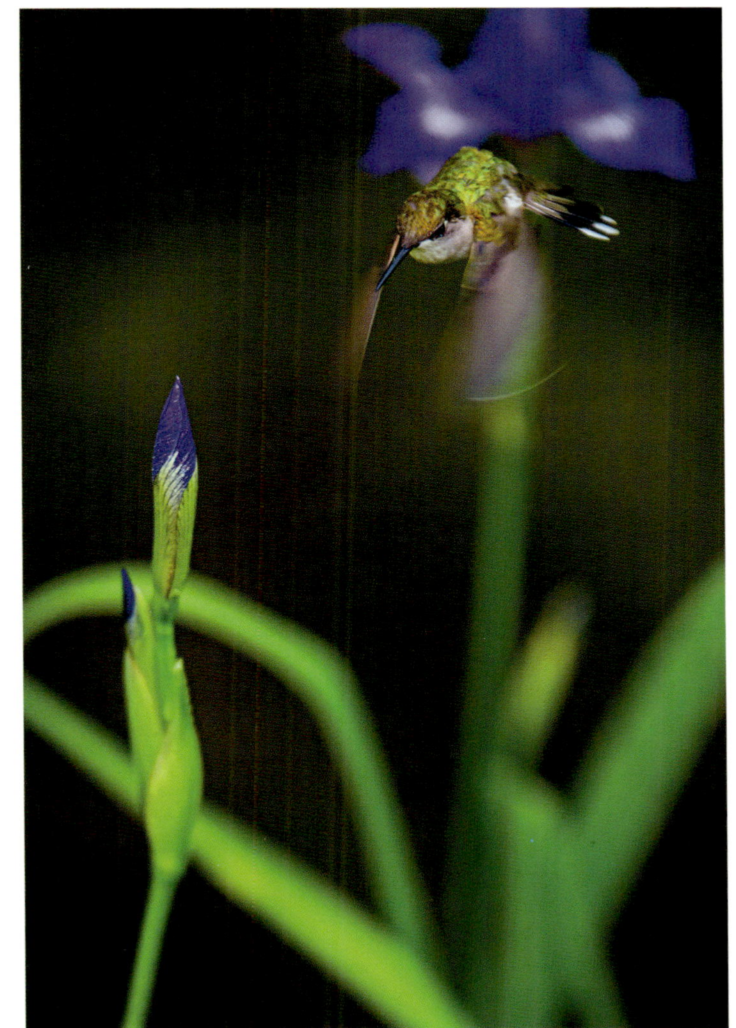

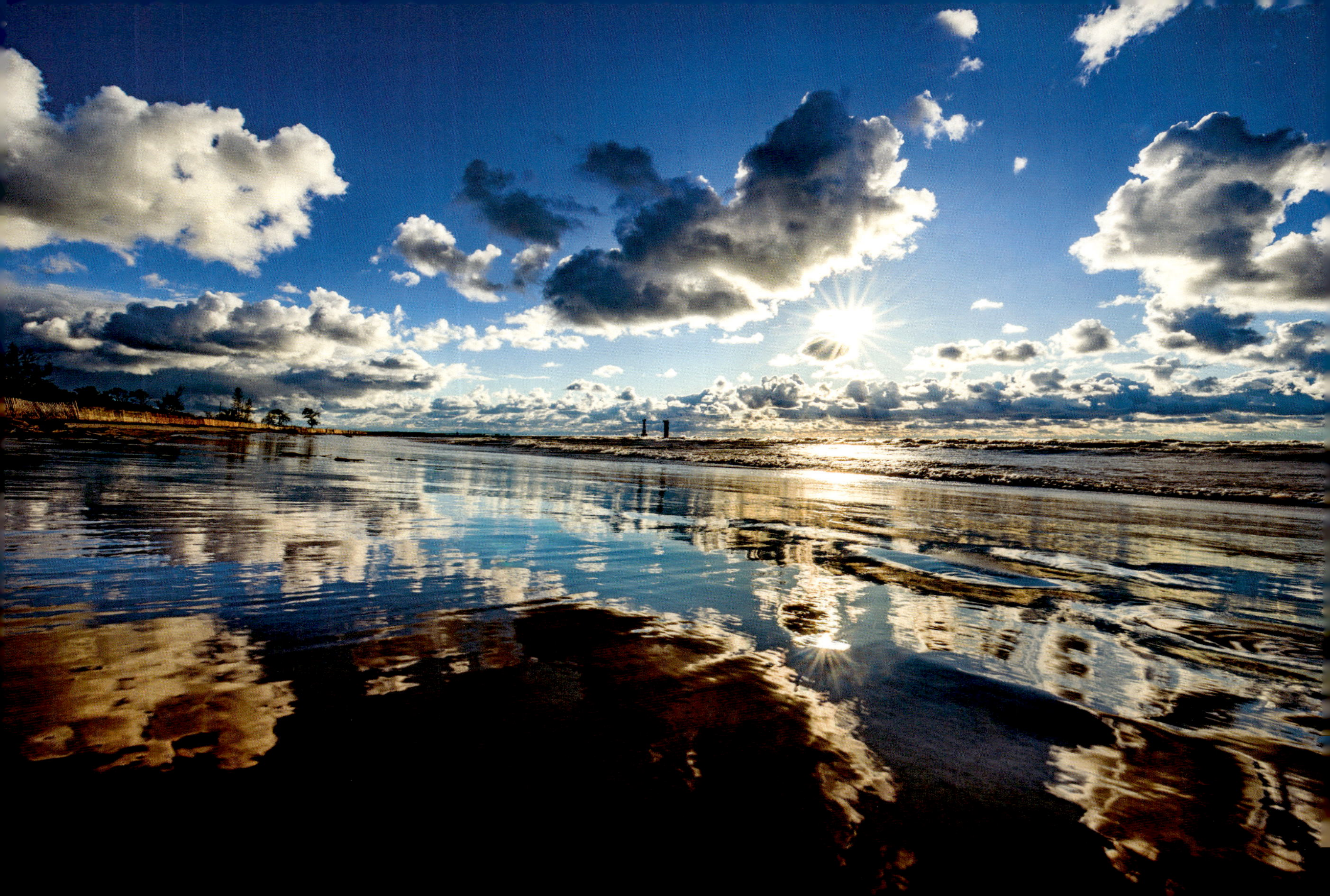

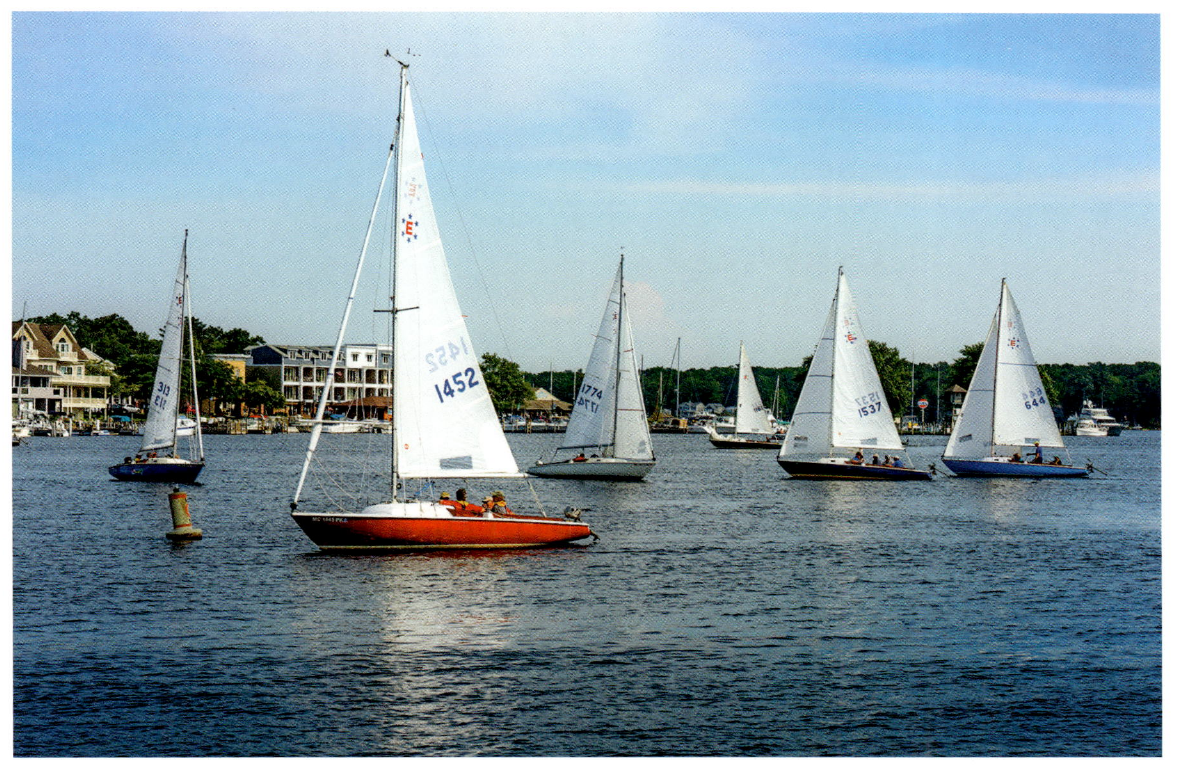
313
1452
1774
1537
644

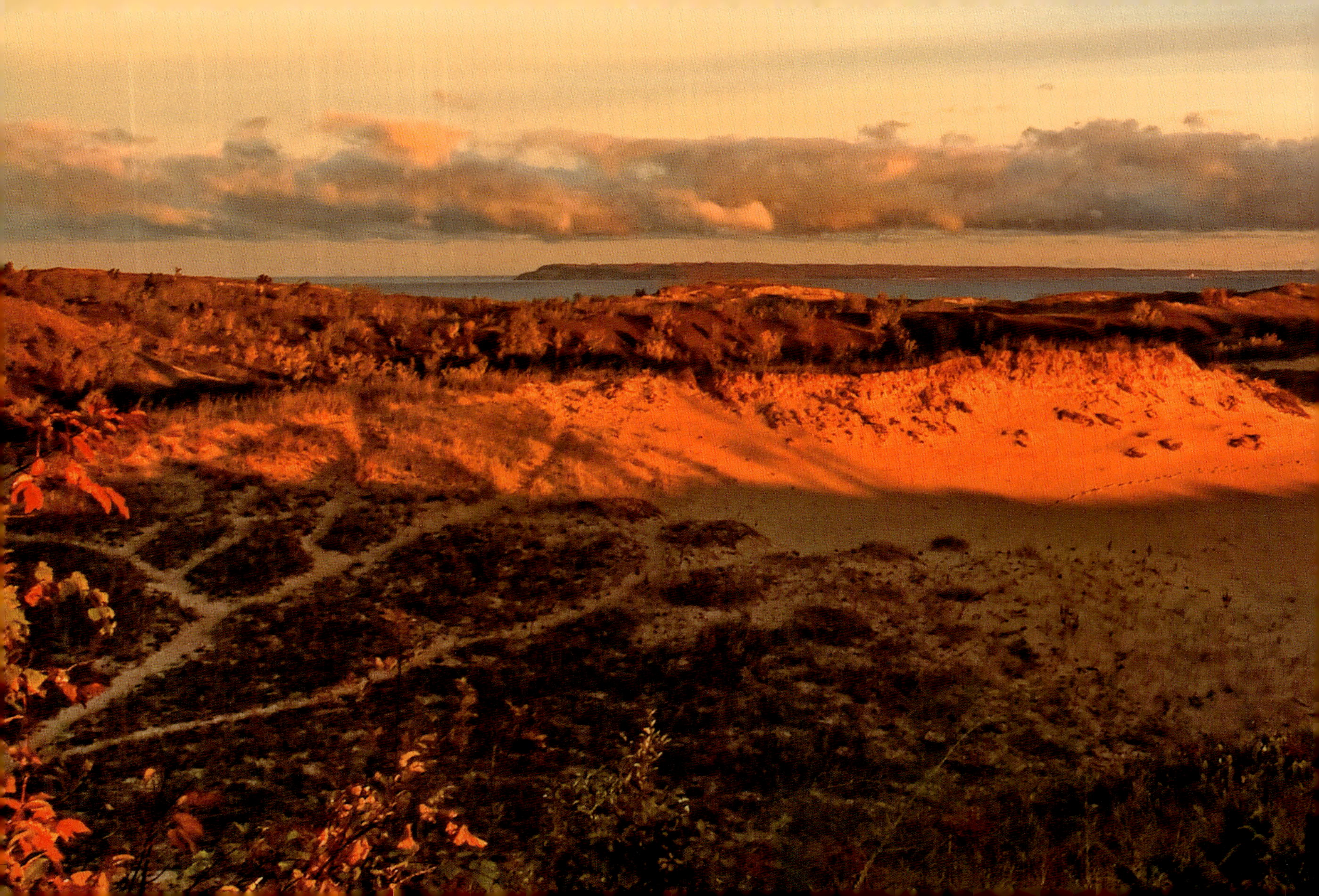

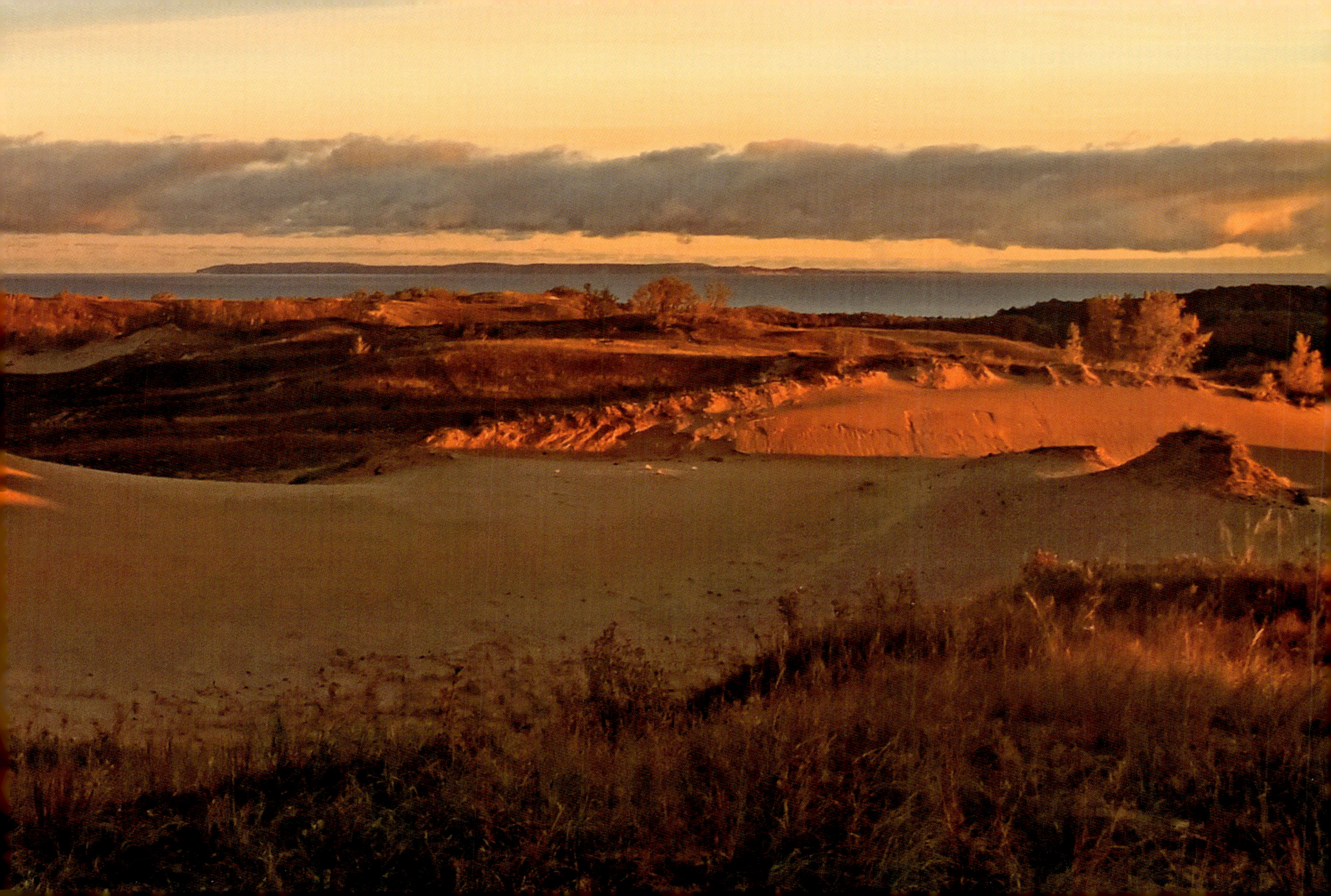

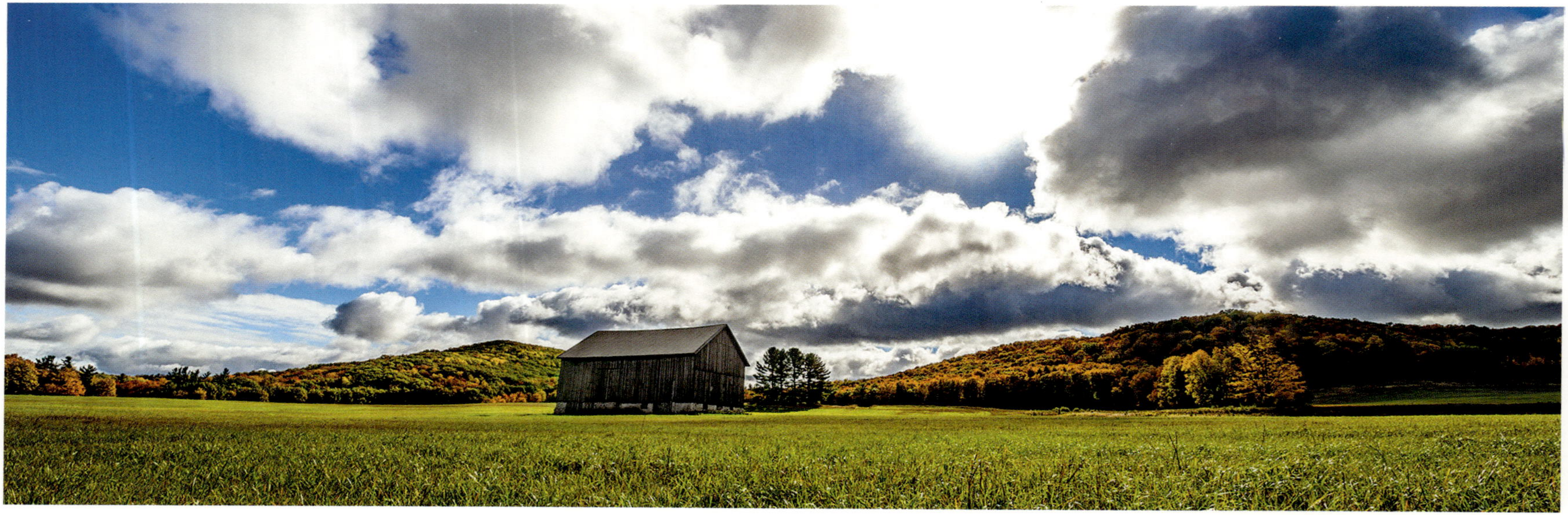

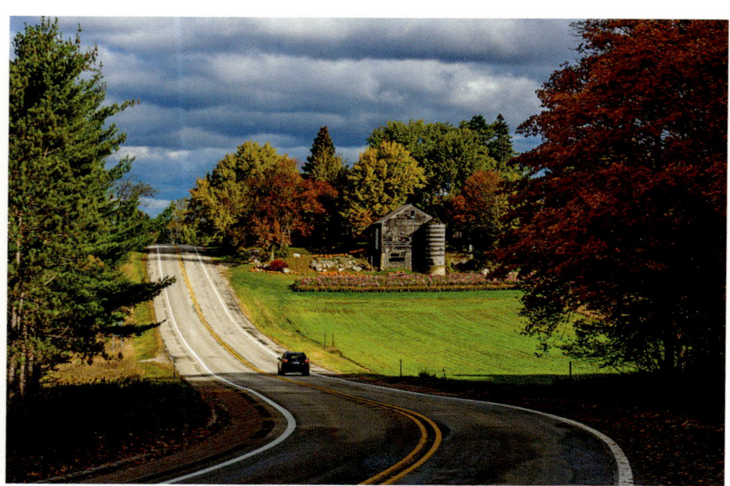

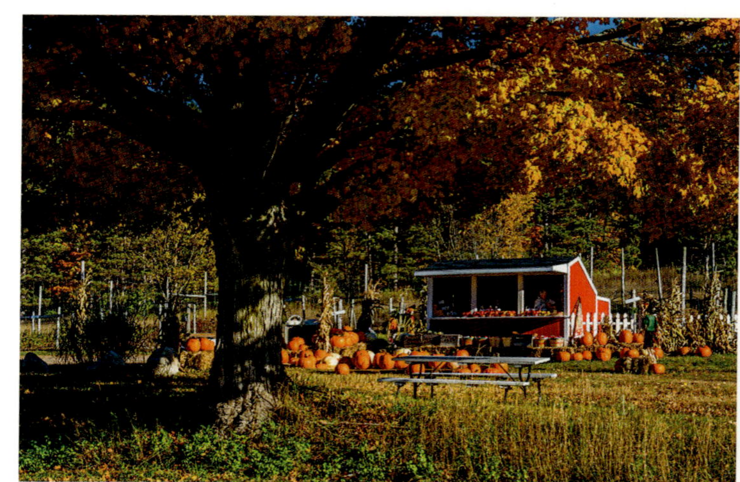

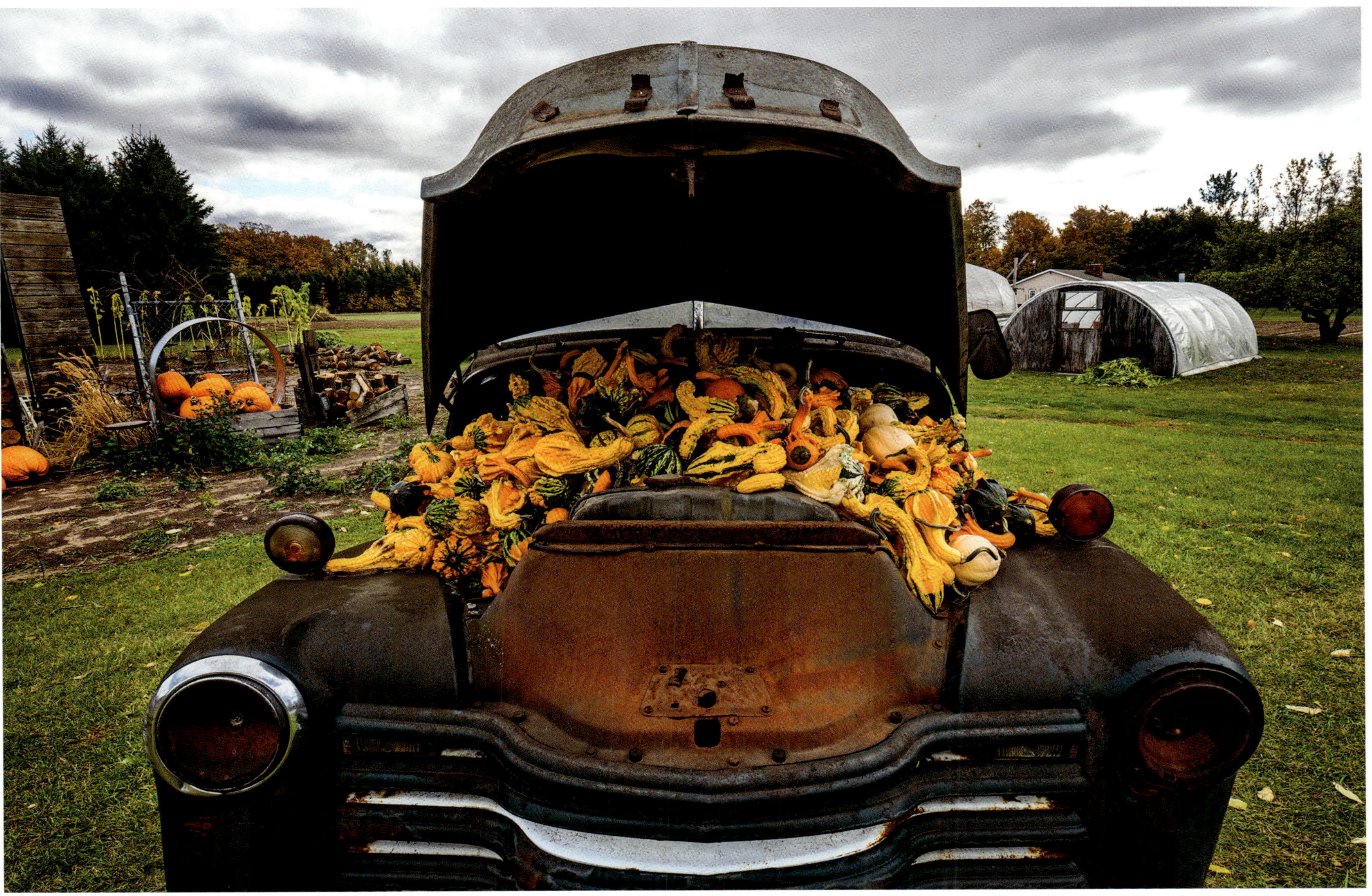

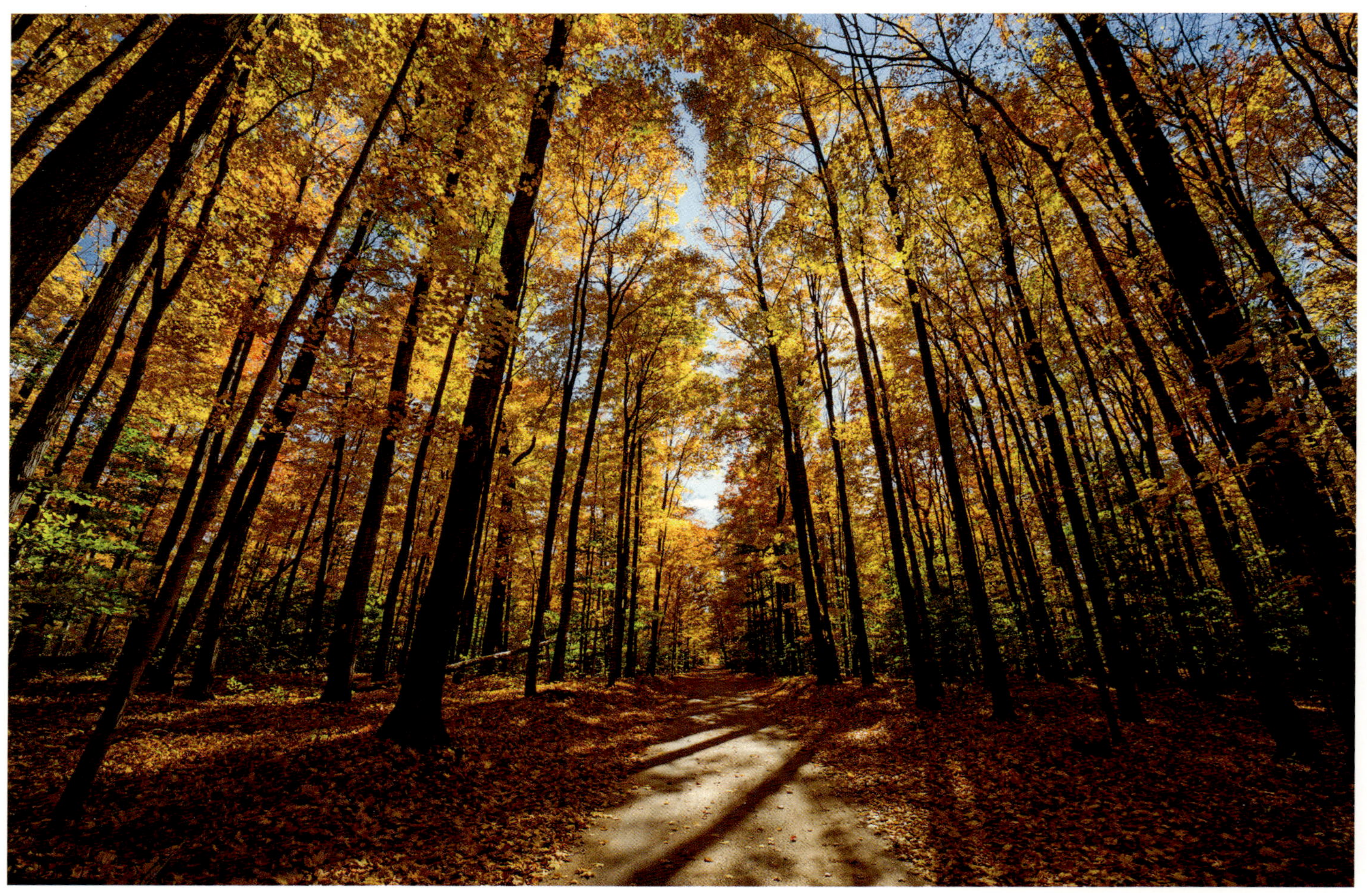

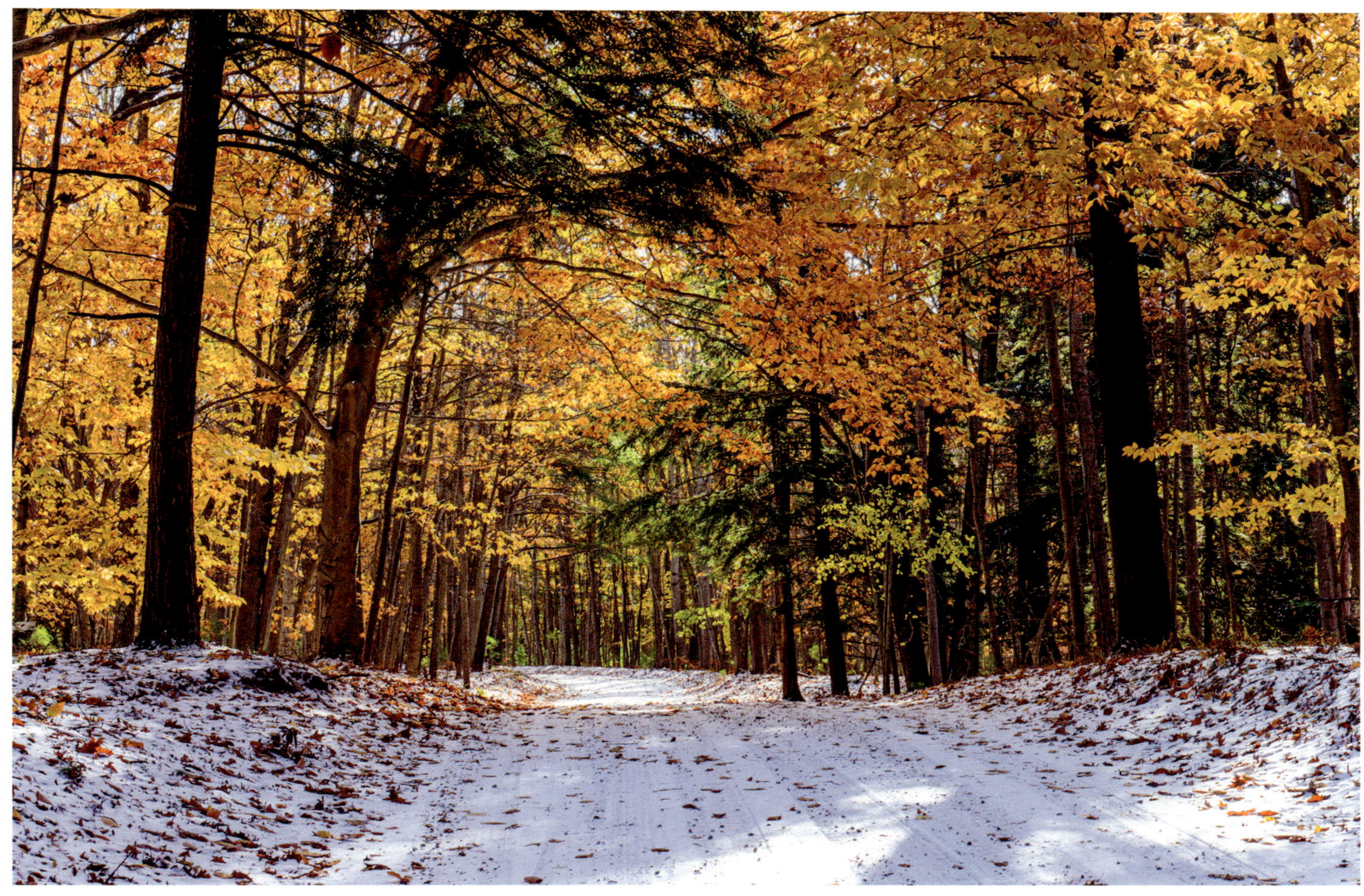

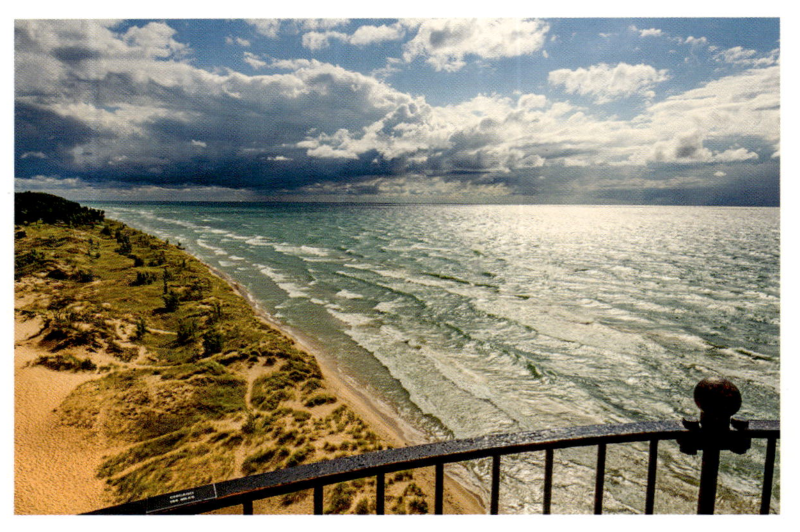

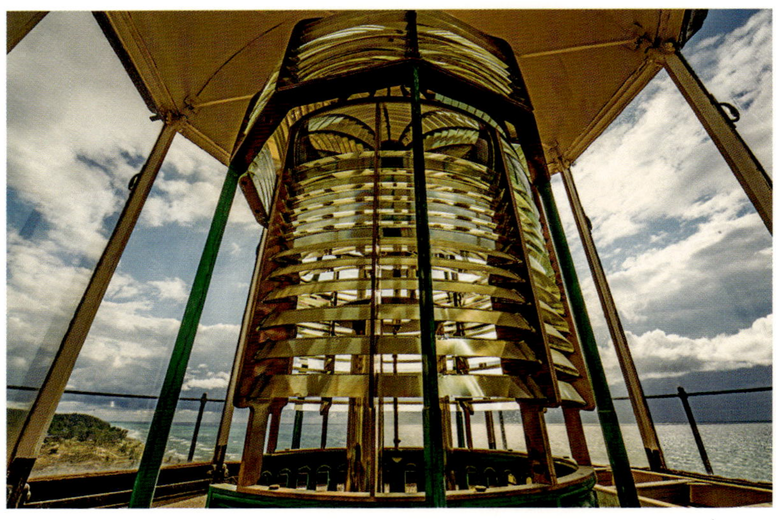

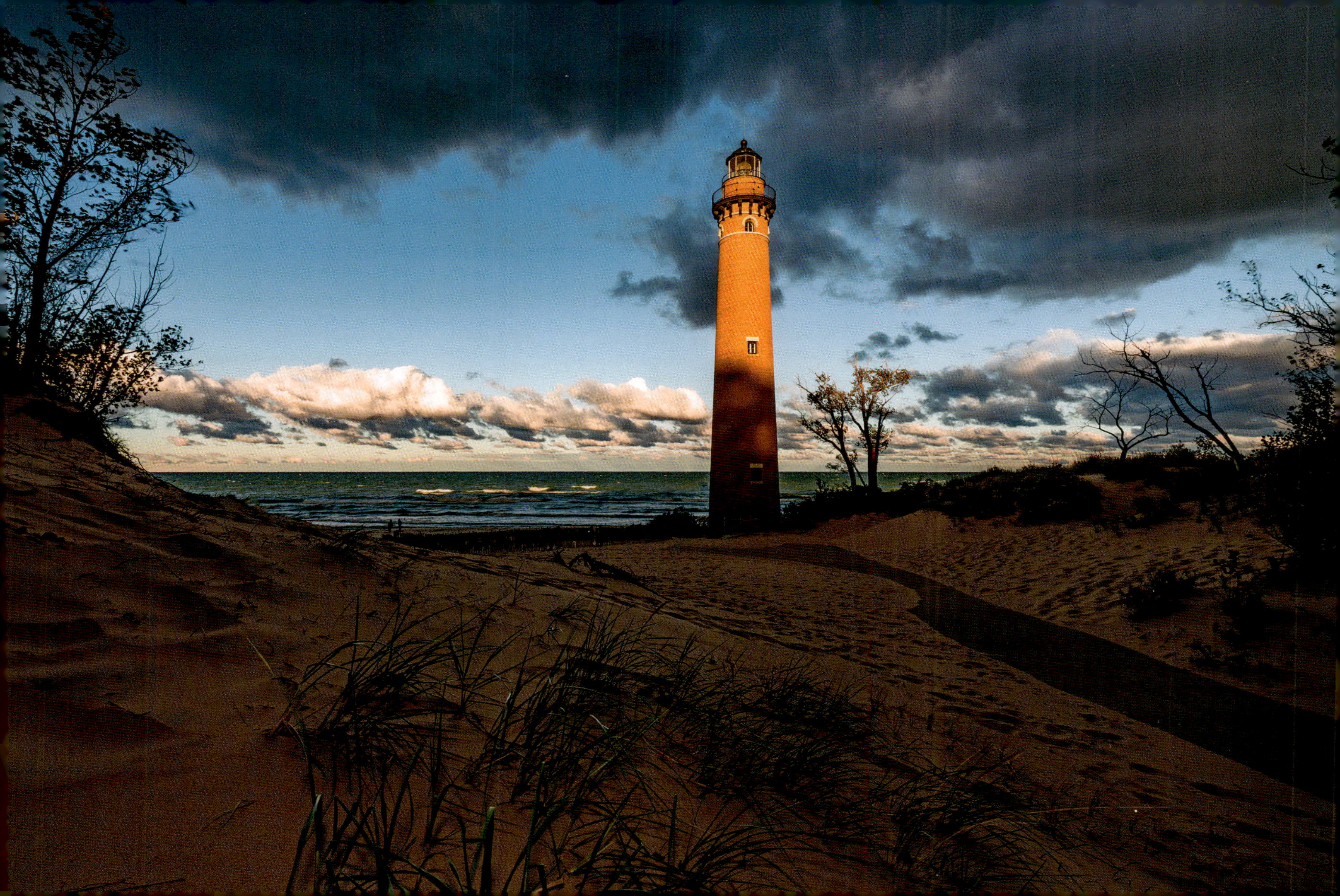

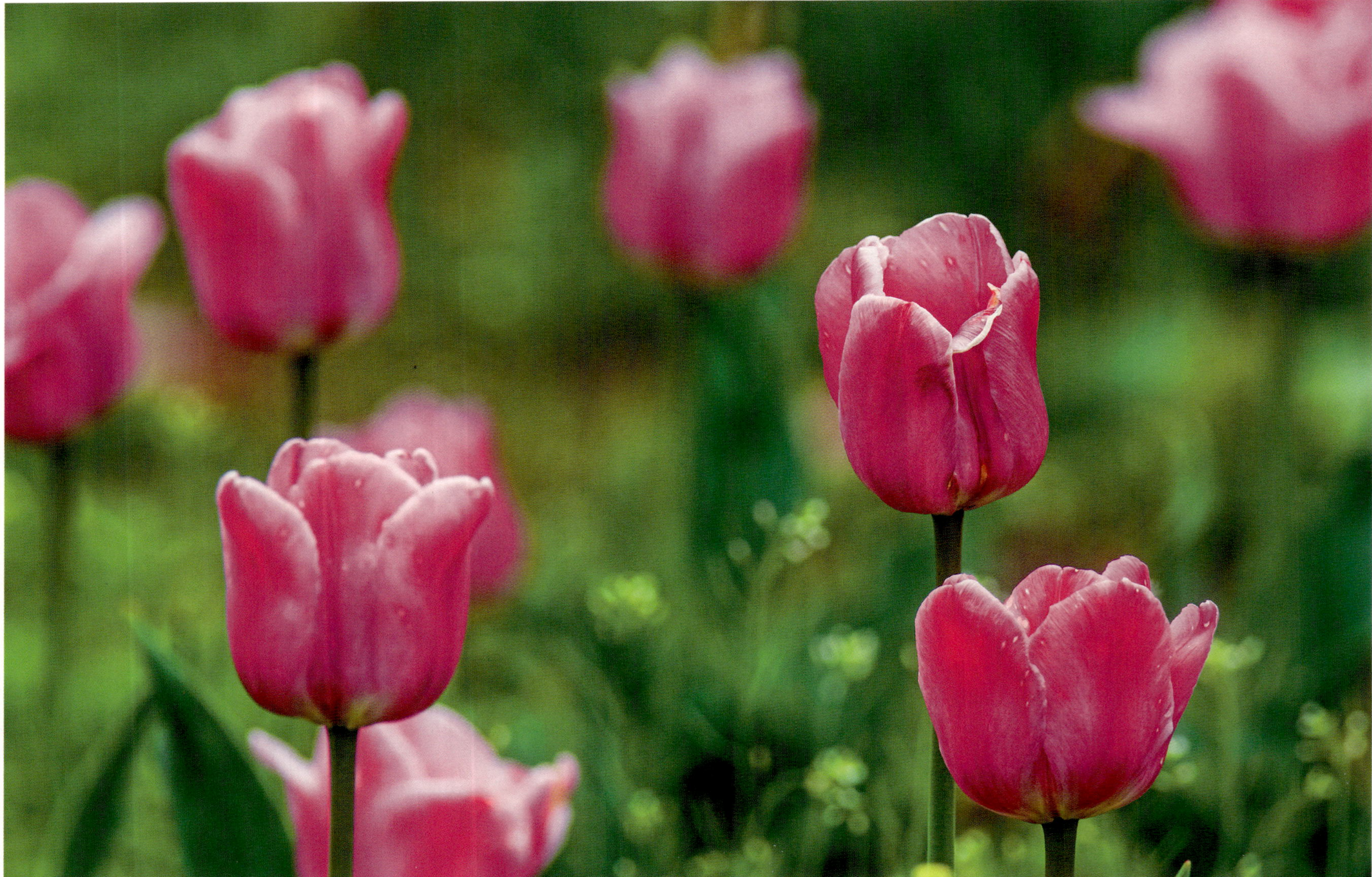

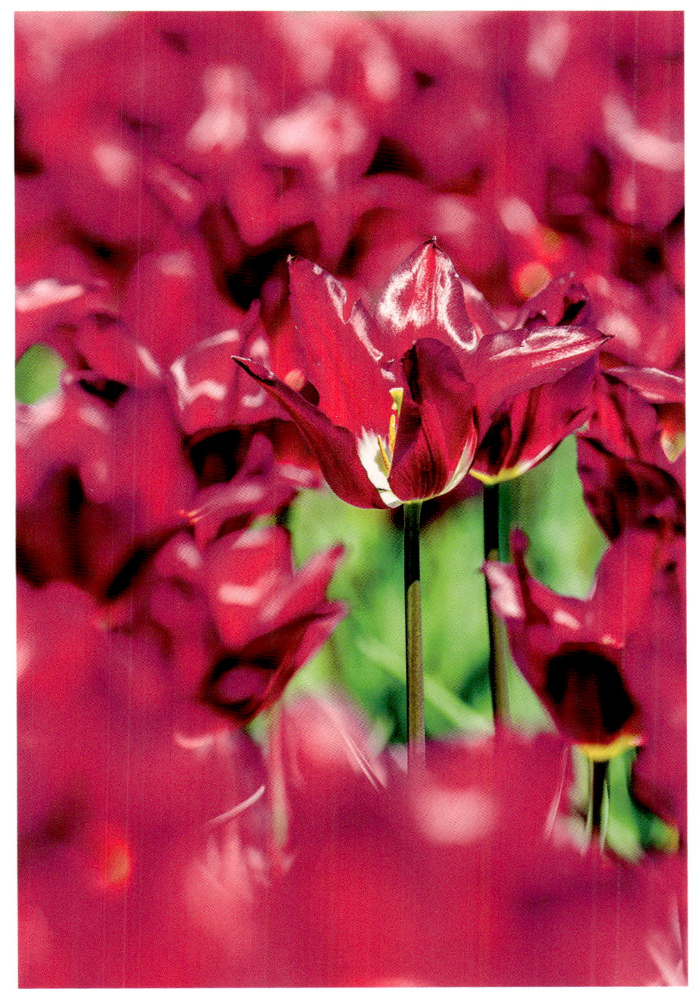

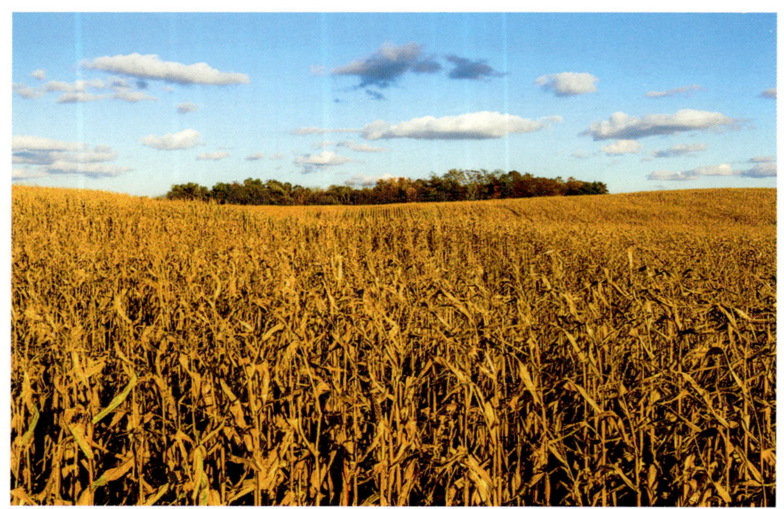

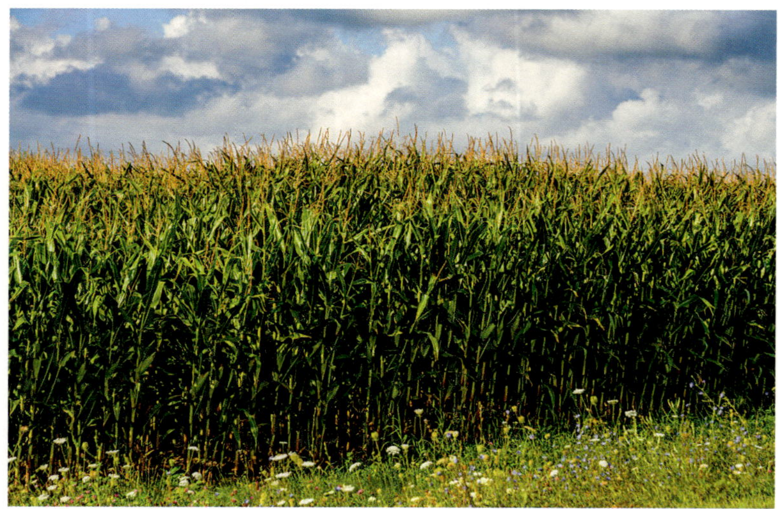

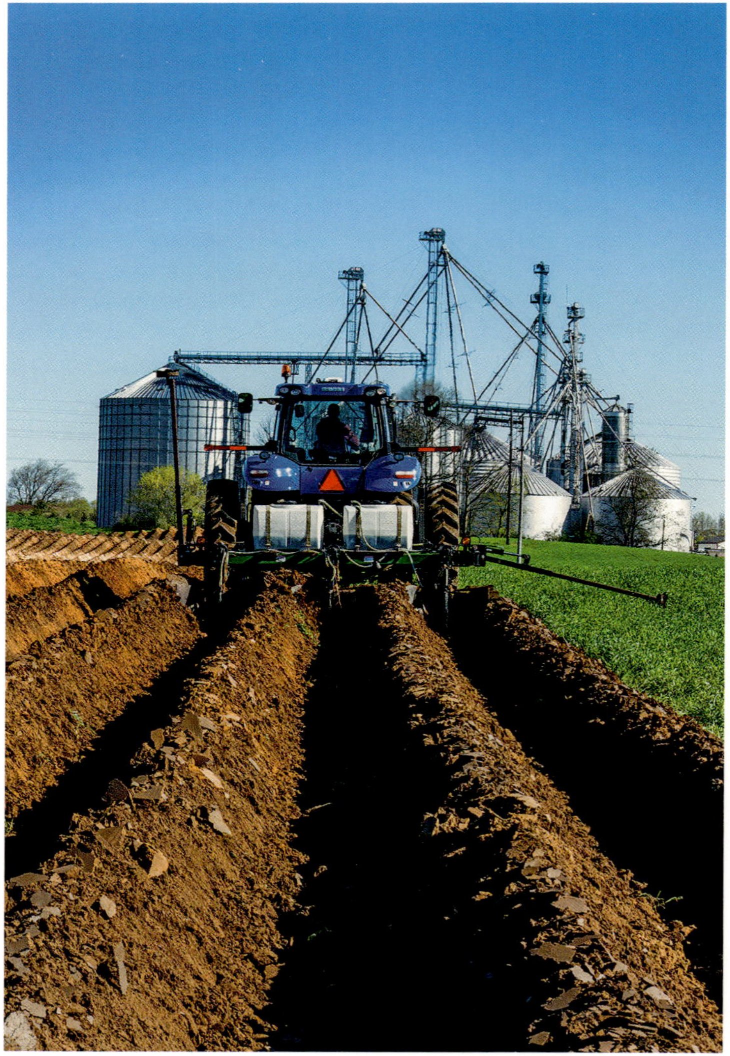

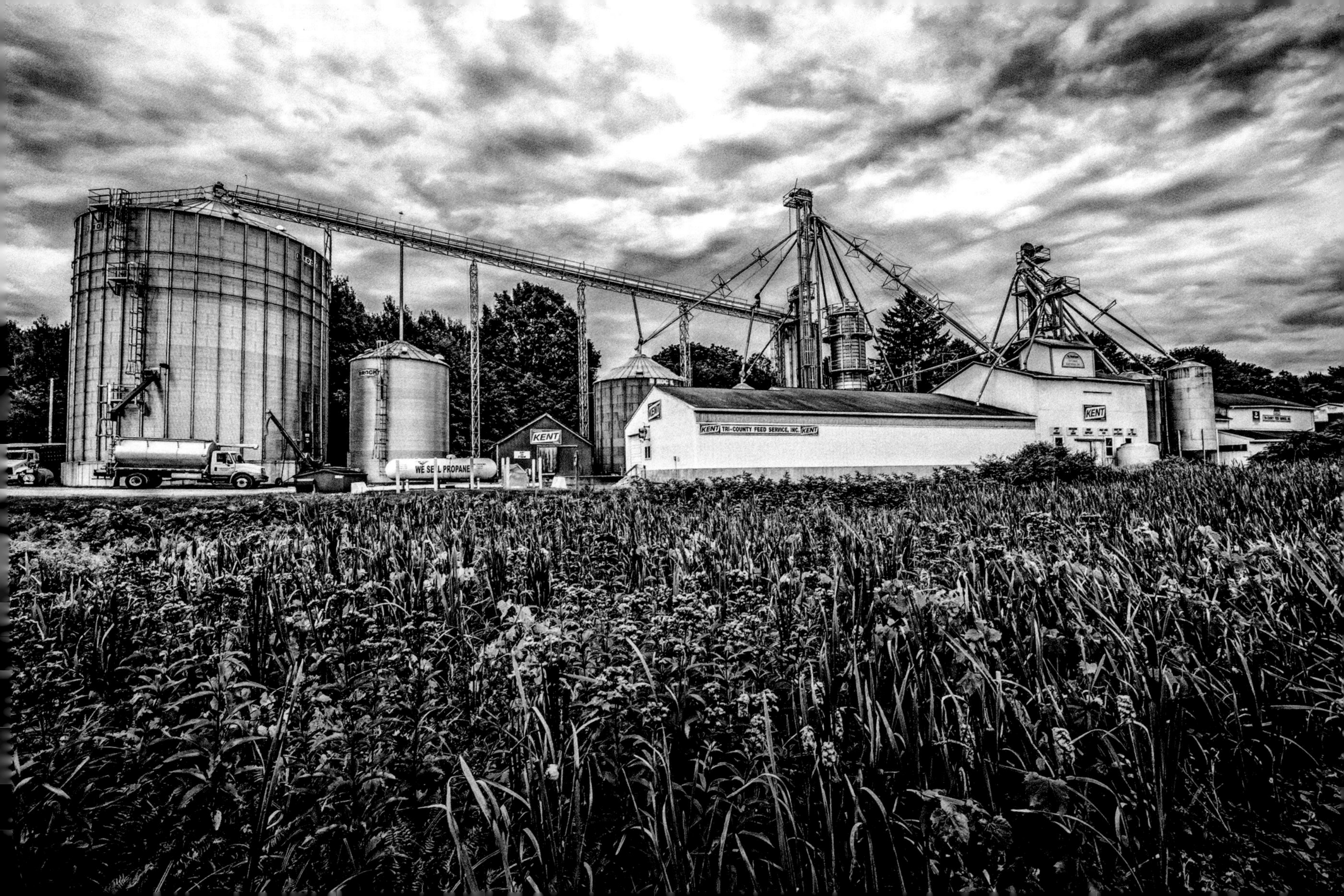
BROCK
KENT
WE SELL PROPANE
KENT
KENT TRI-COUNTY FEED SERVICE, INC. KENT
KENT

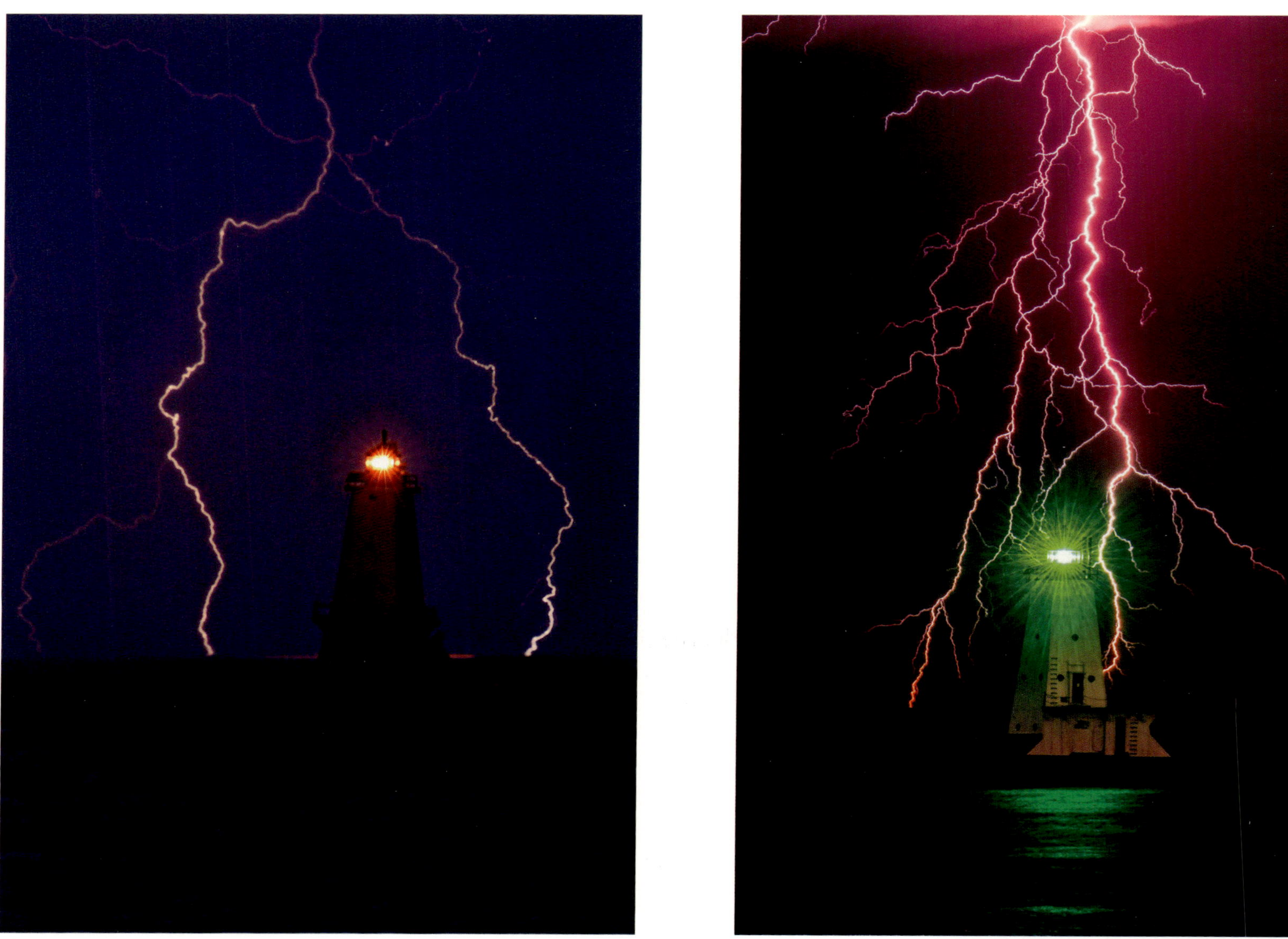

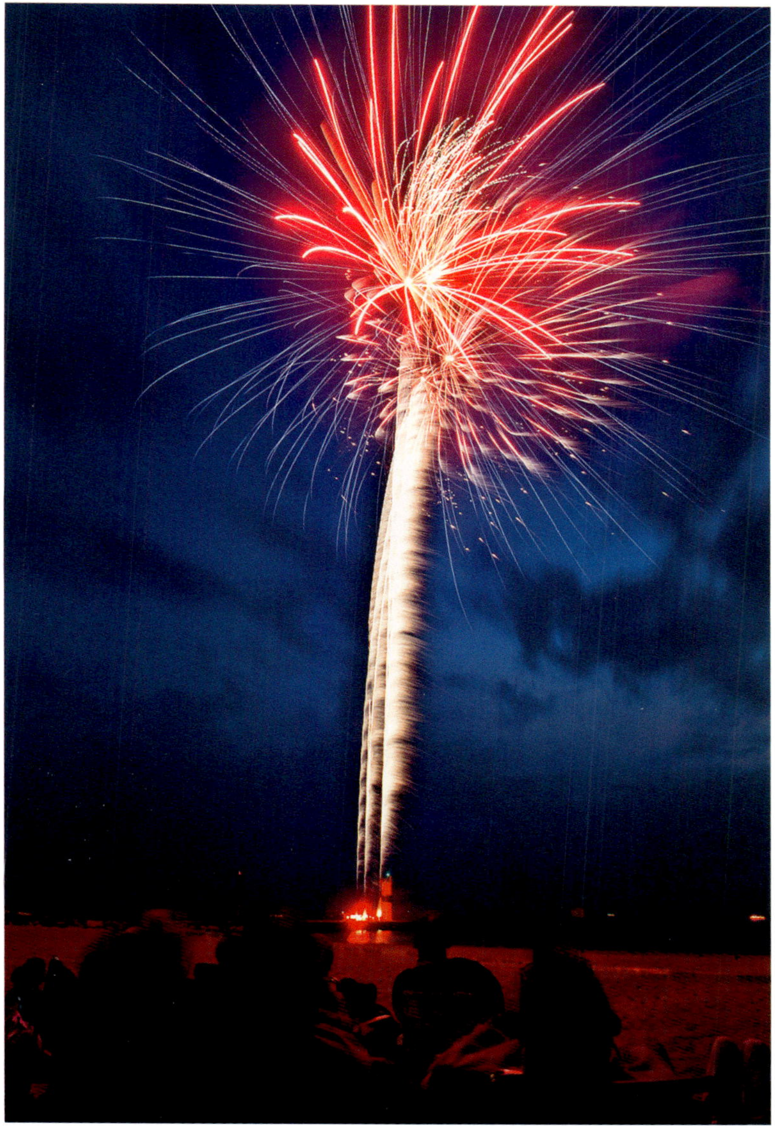

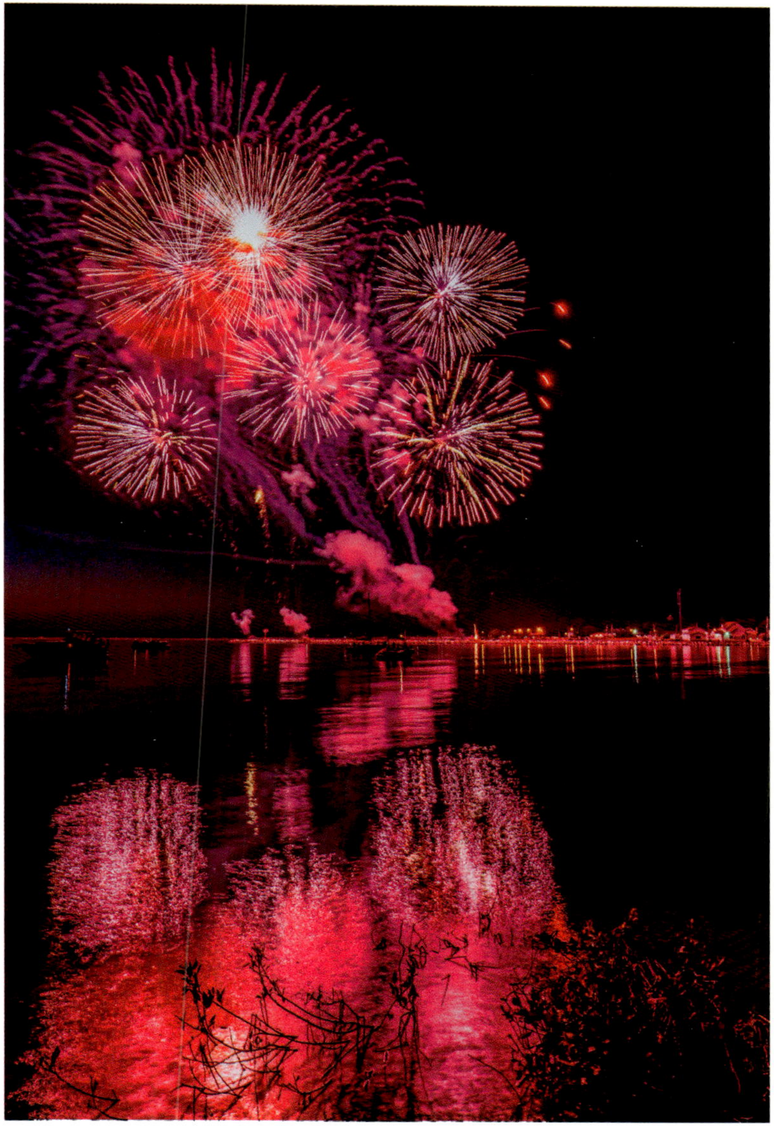

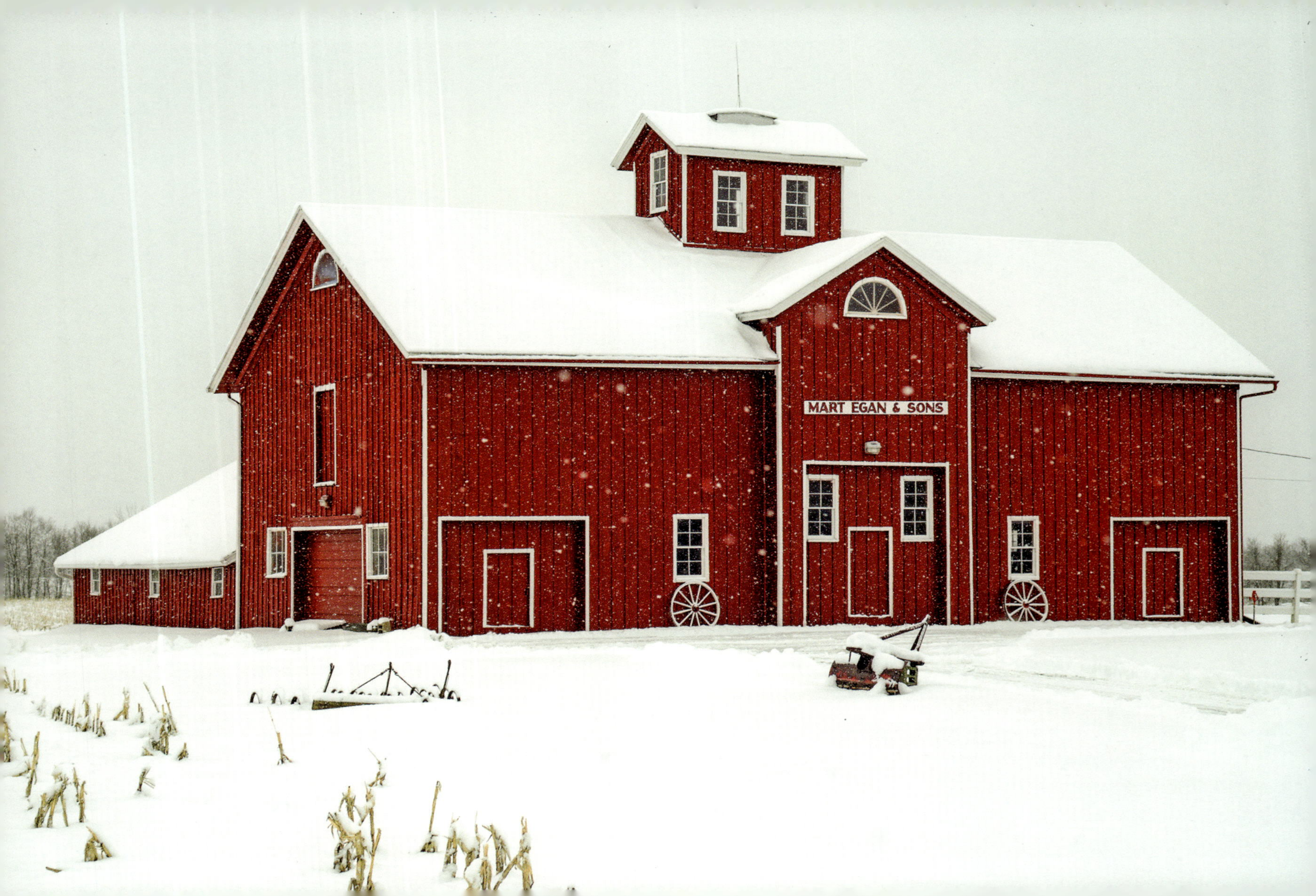
MART EGAN & SONS

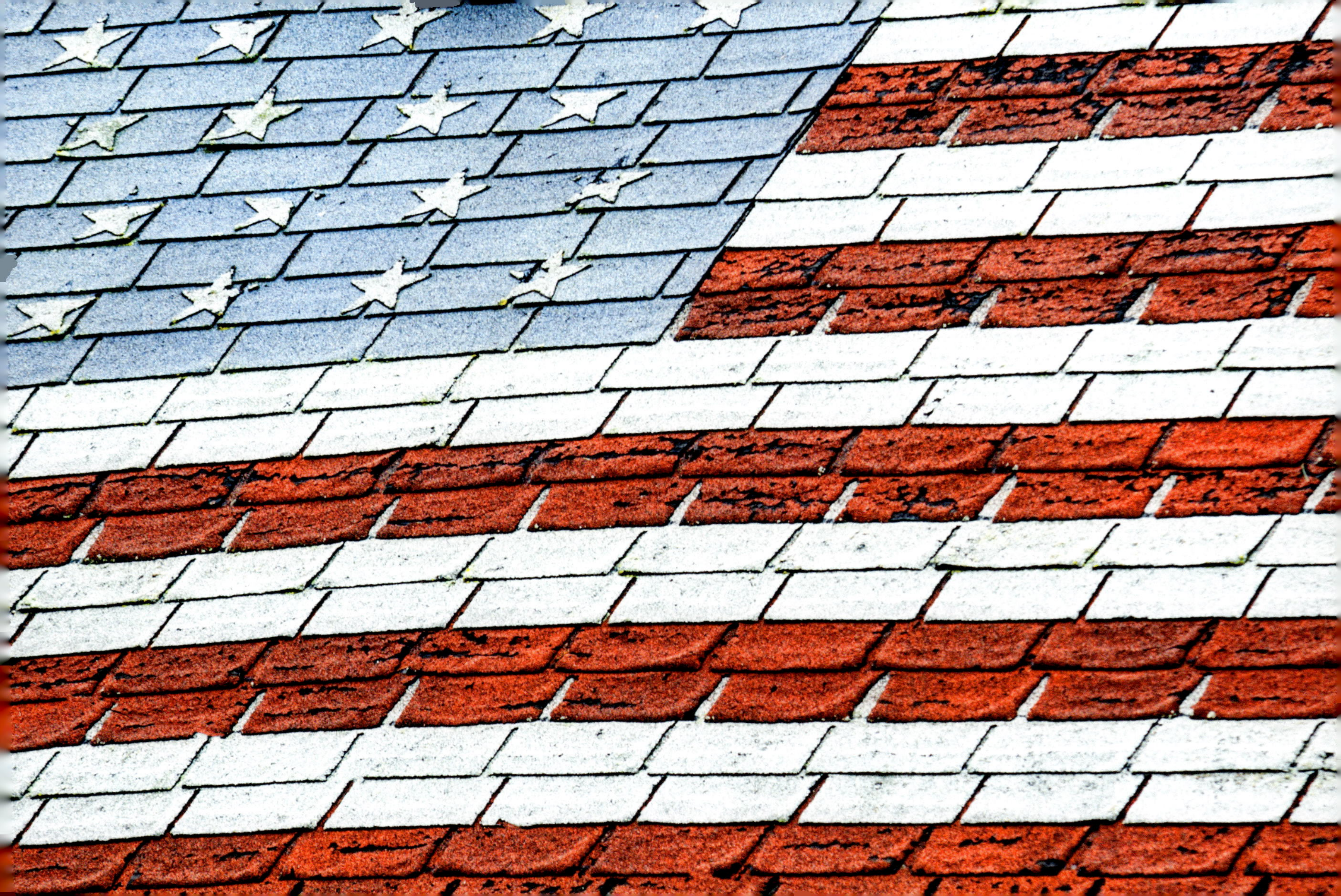

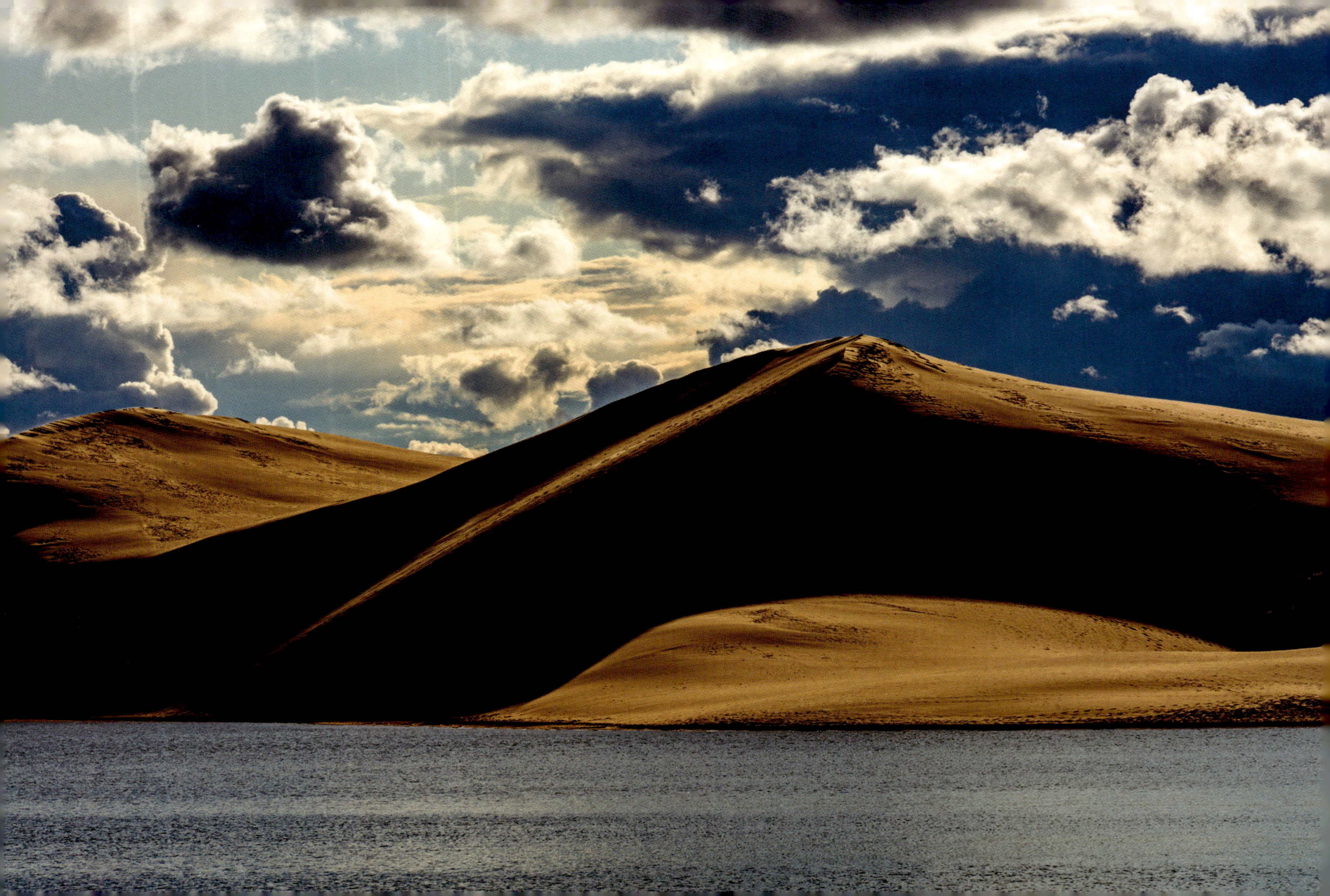

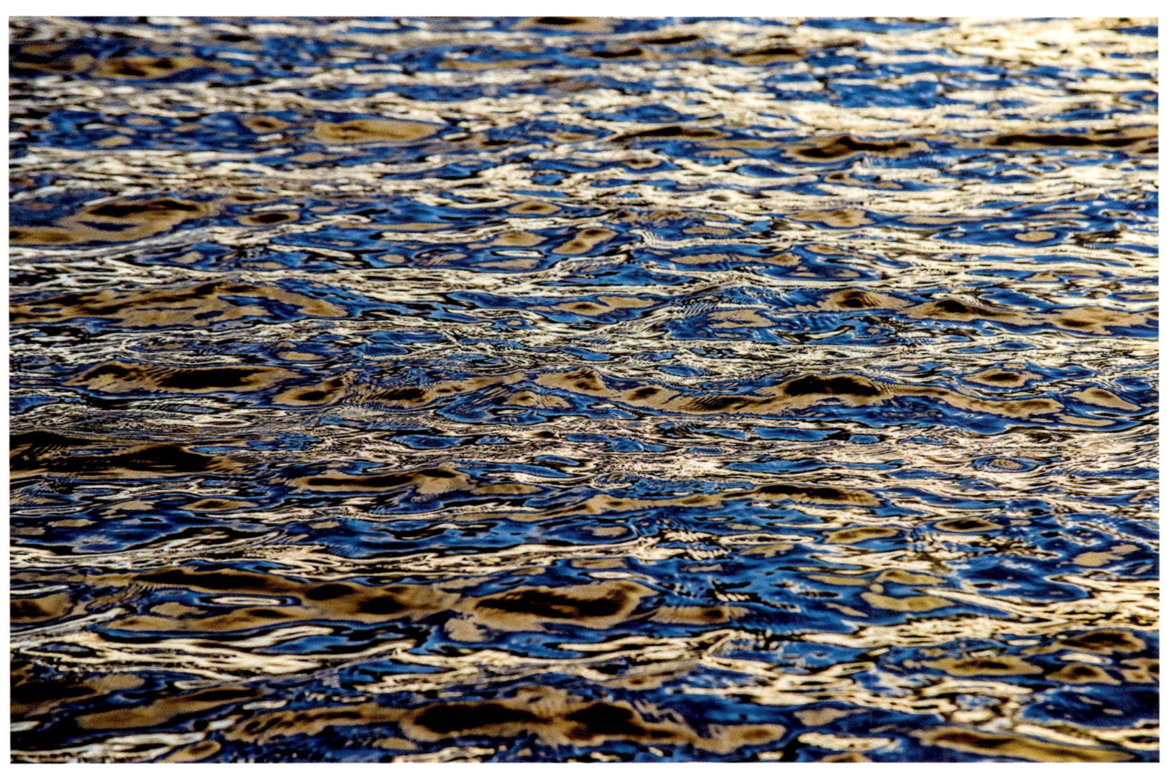

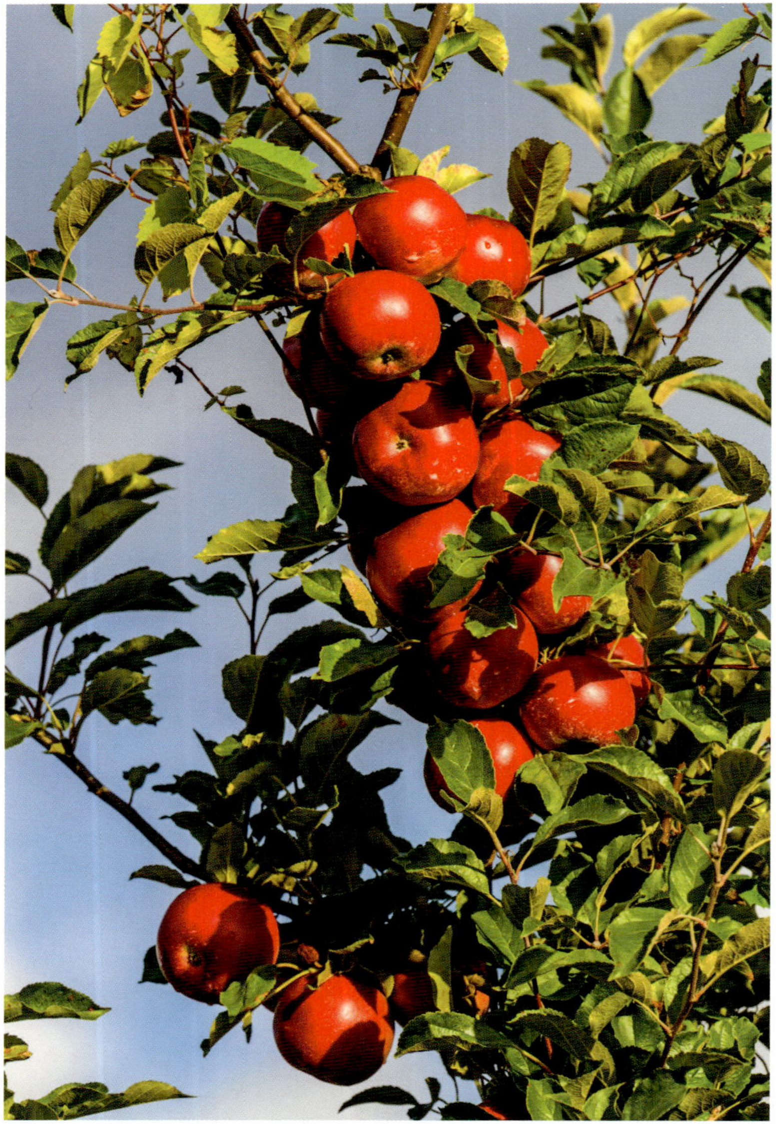

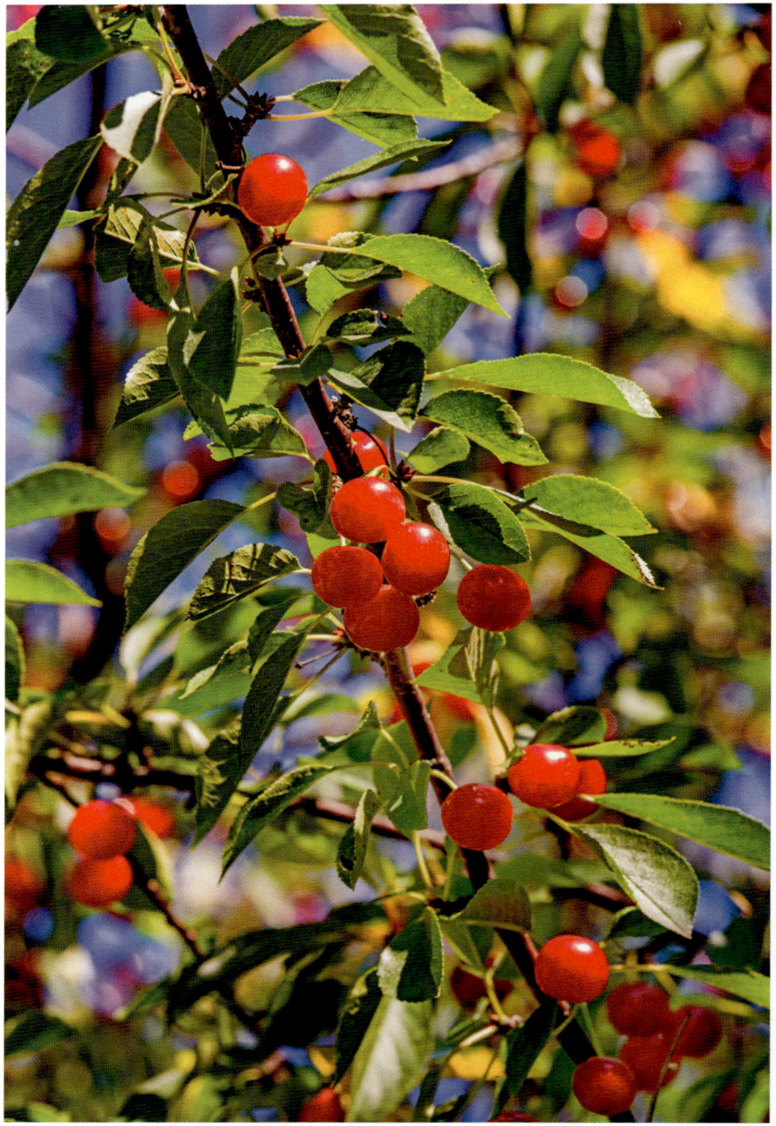

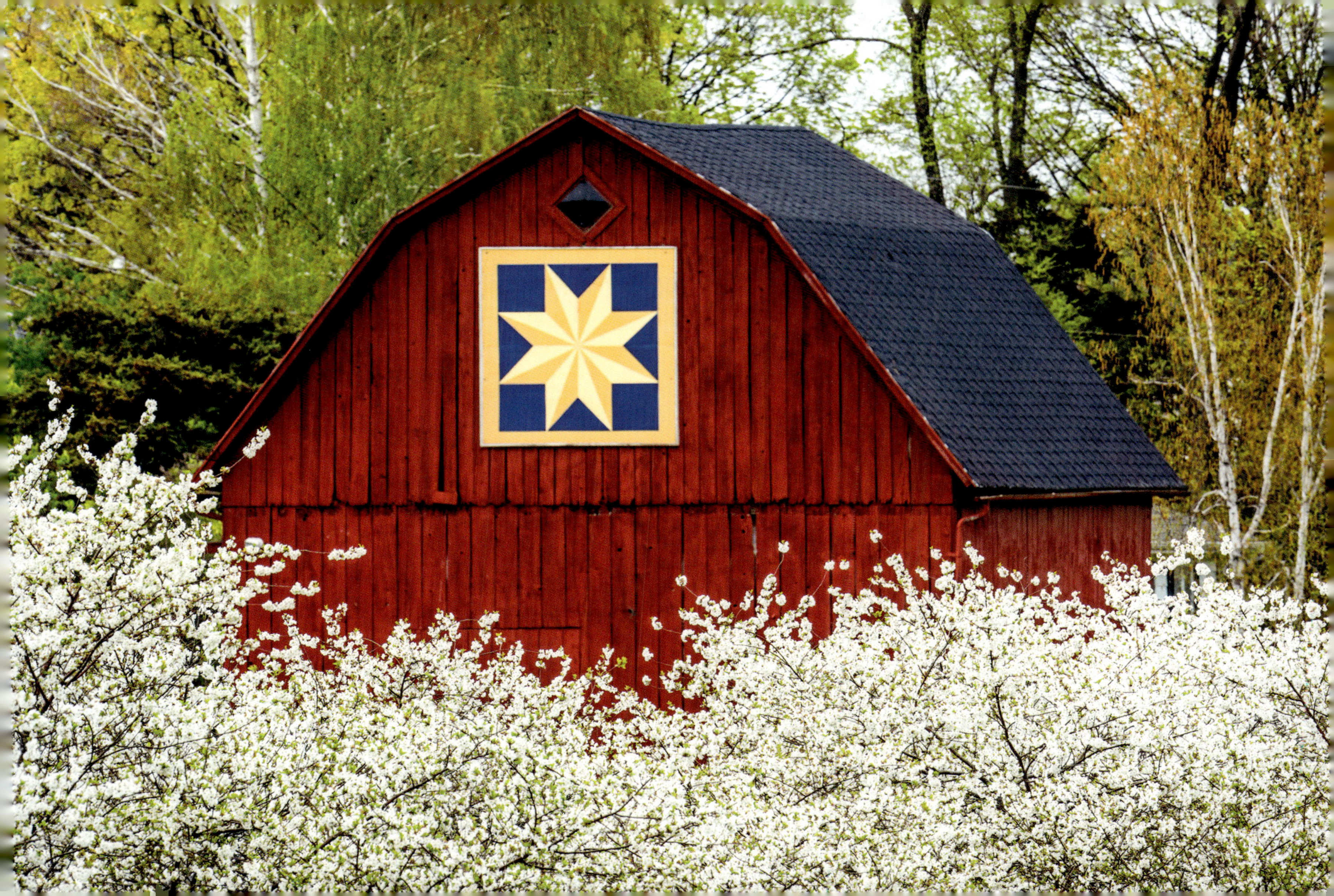

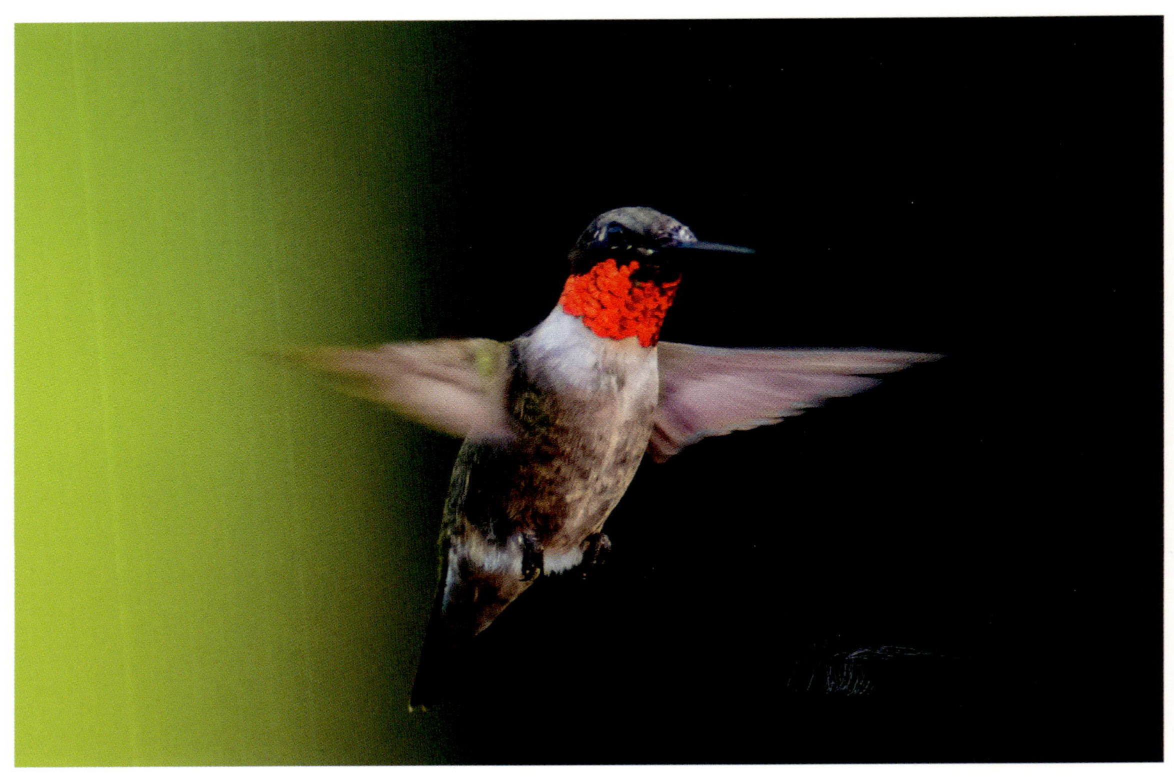

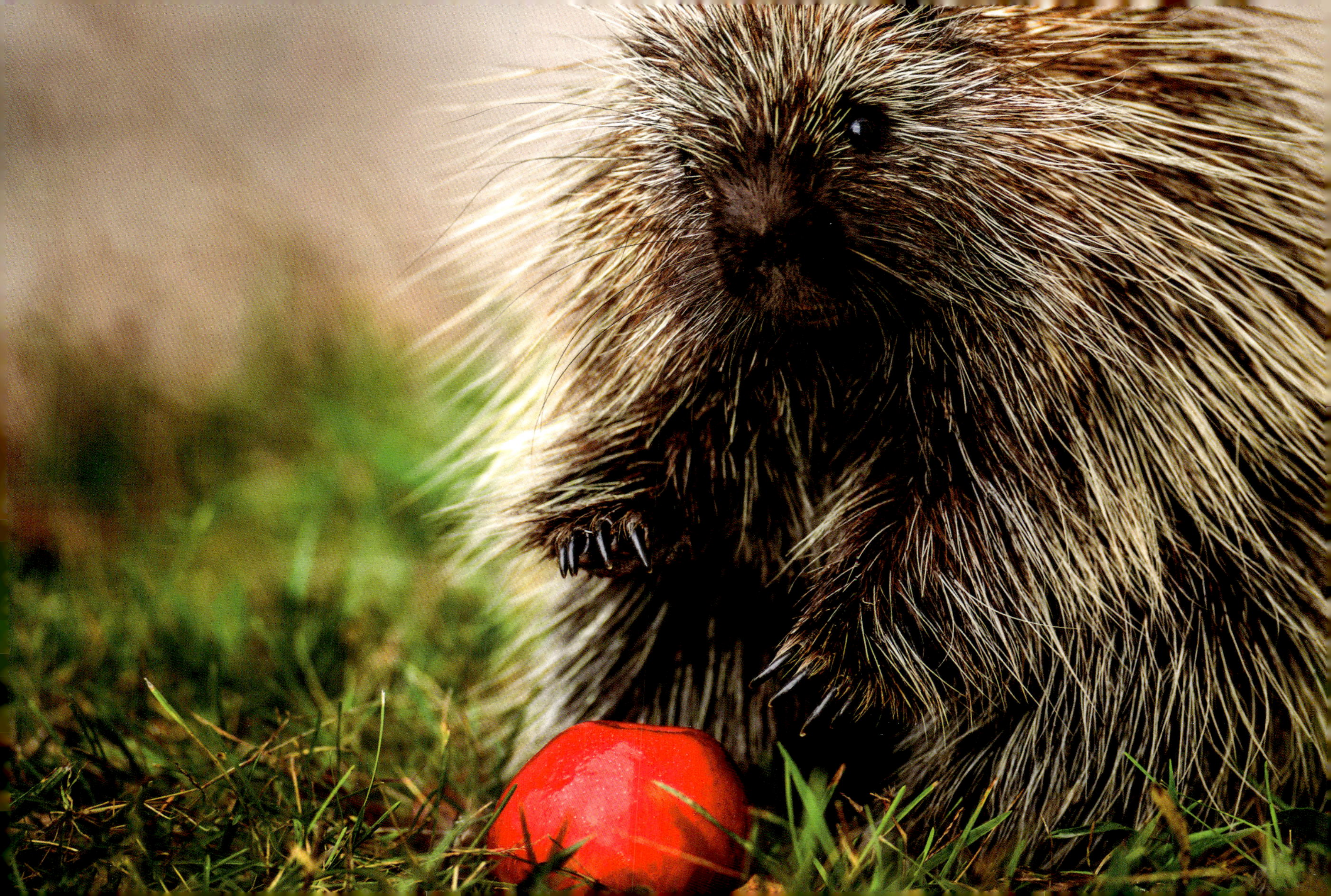

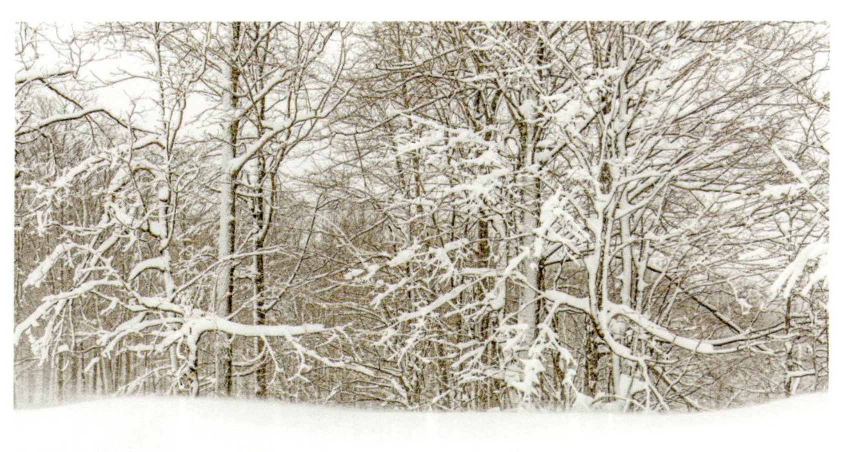

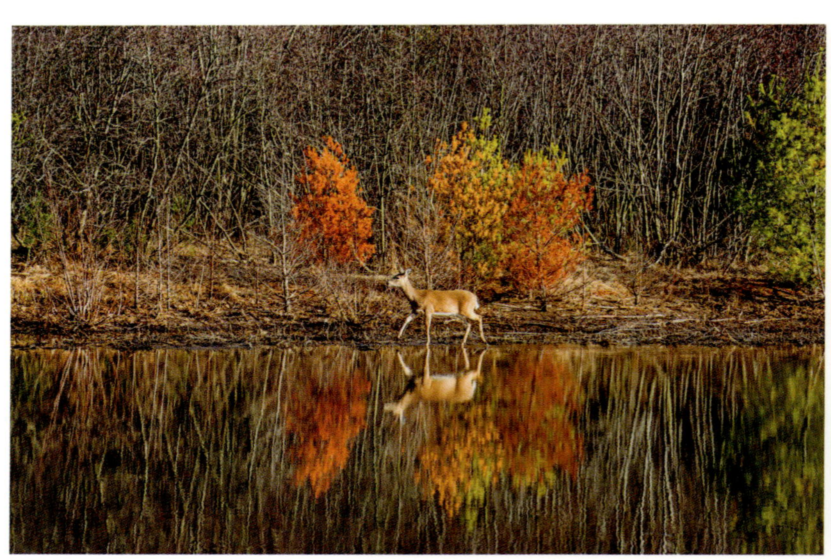

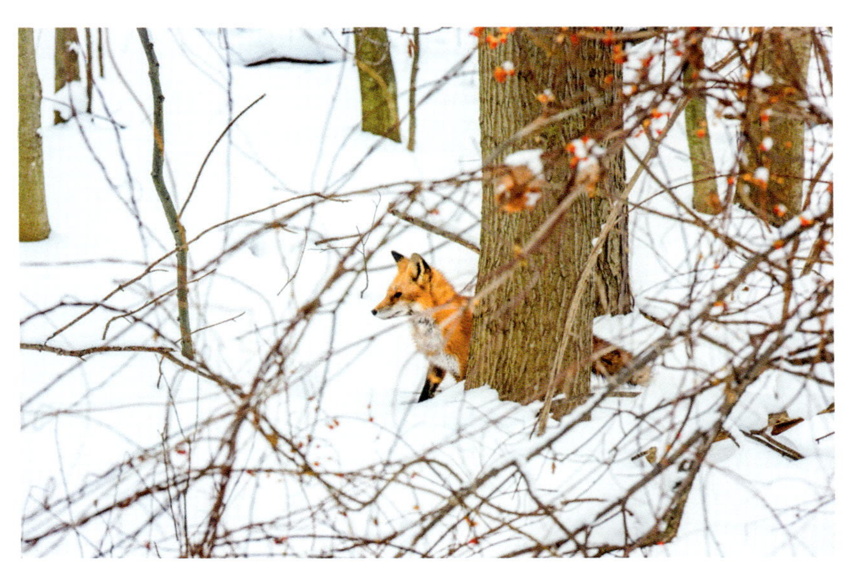

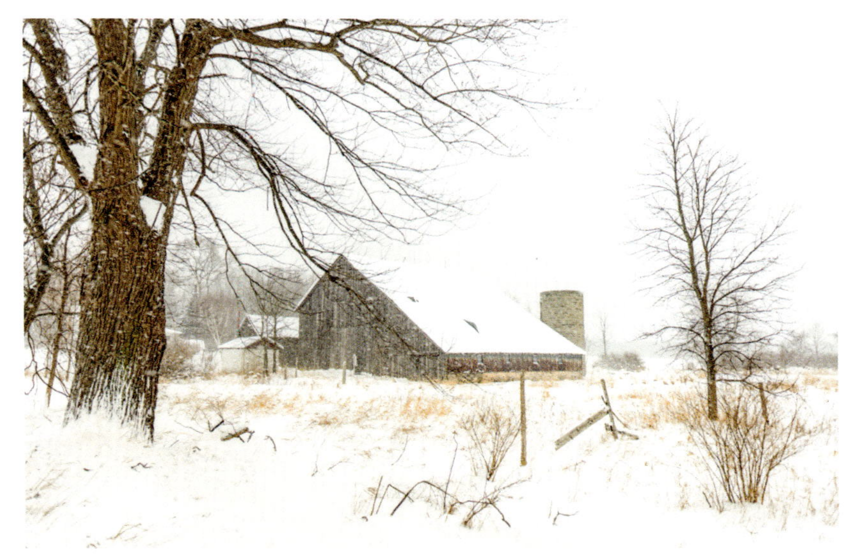

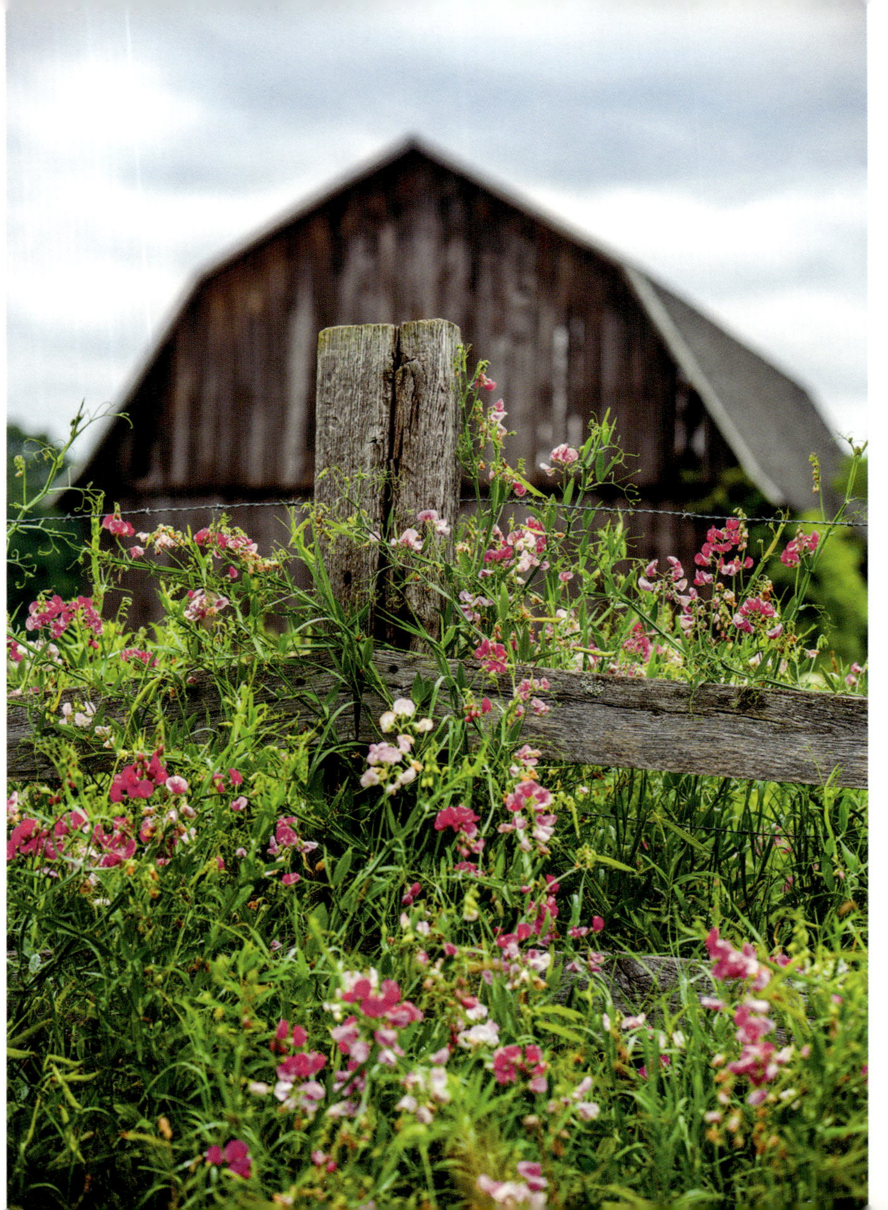

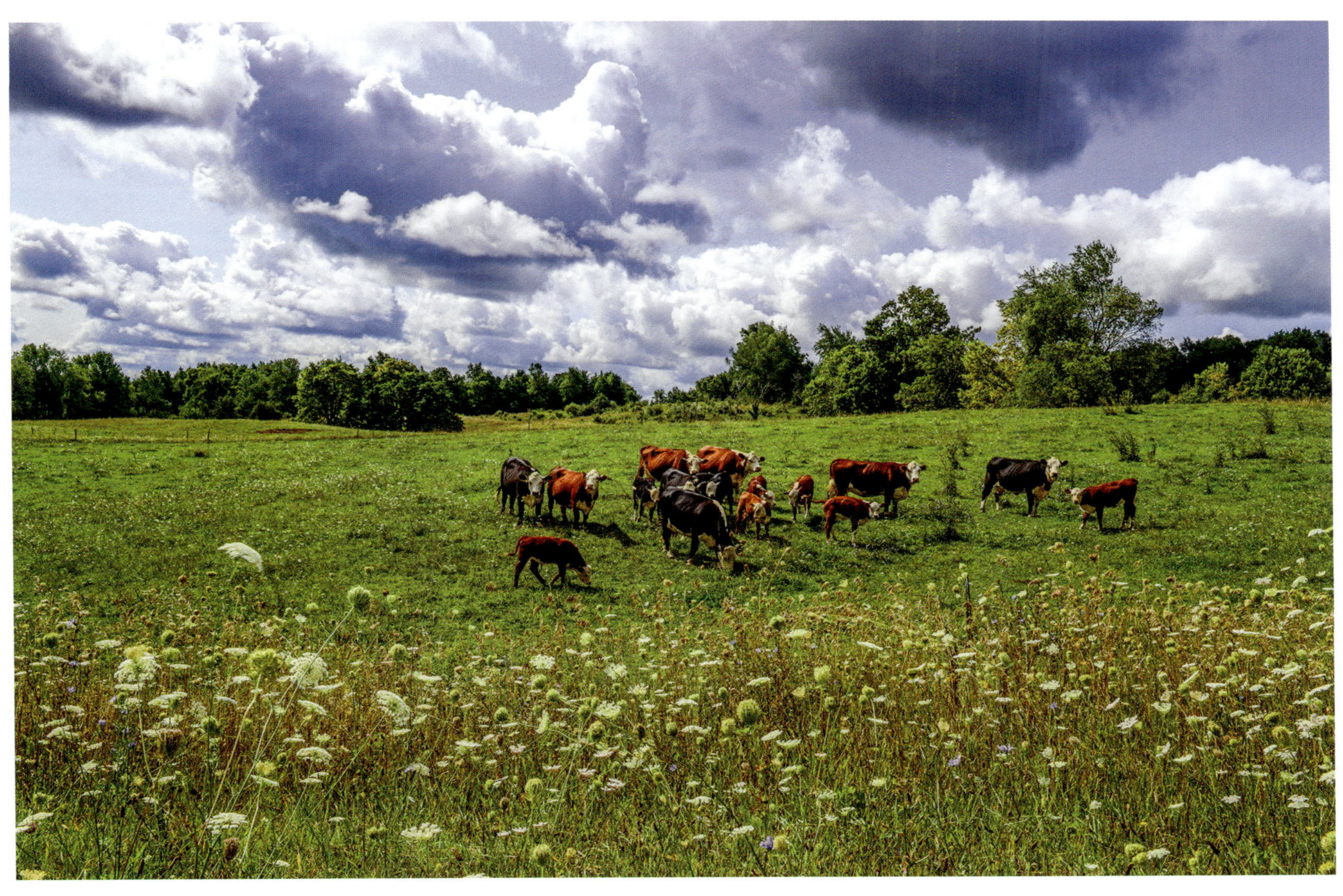

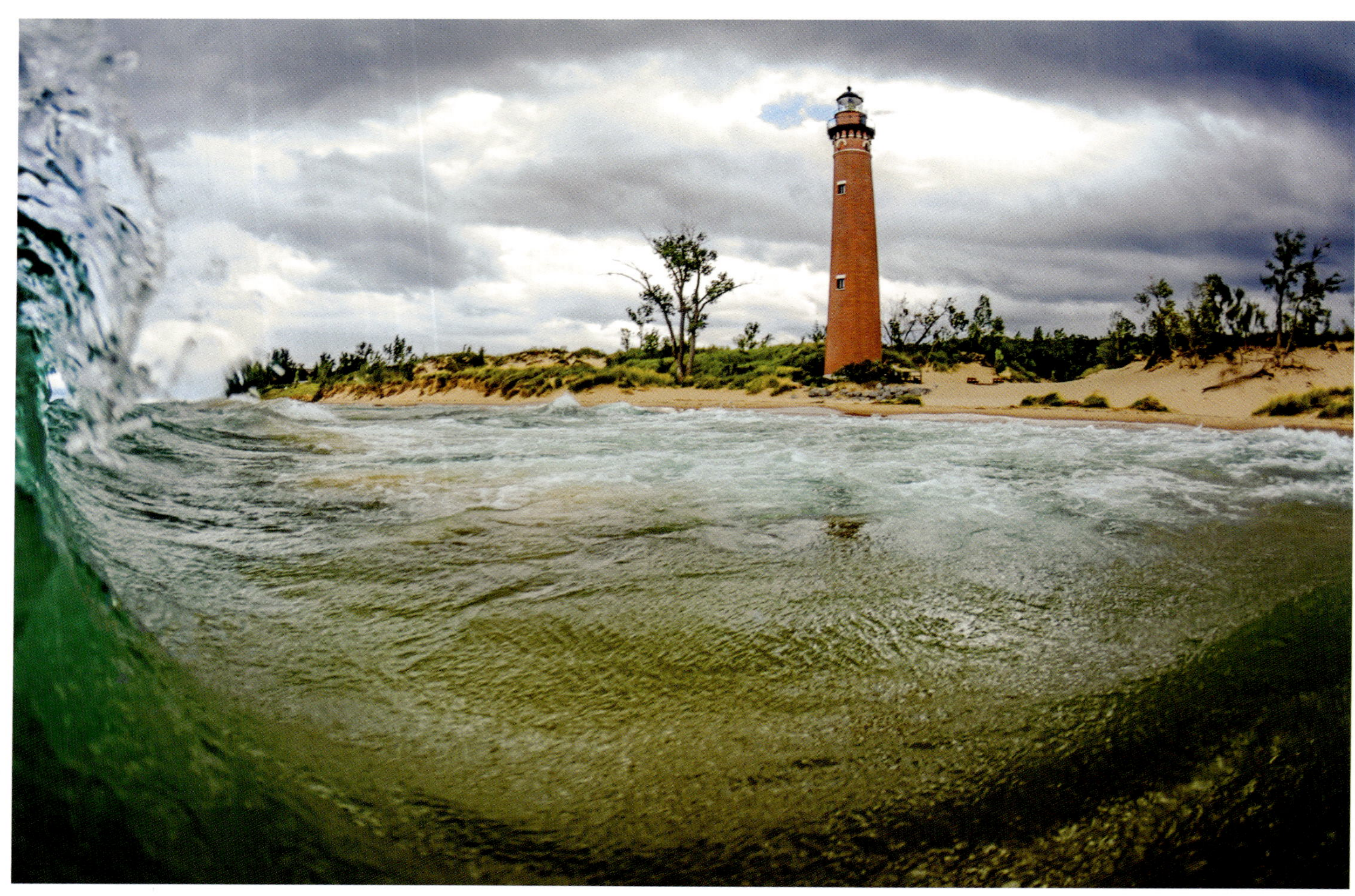

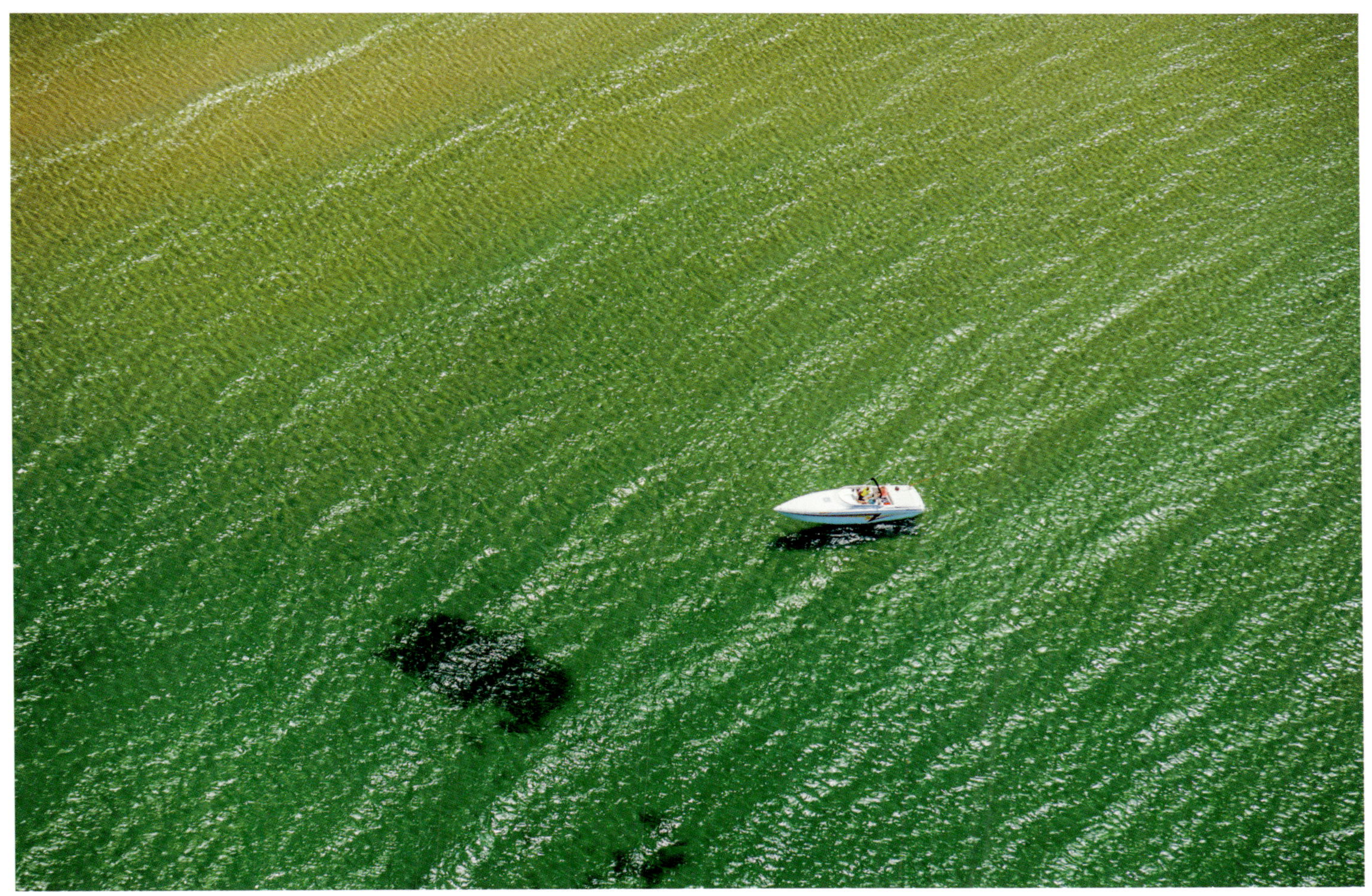

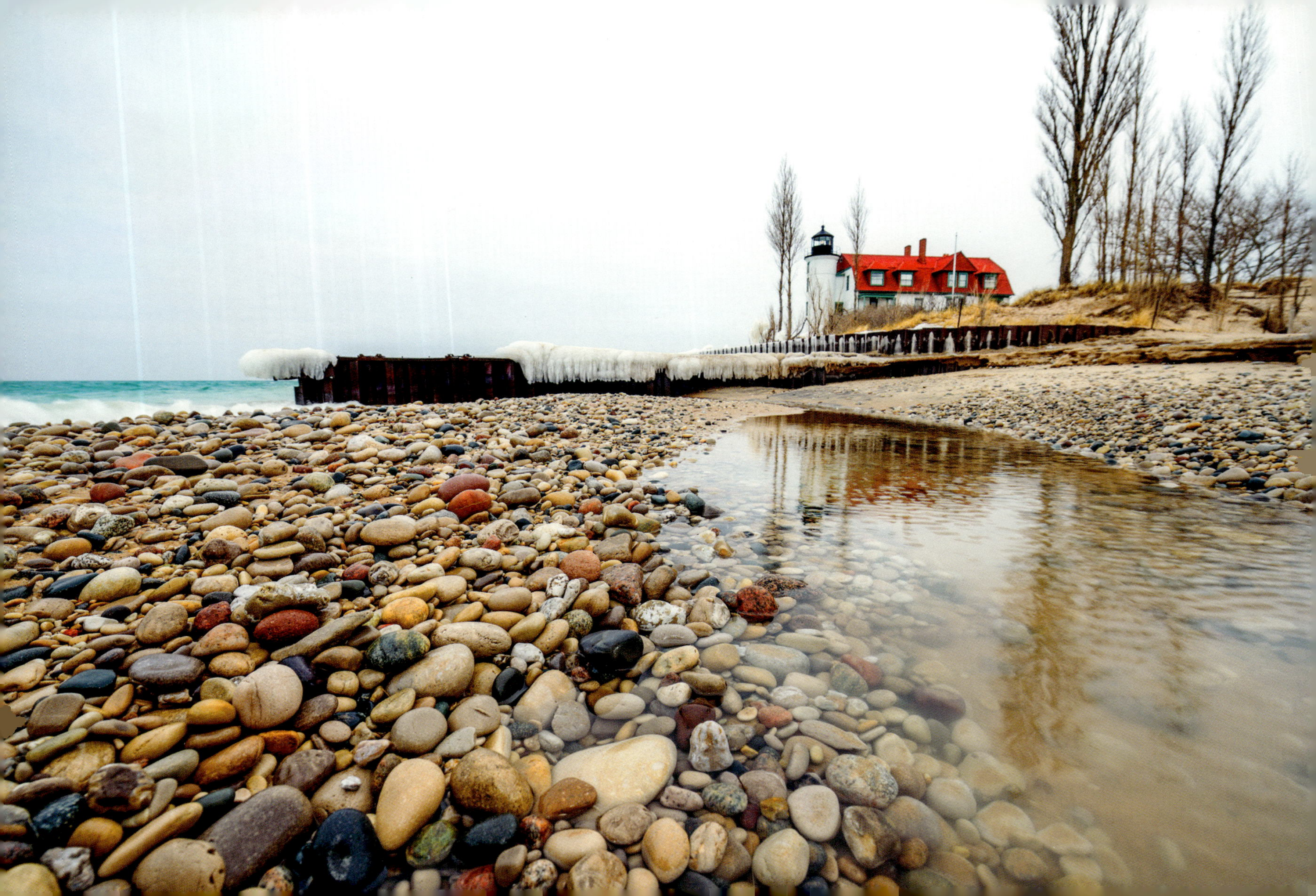

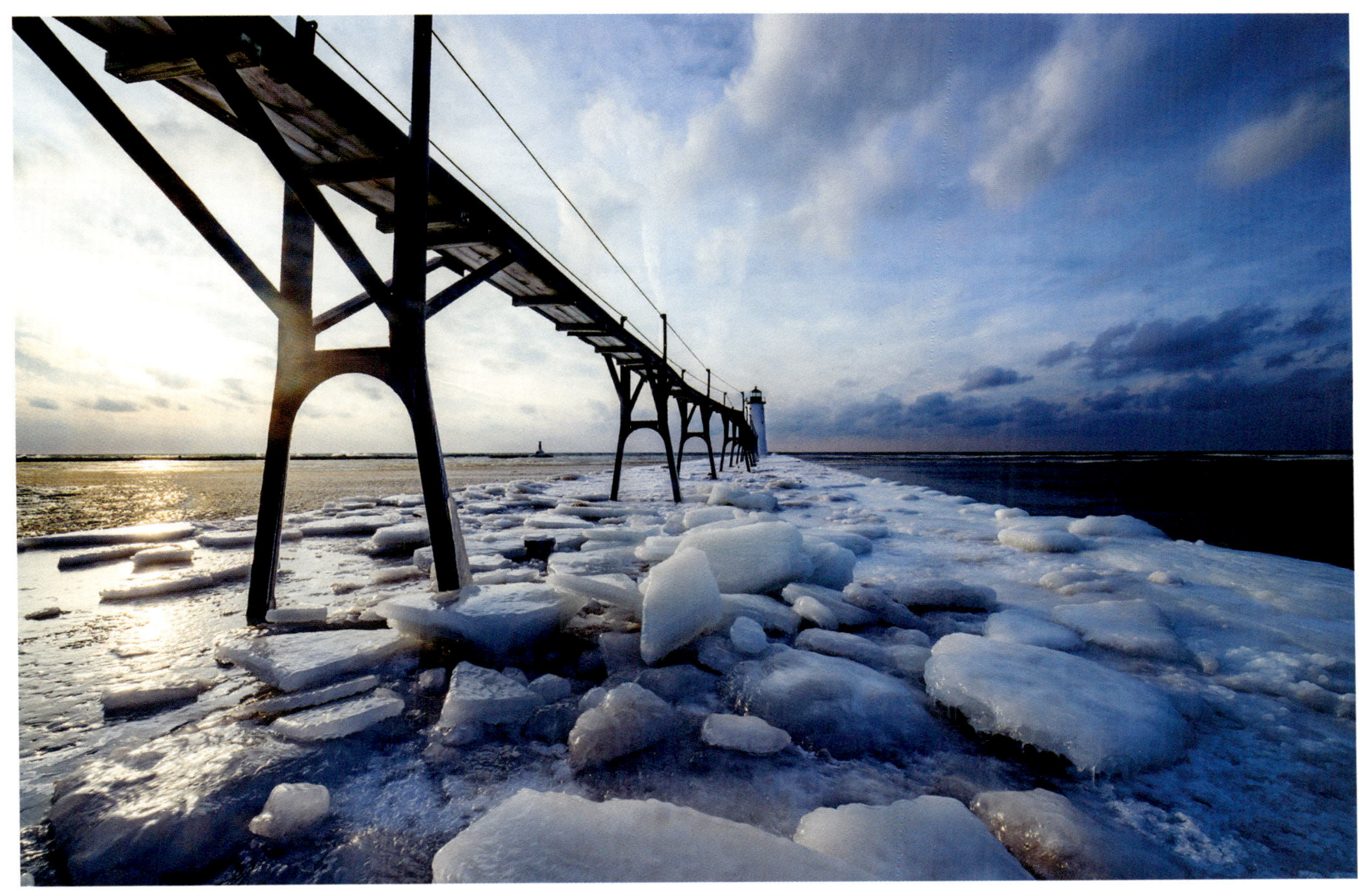

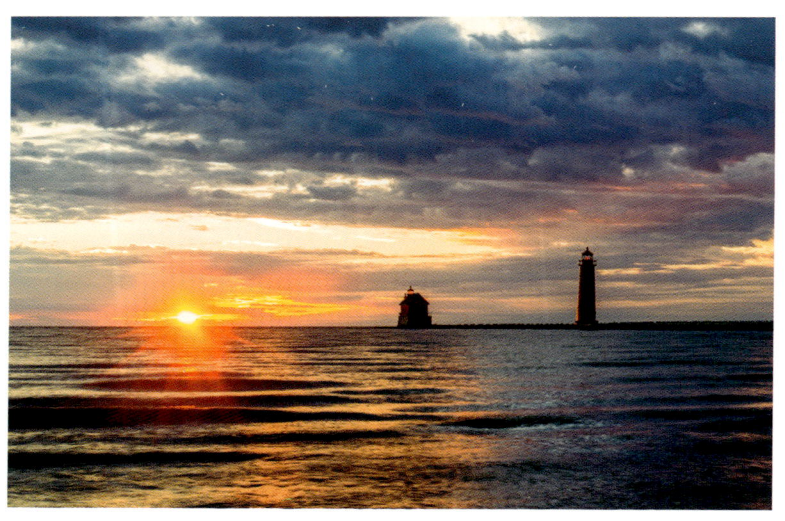

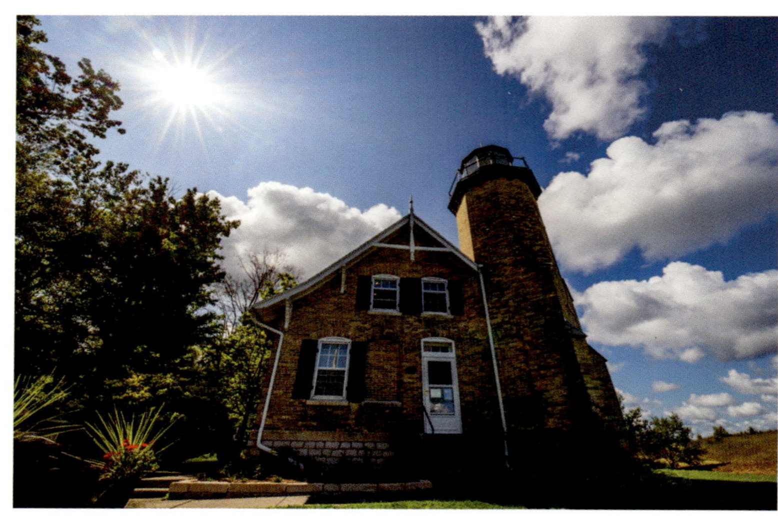

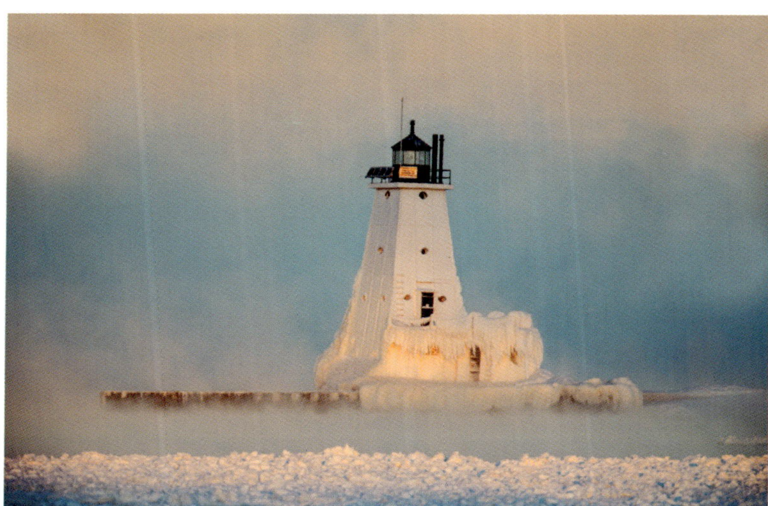

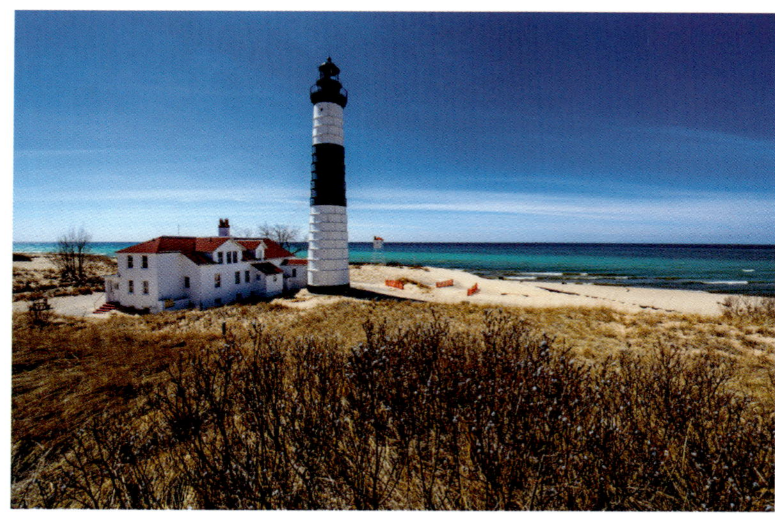

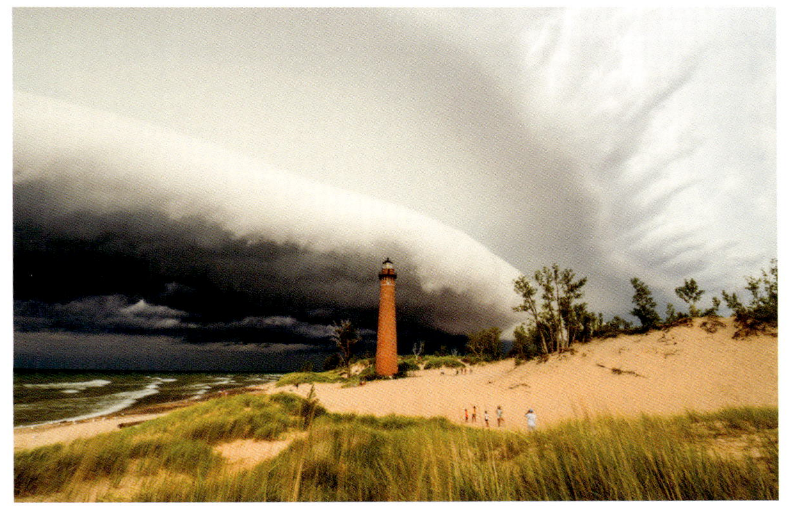
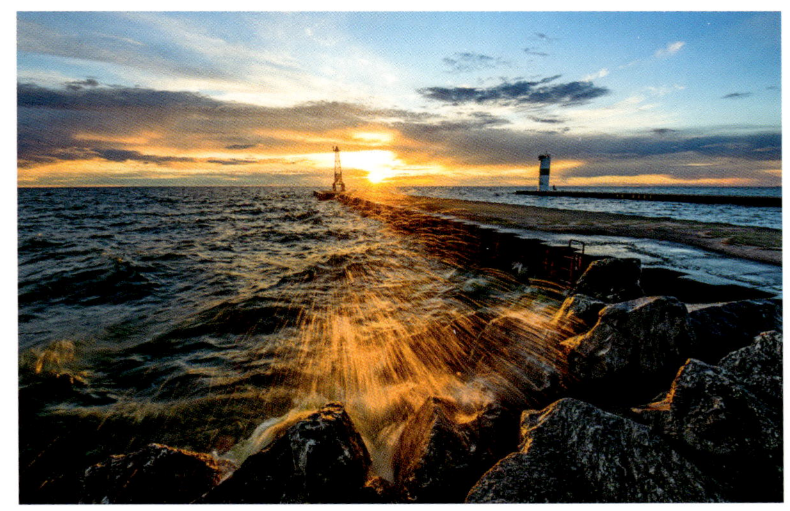
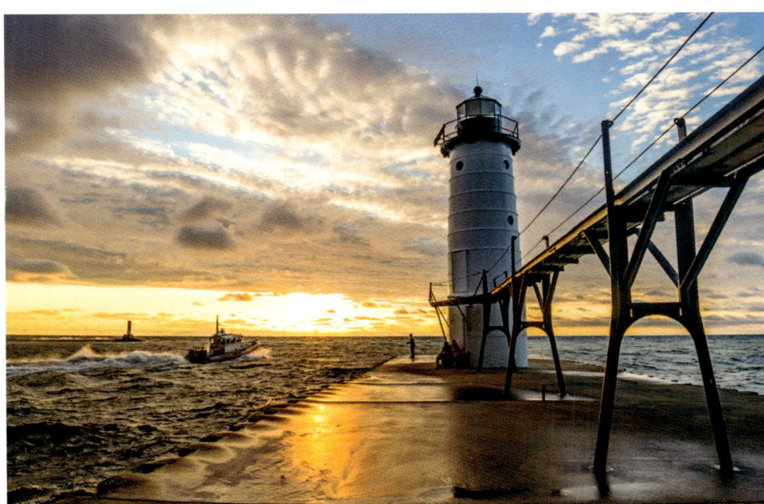
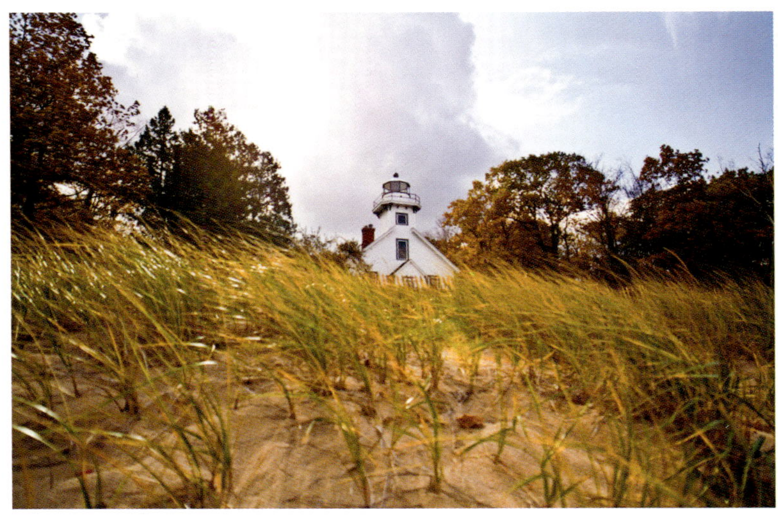

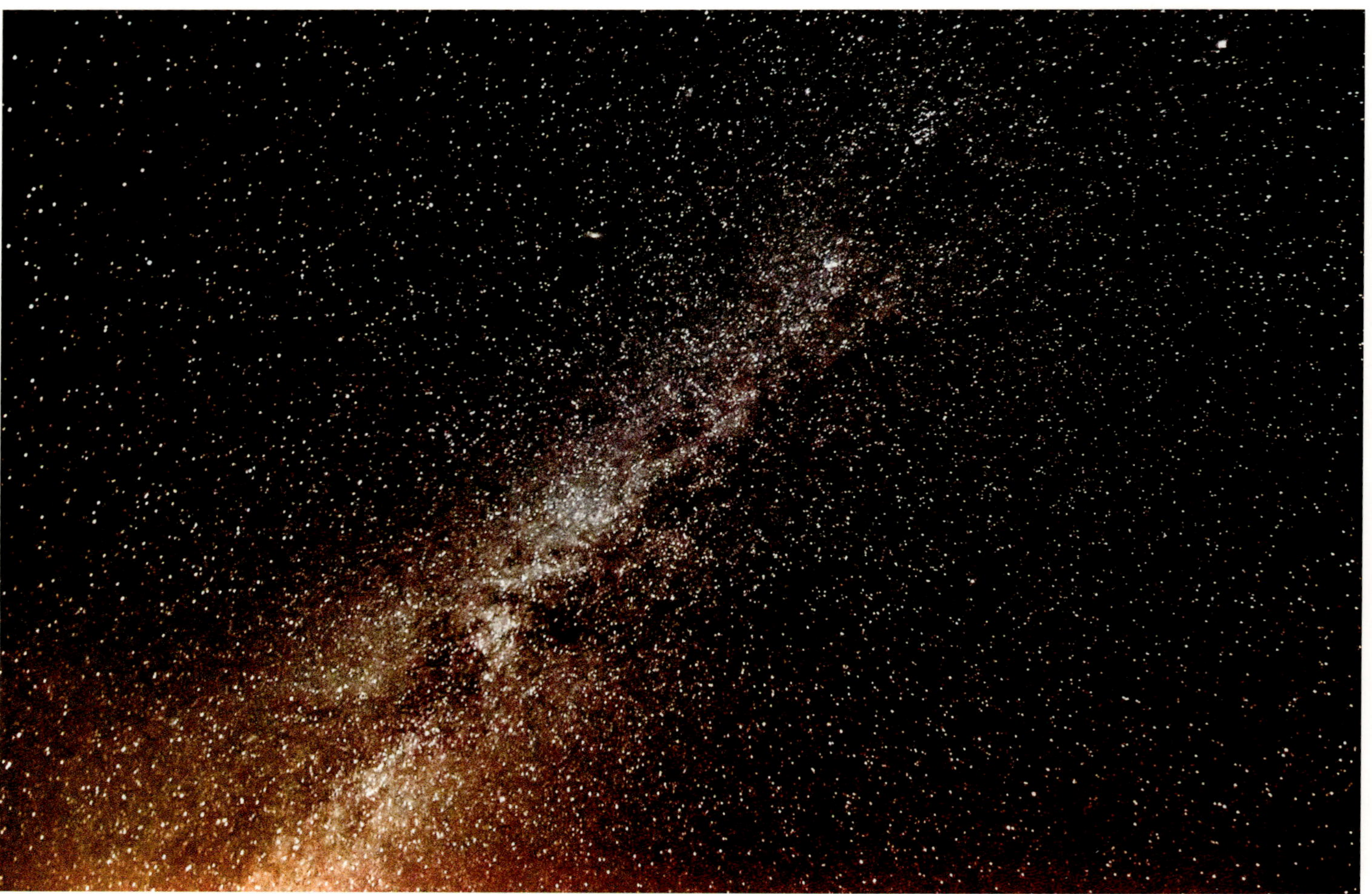

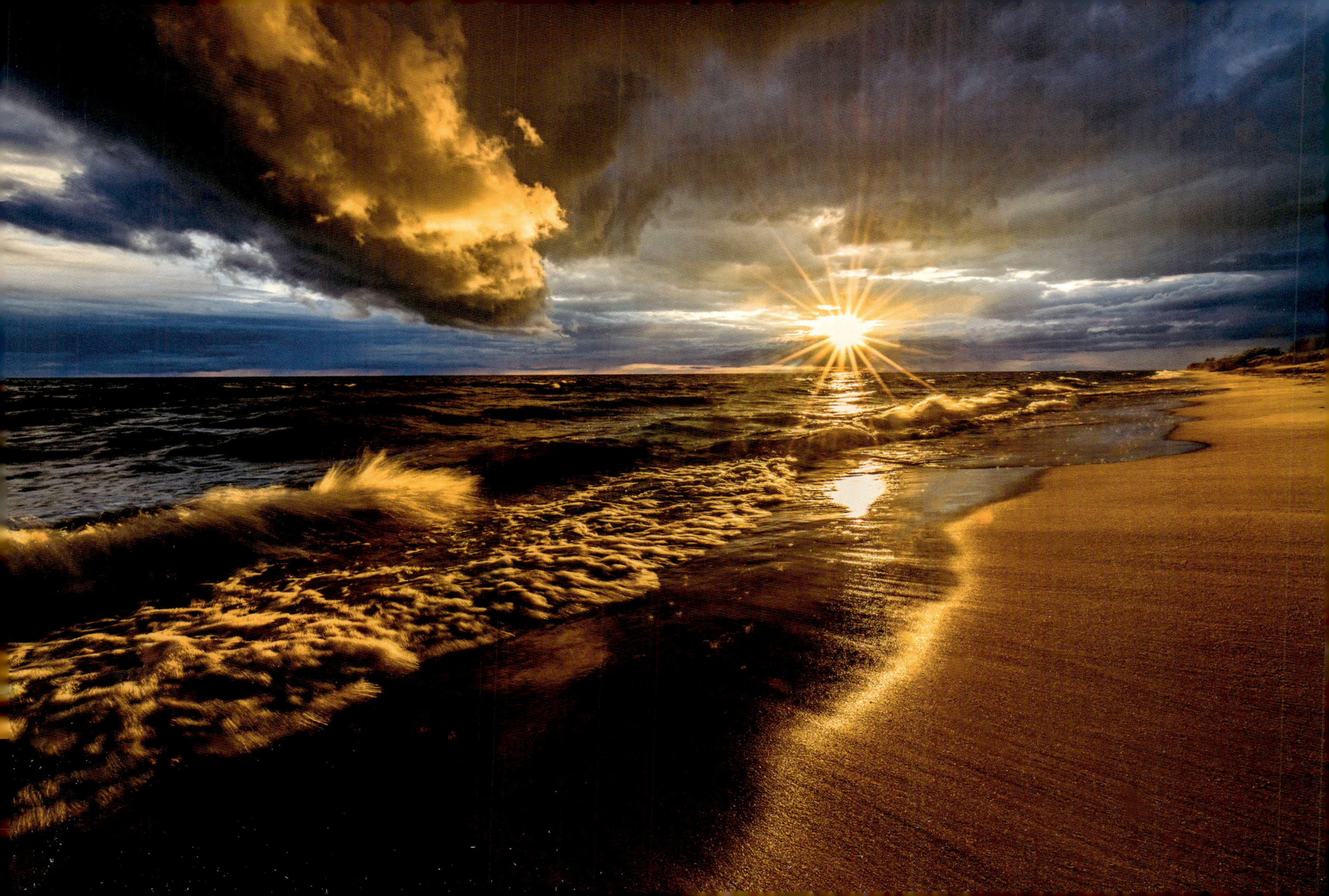

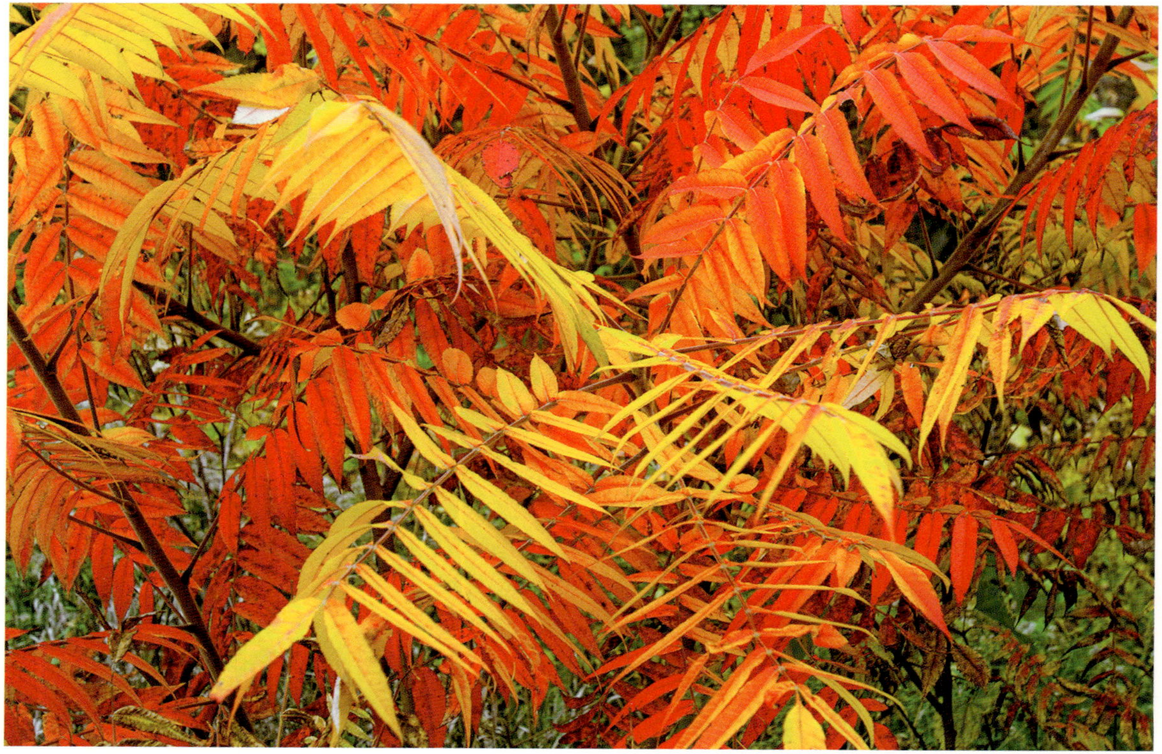

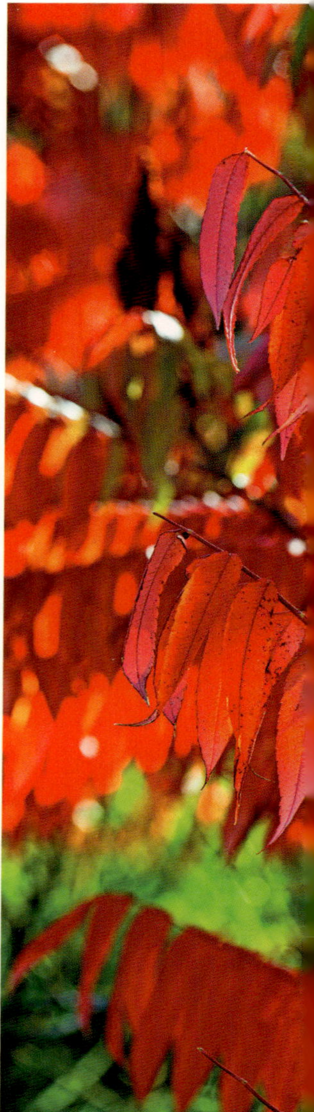

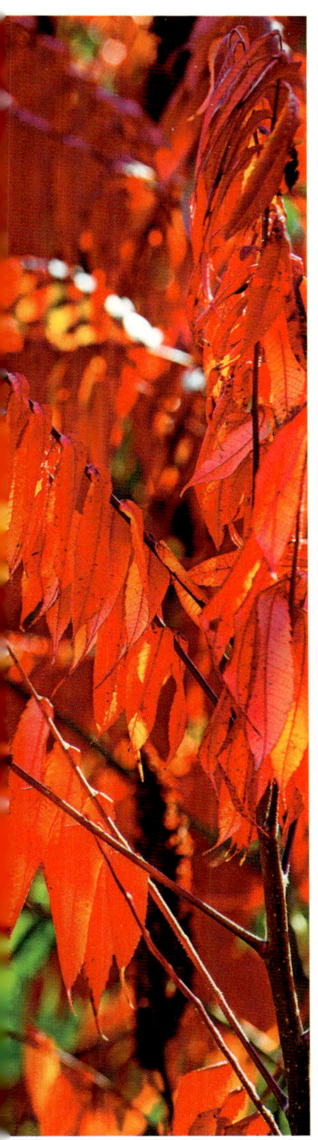

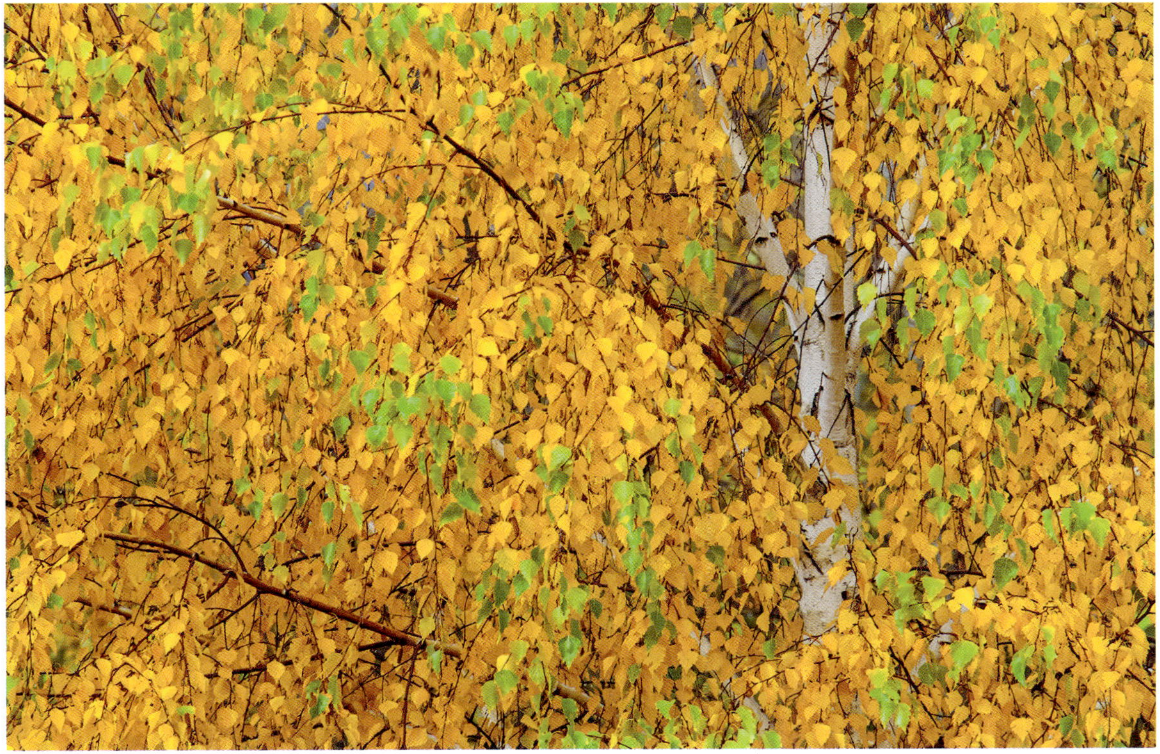

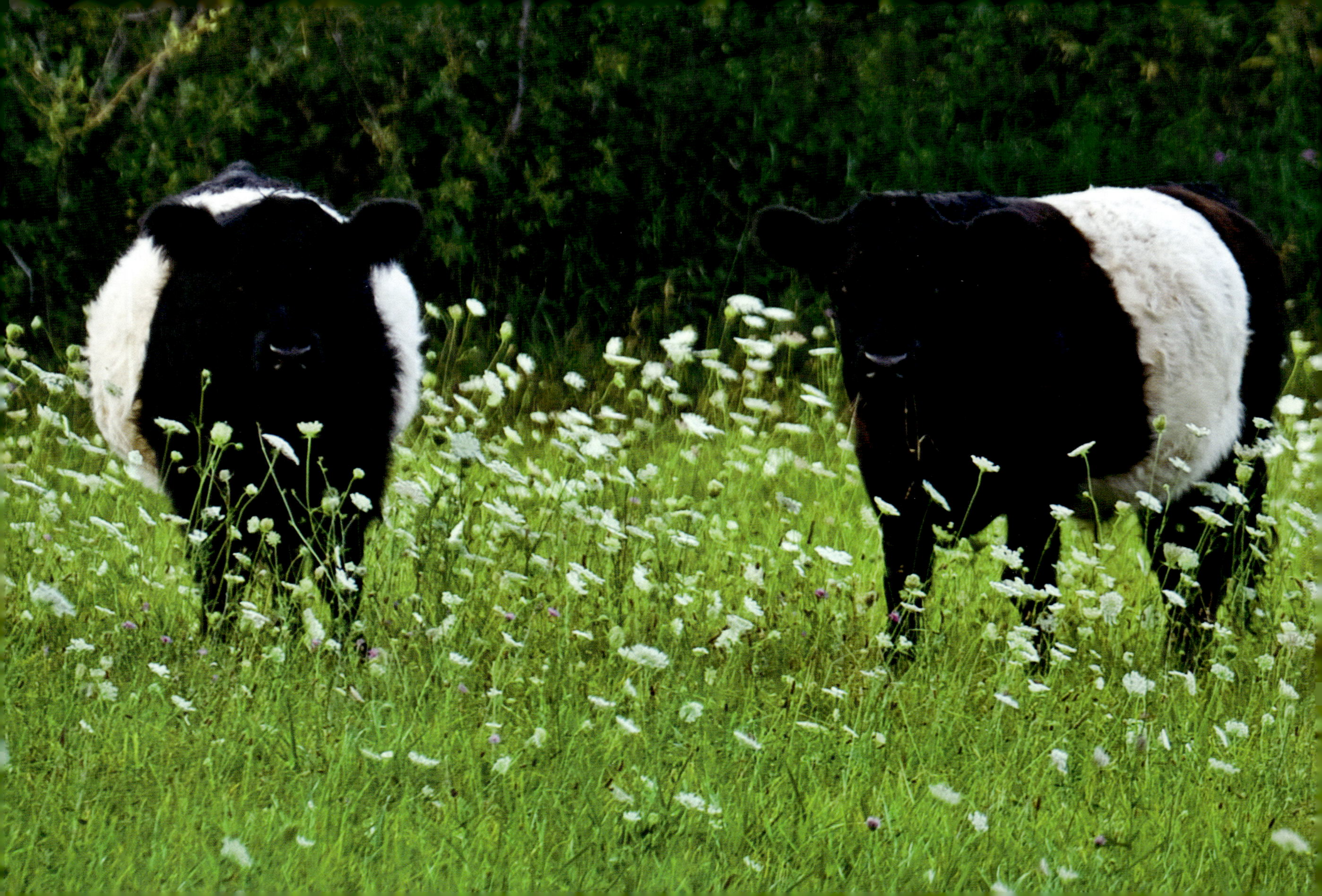

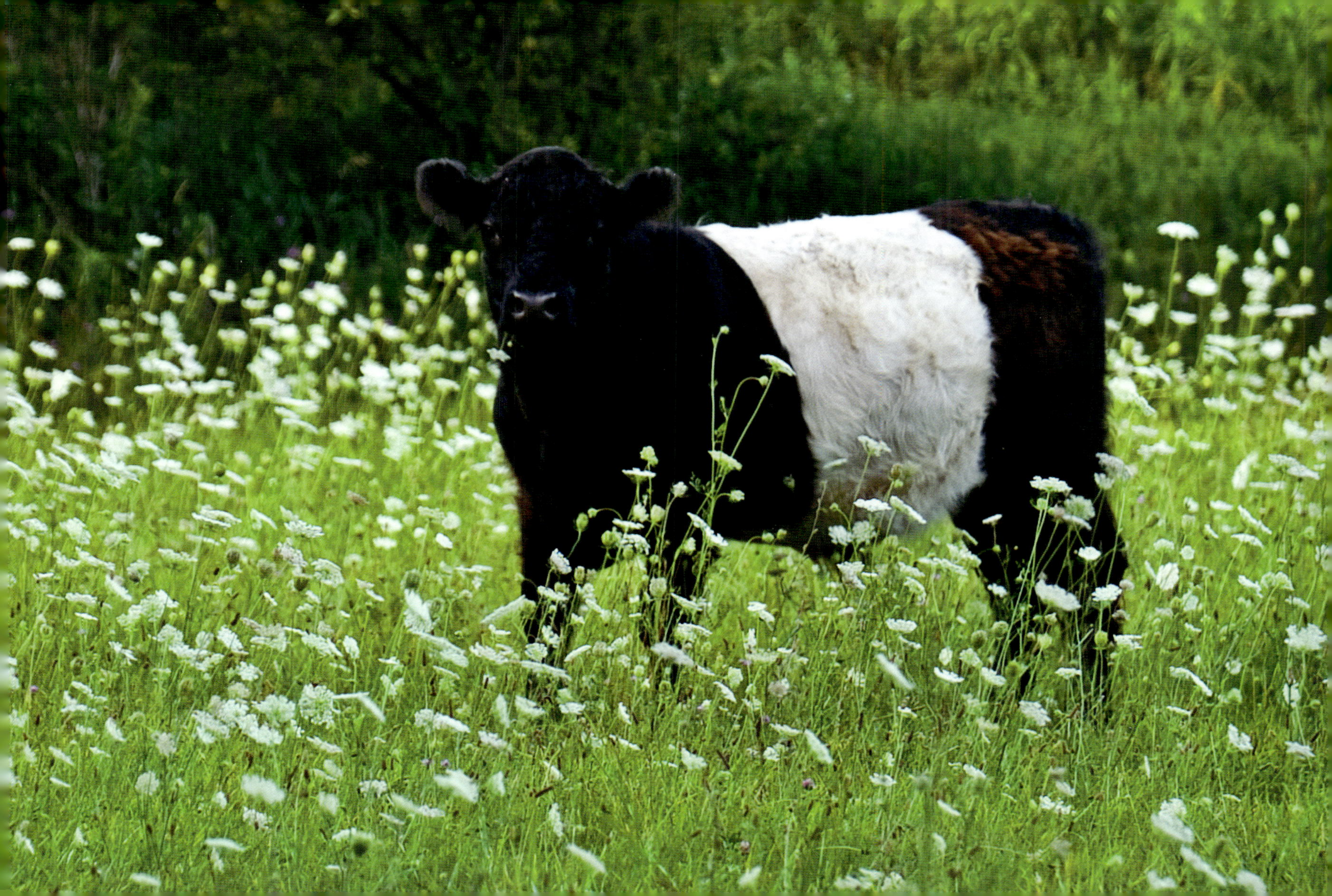

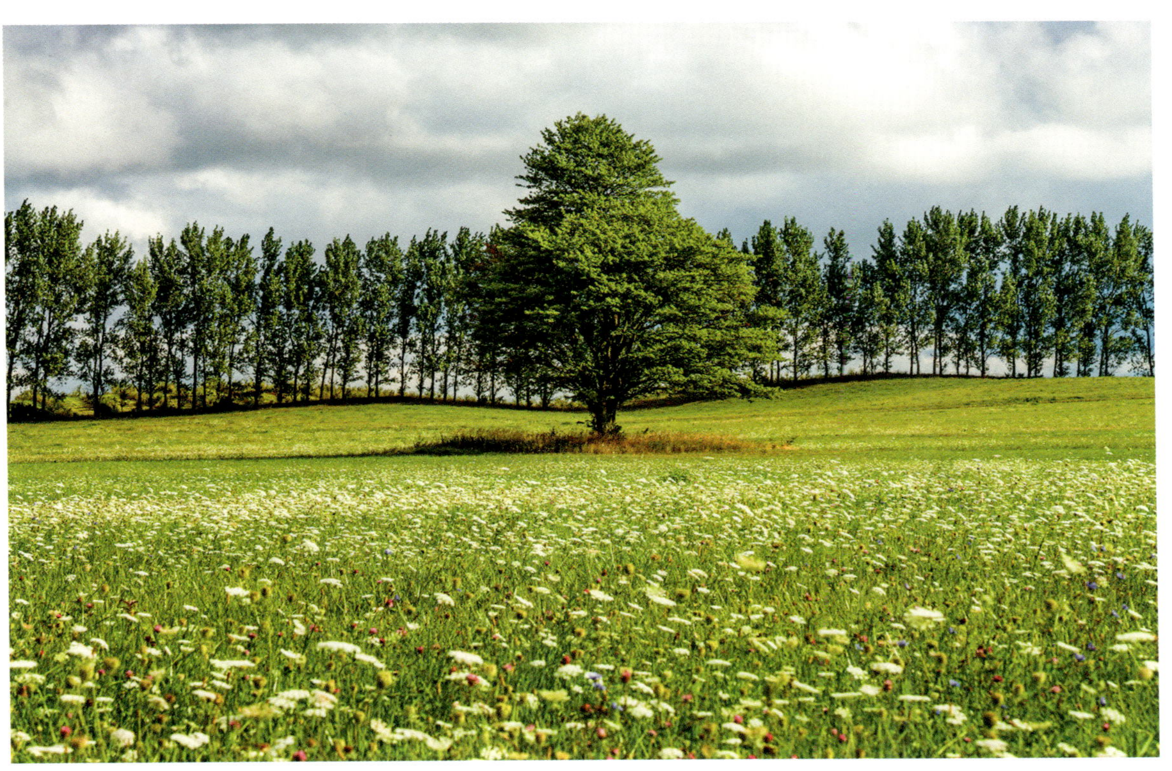

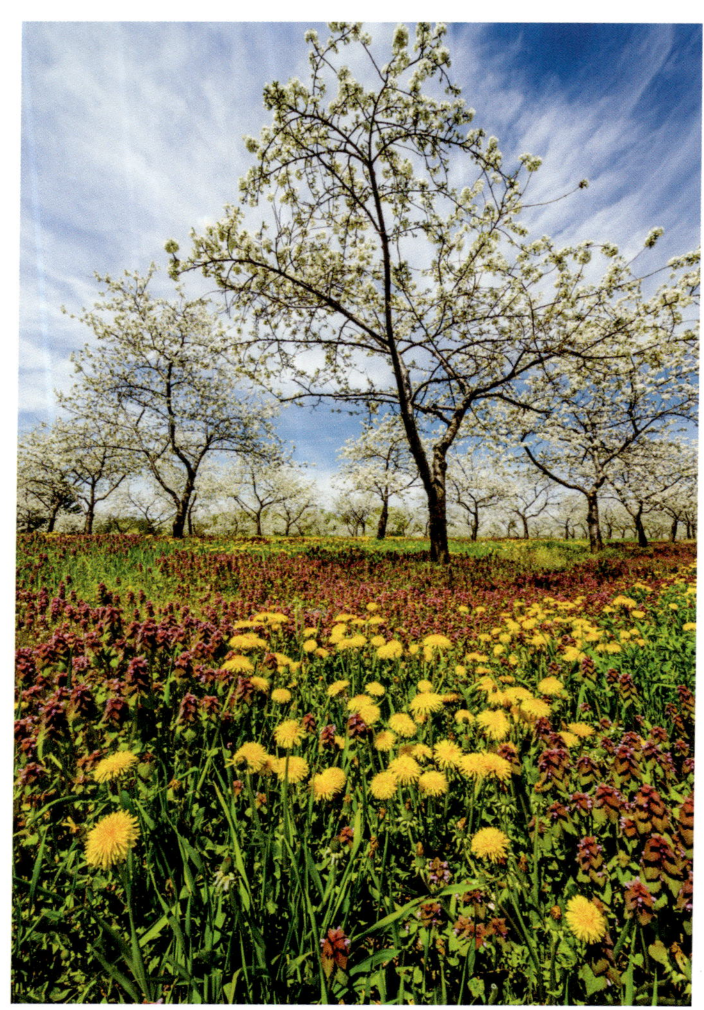

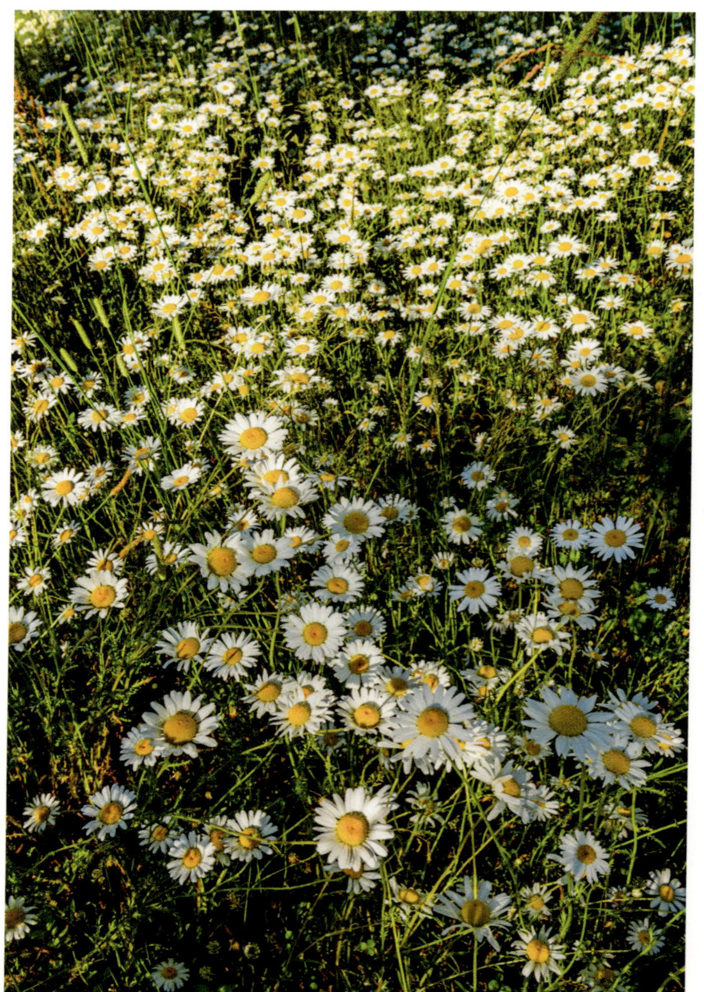

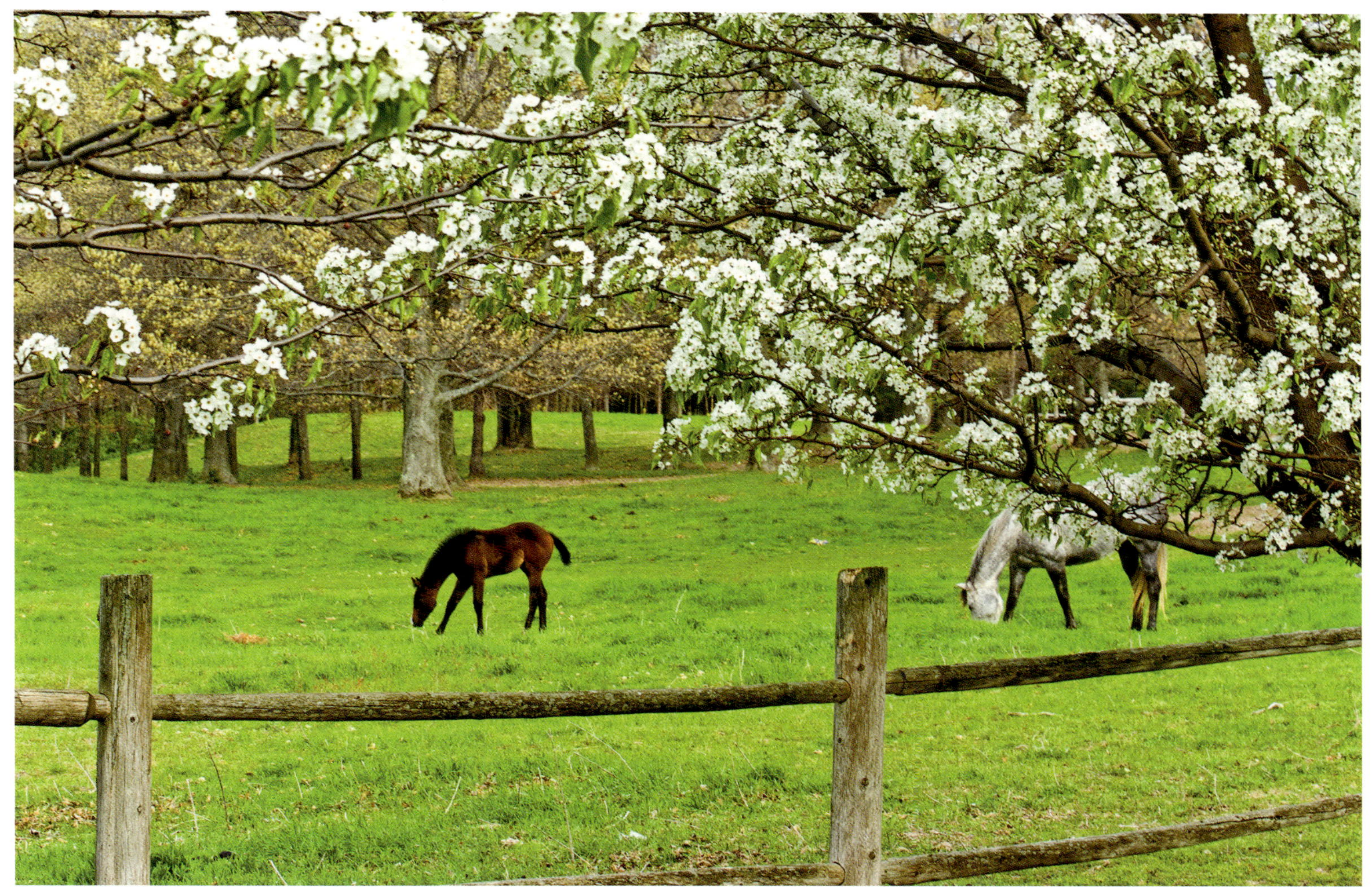

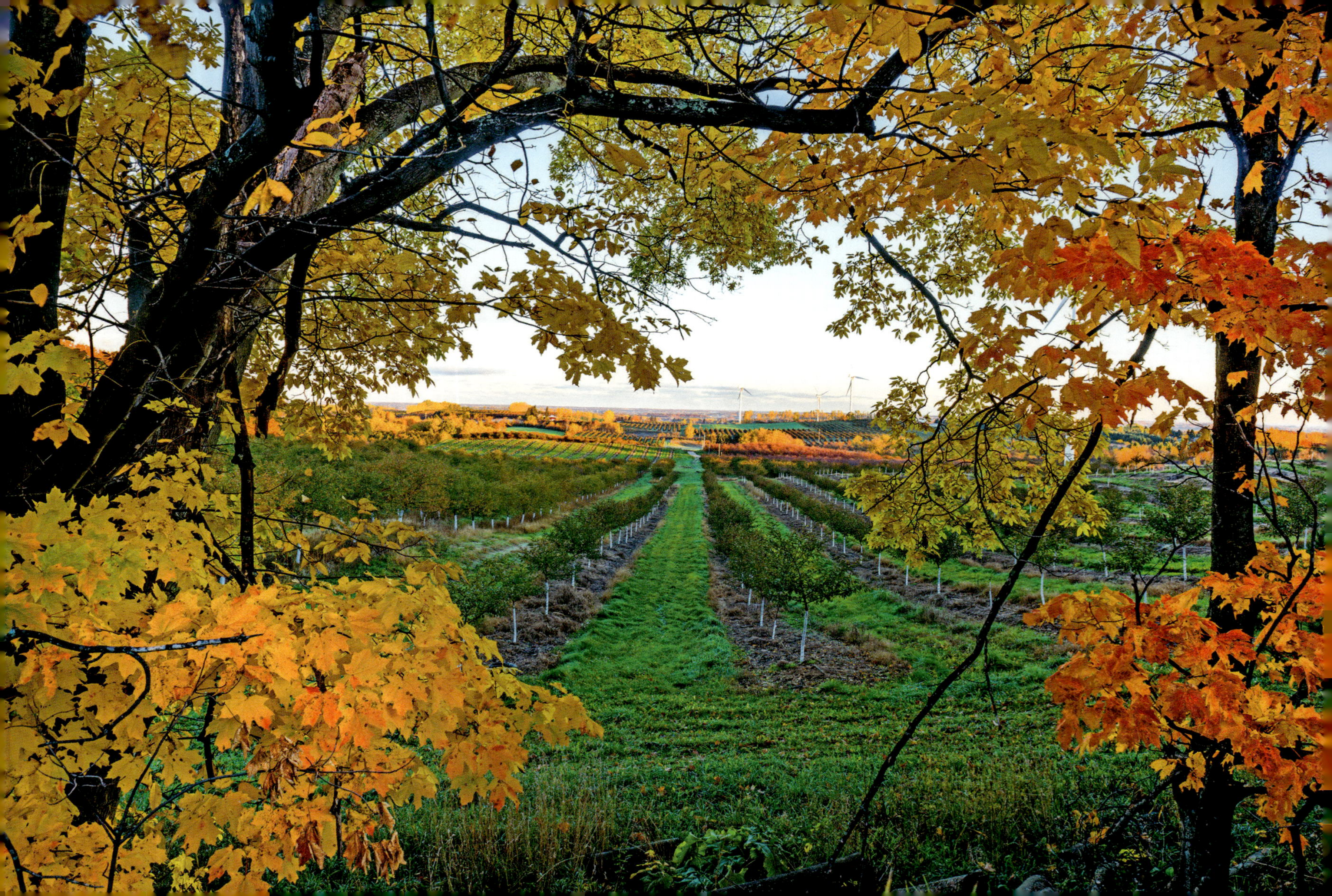

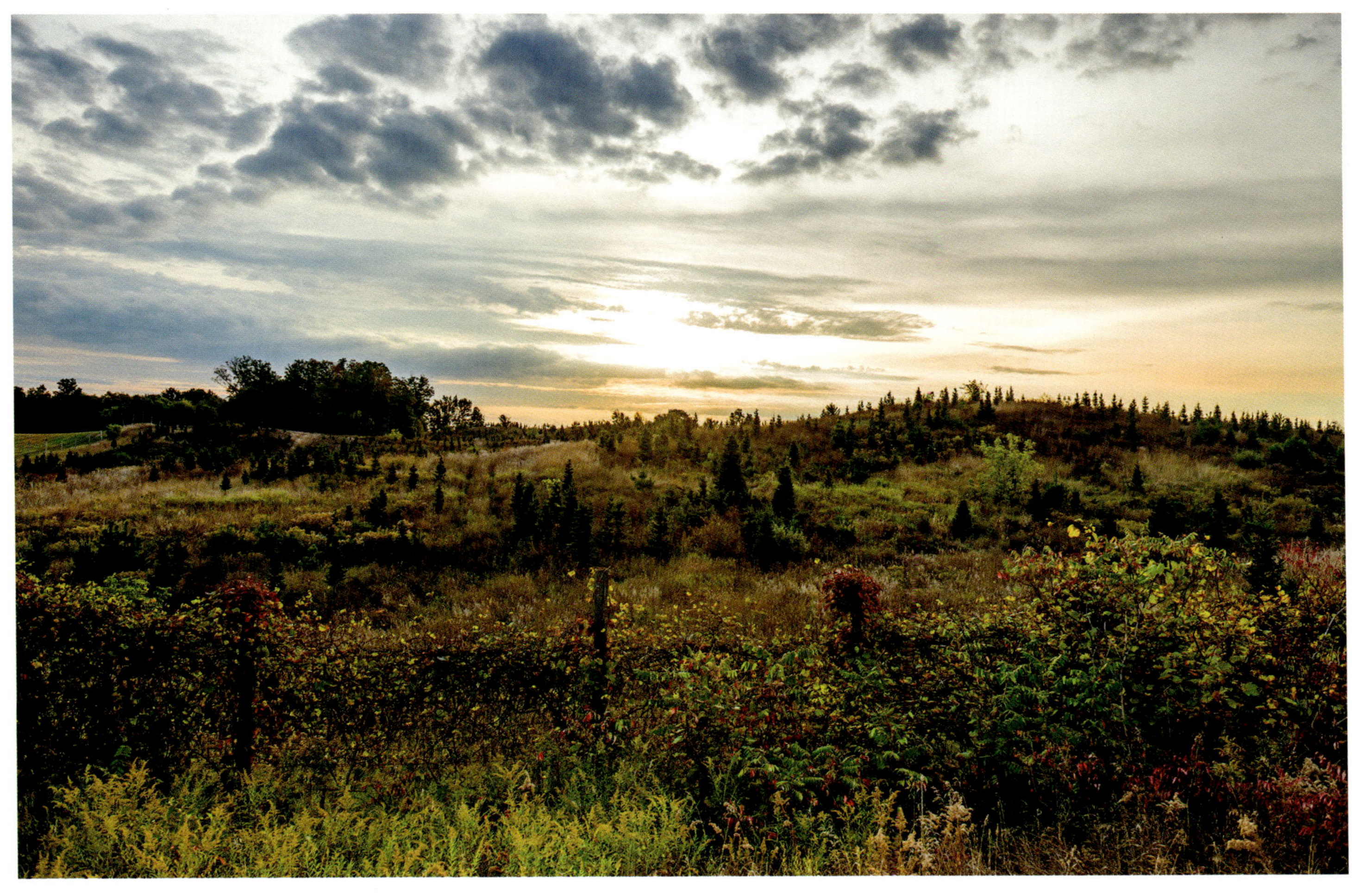

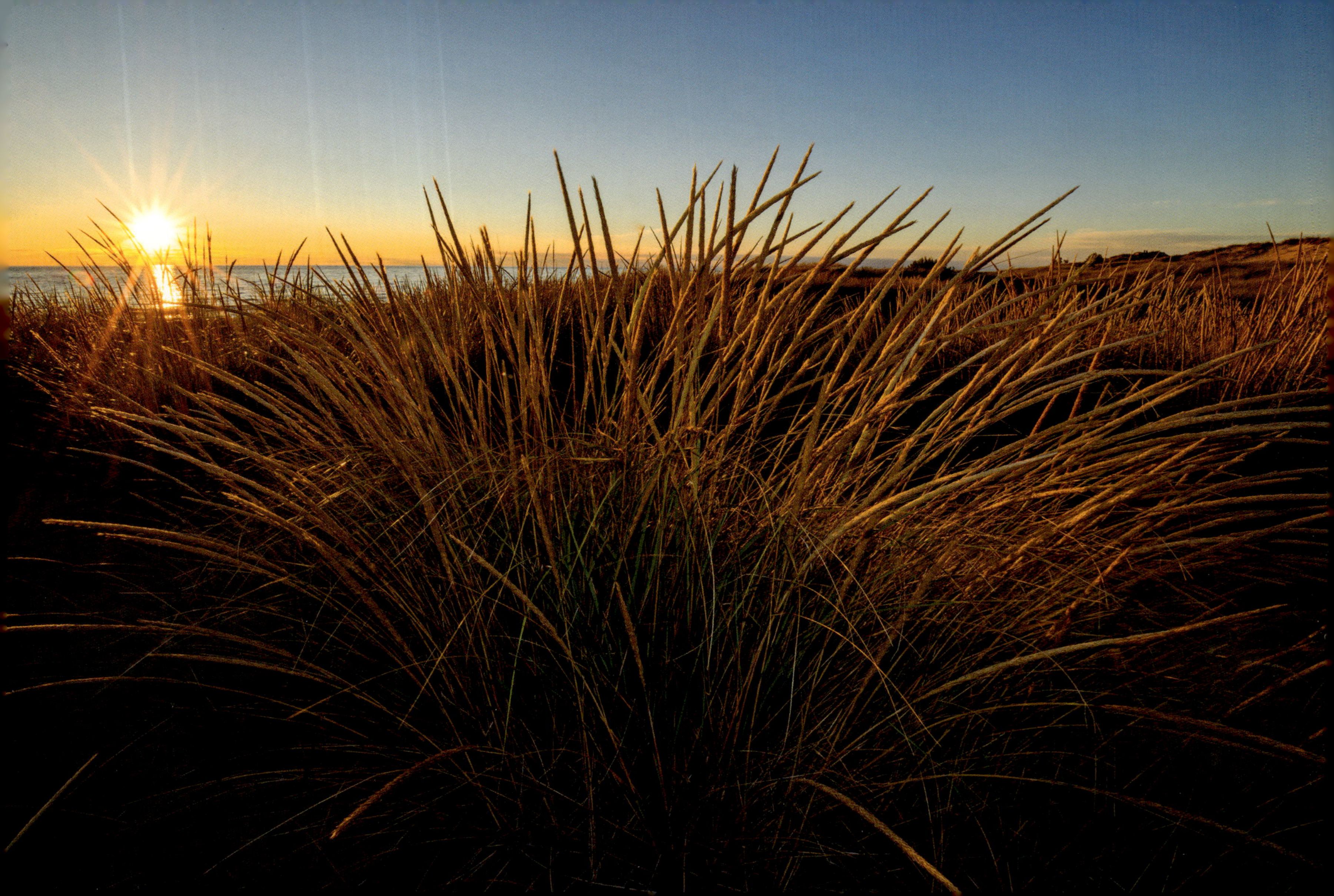

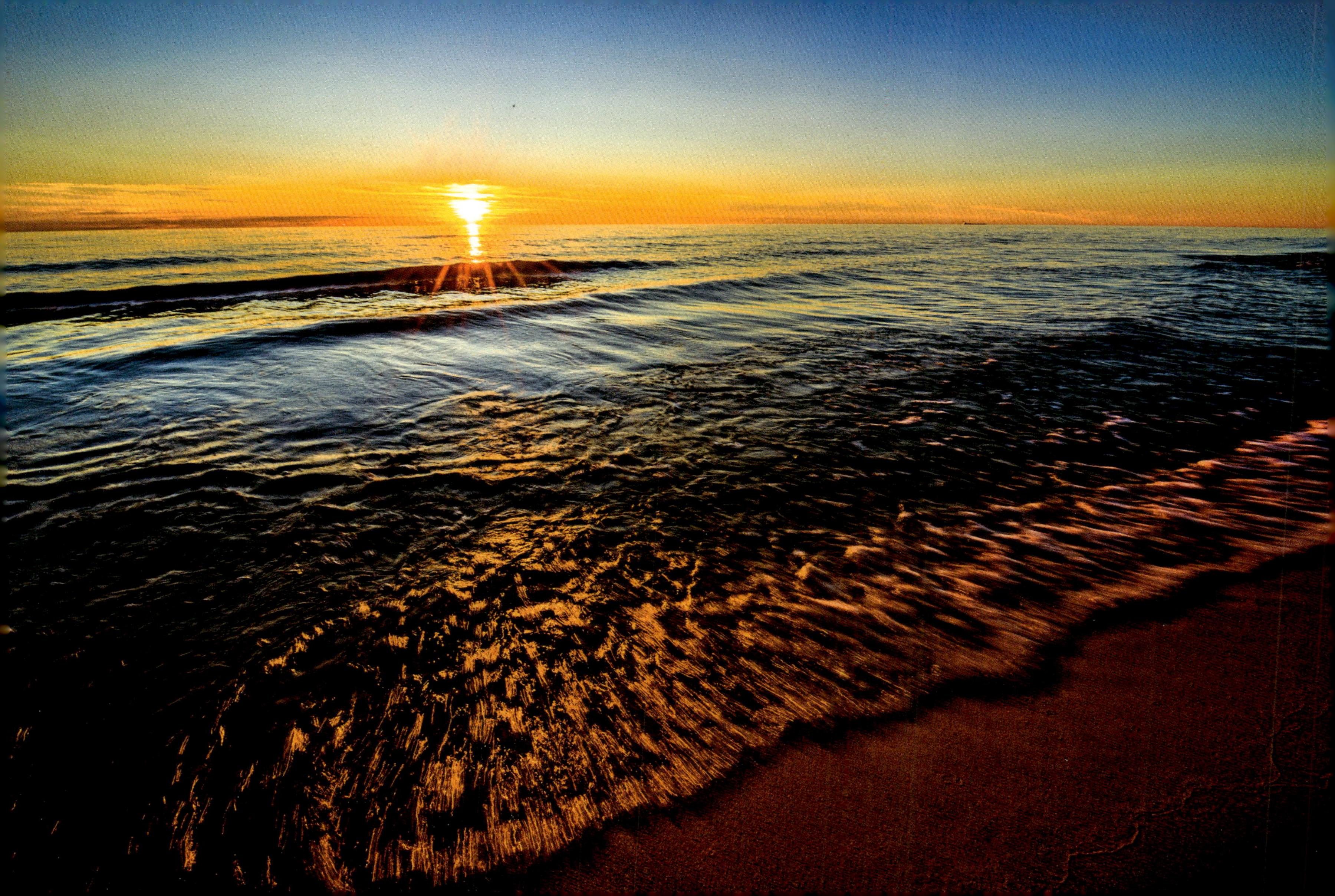

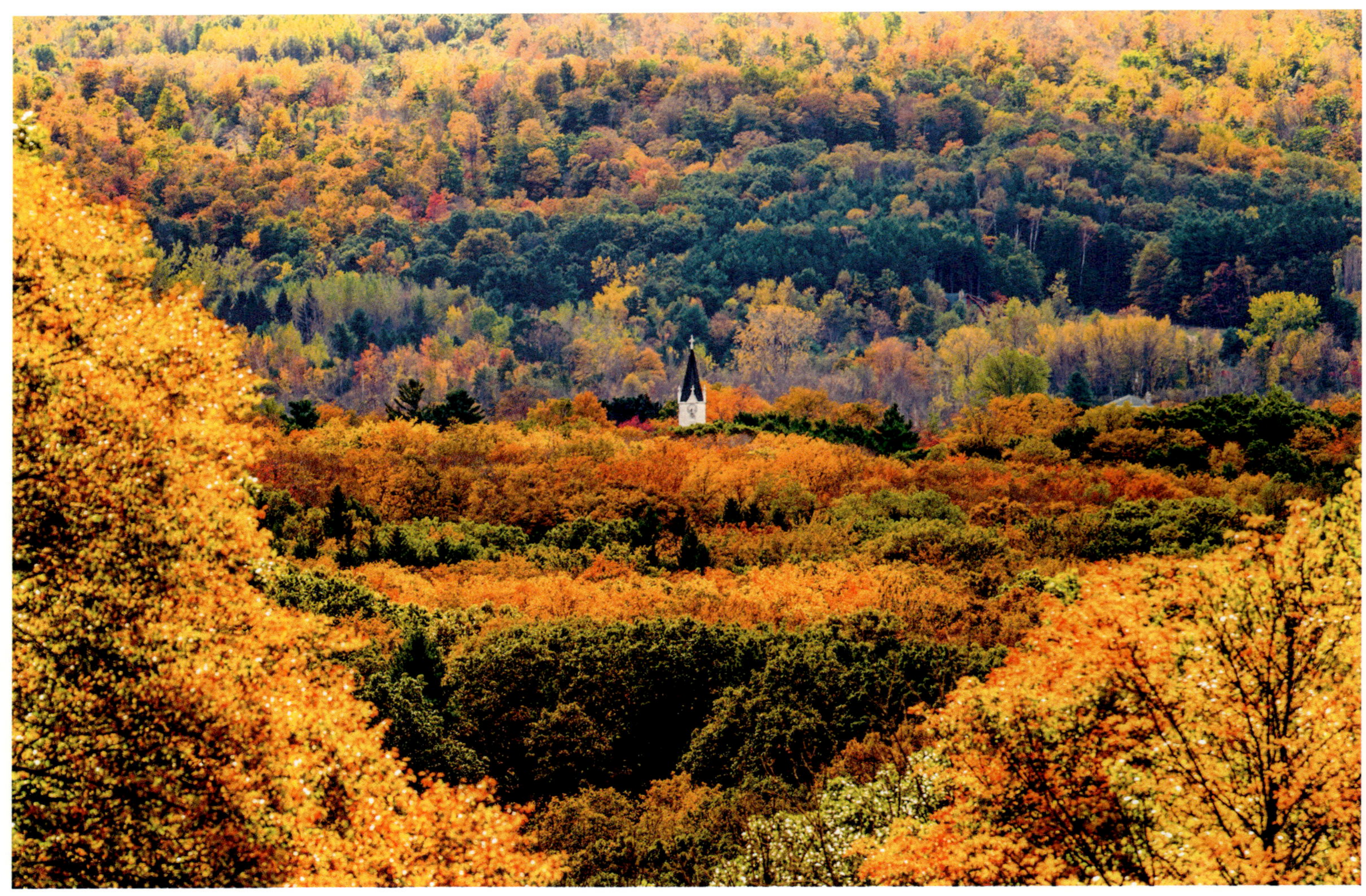

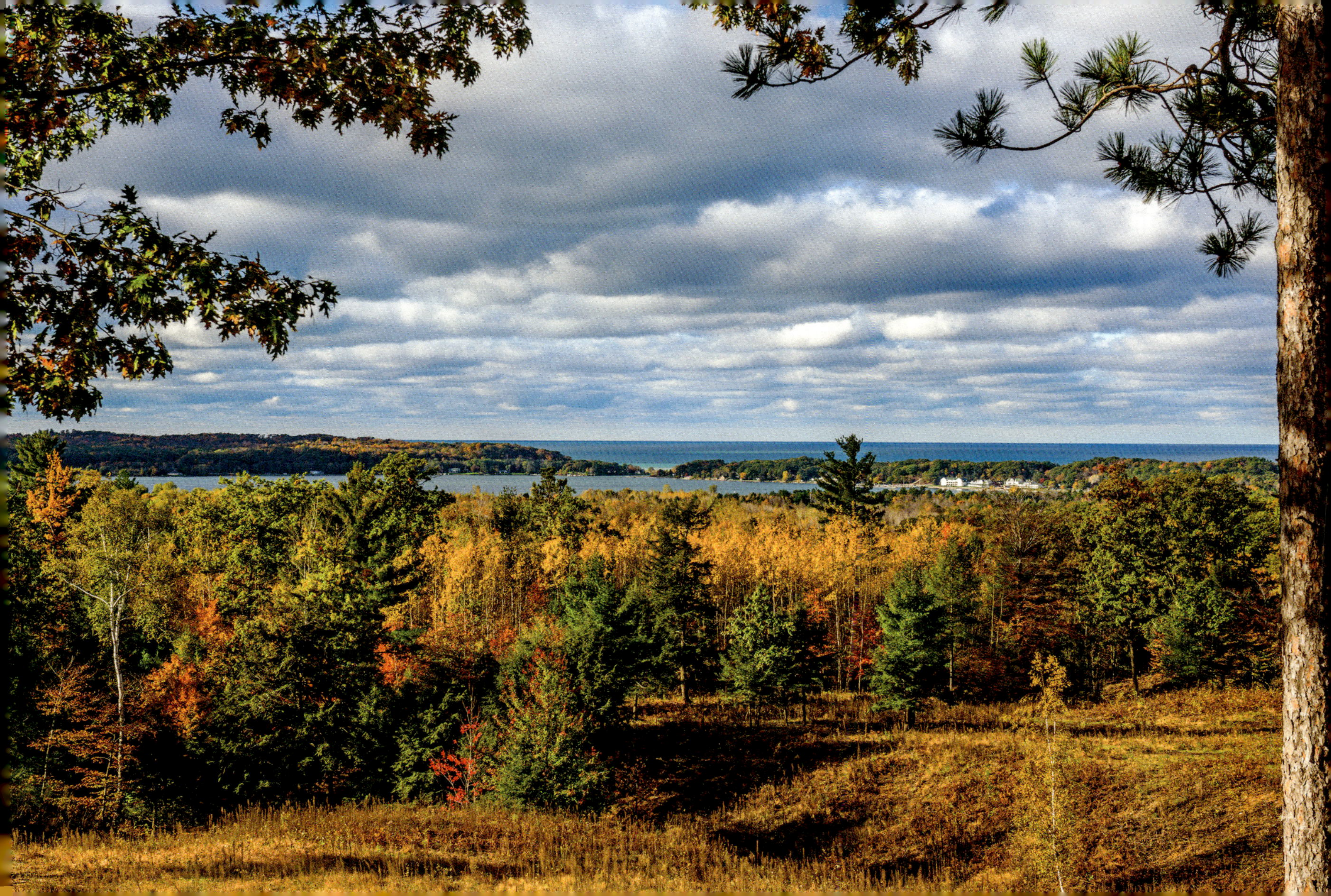

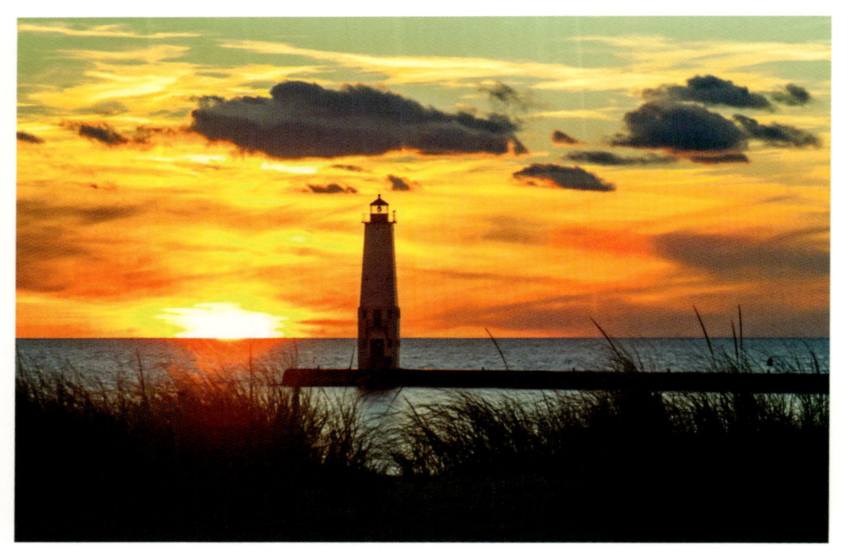

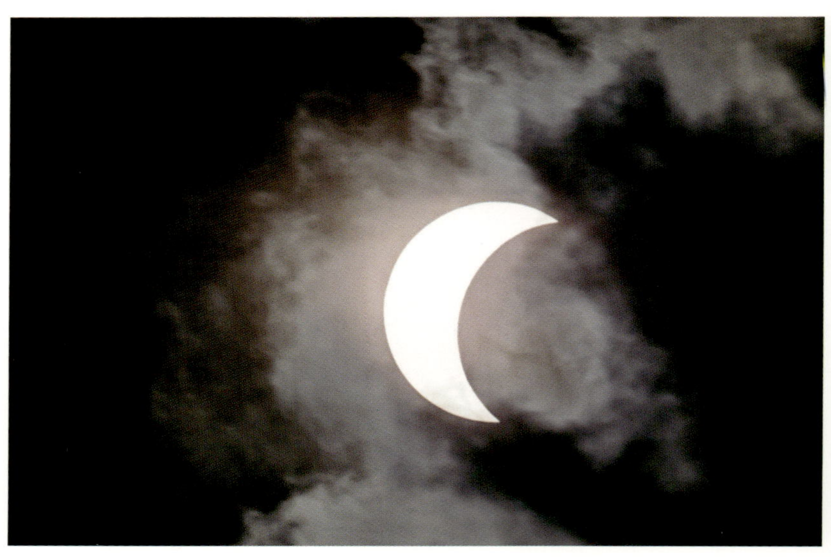

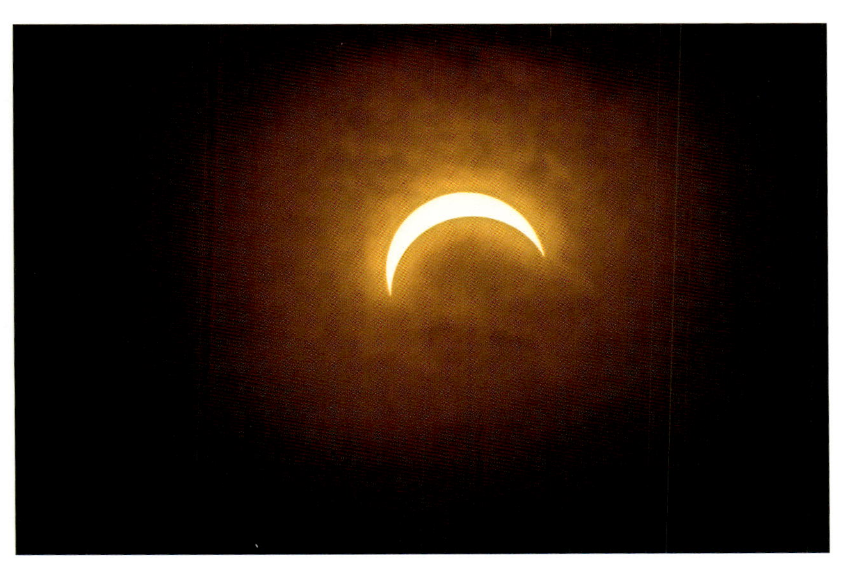

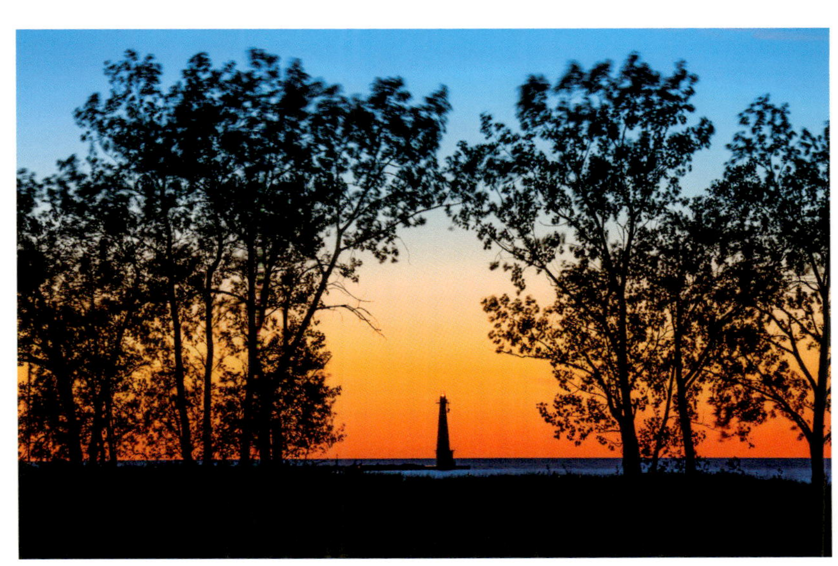

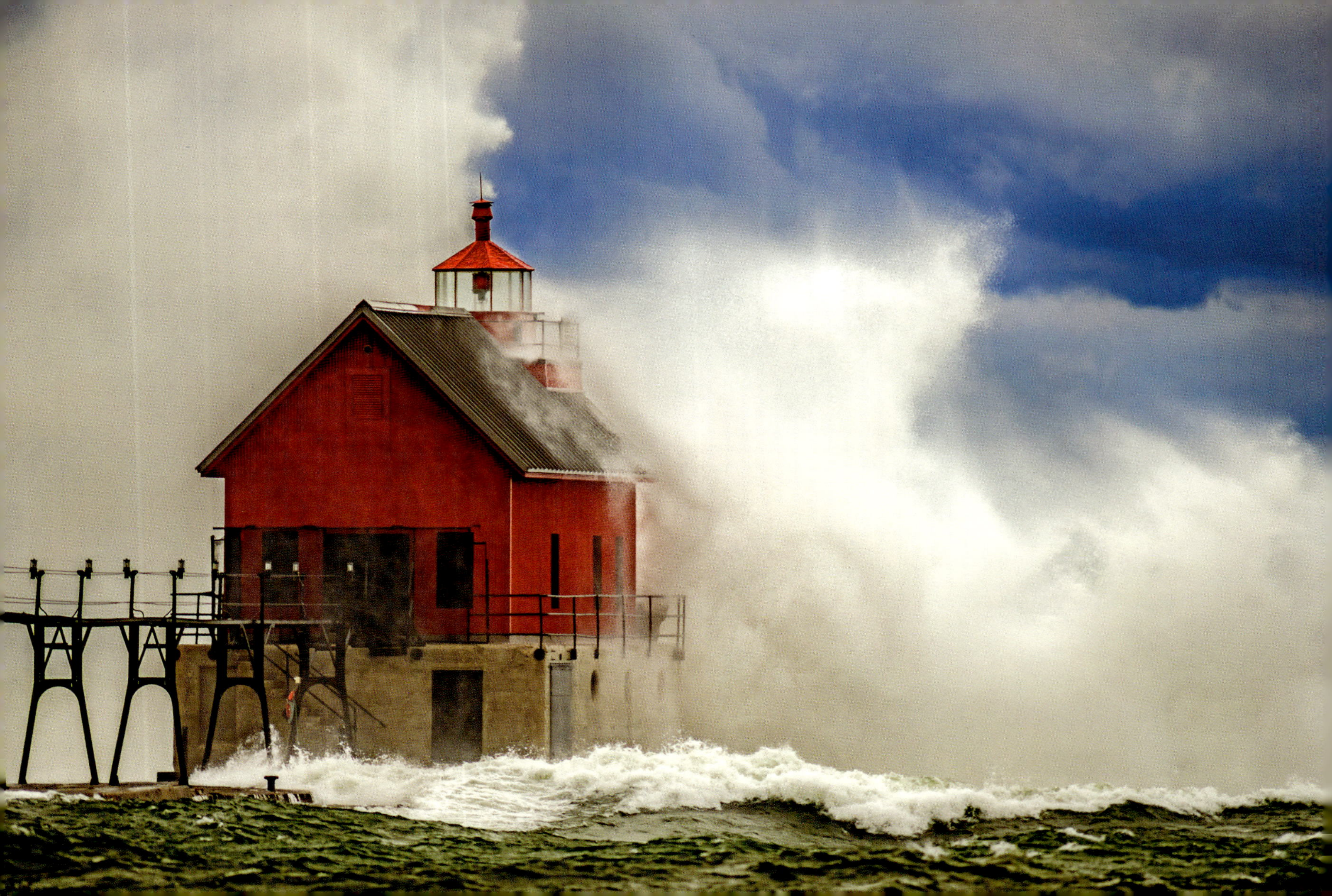

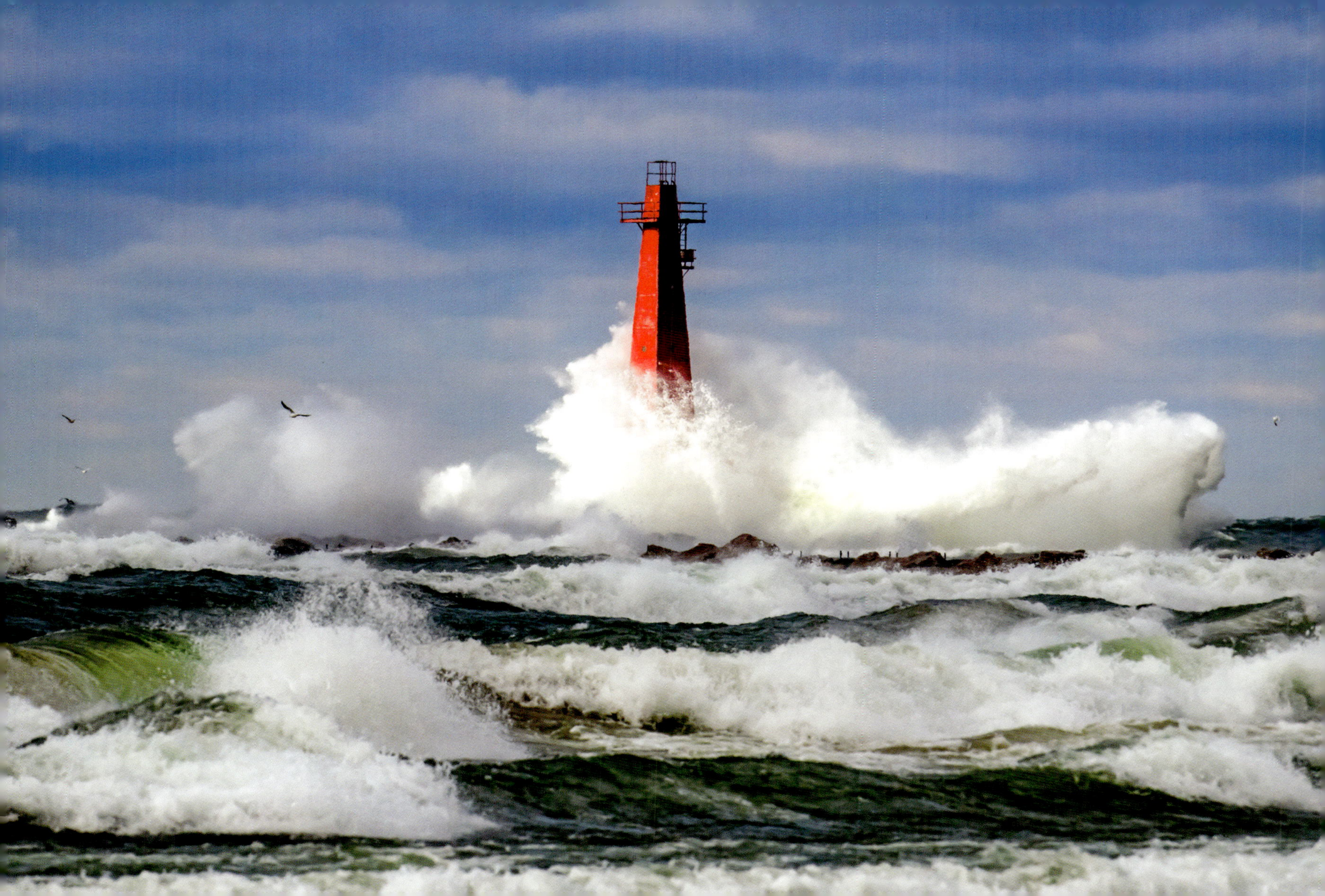

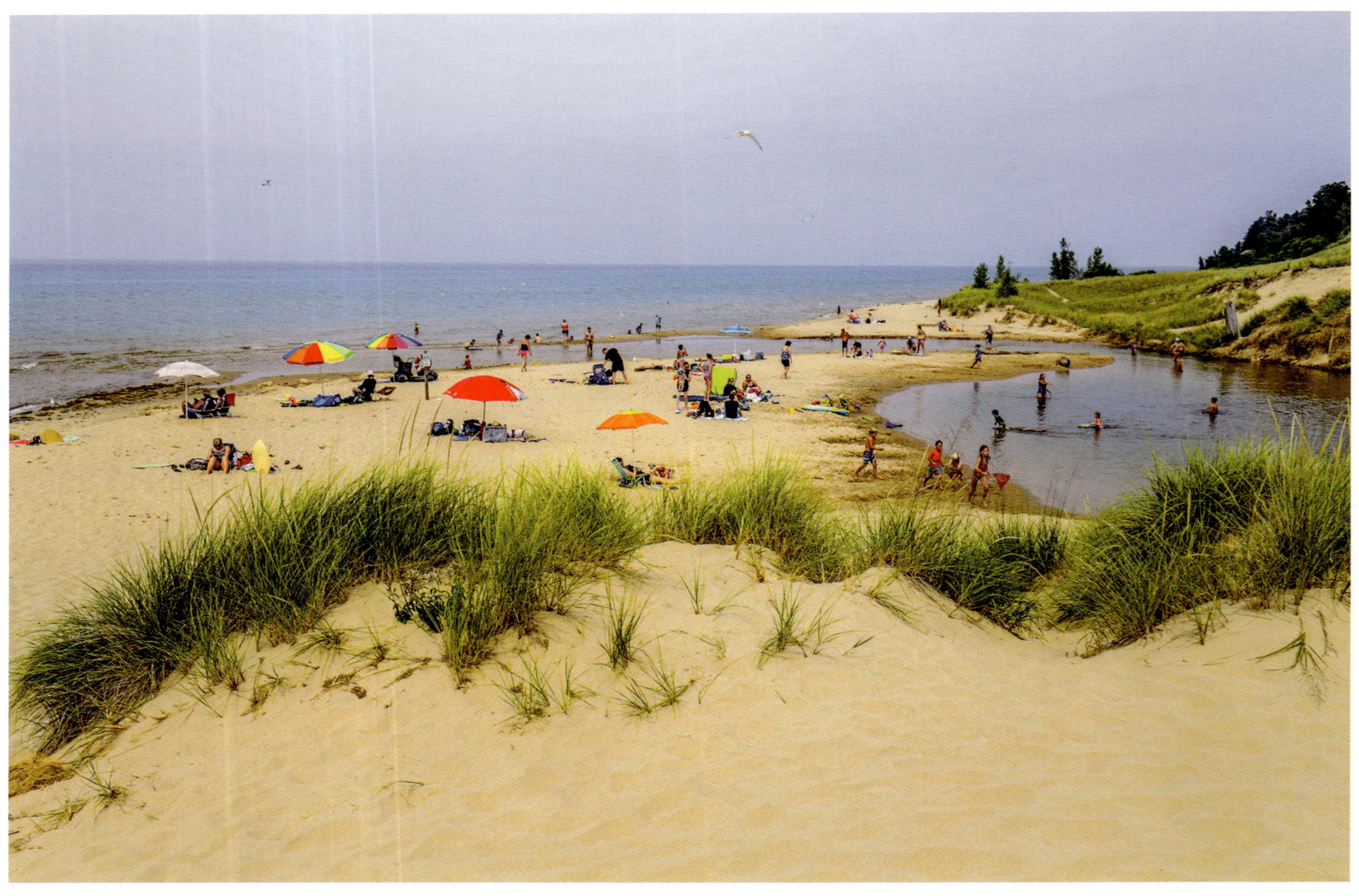

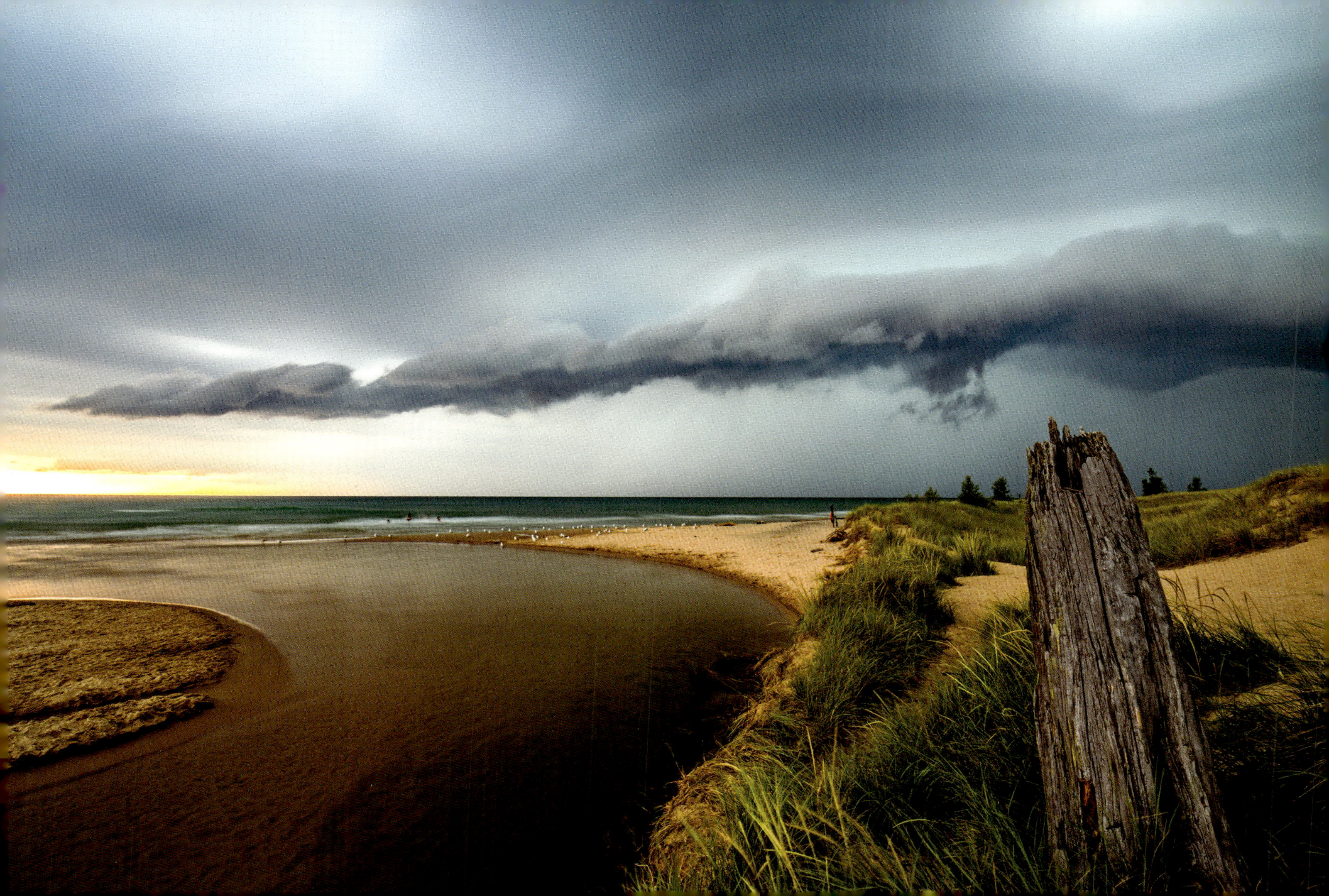

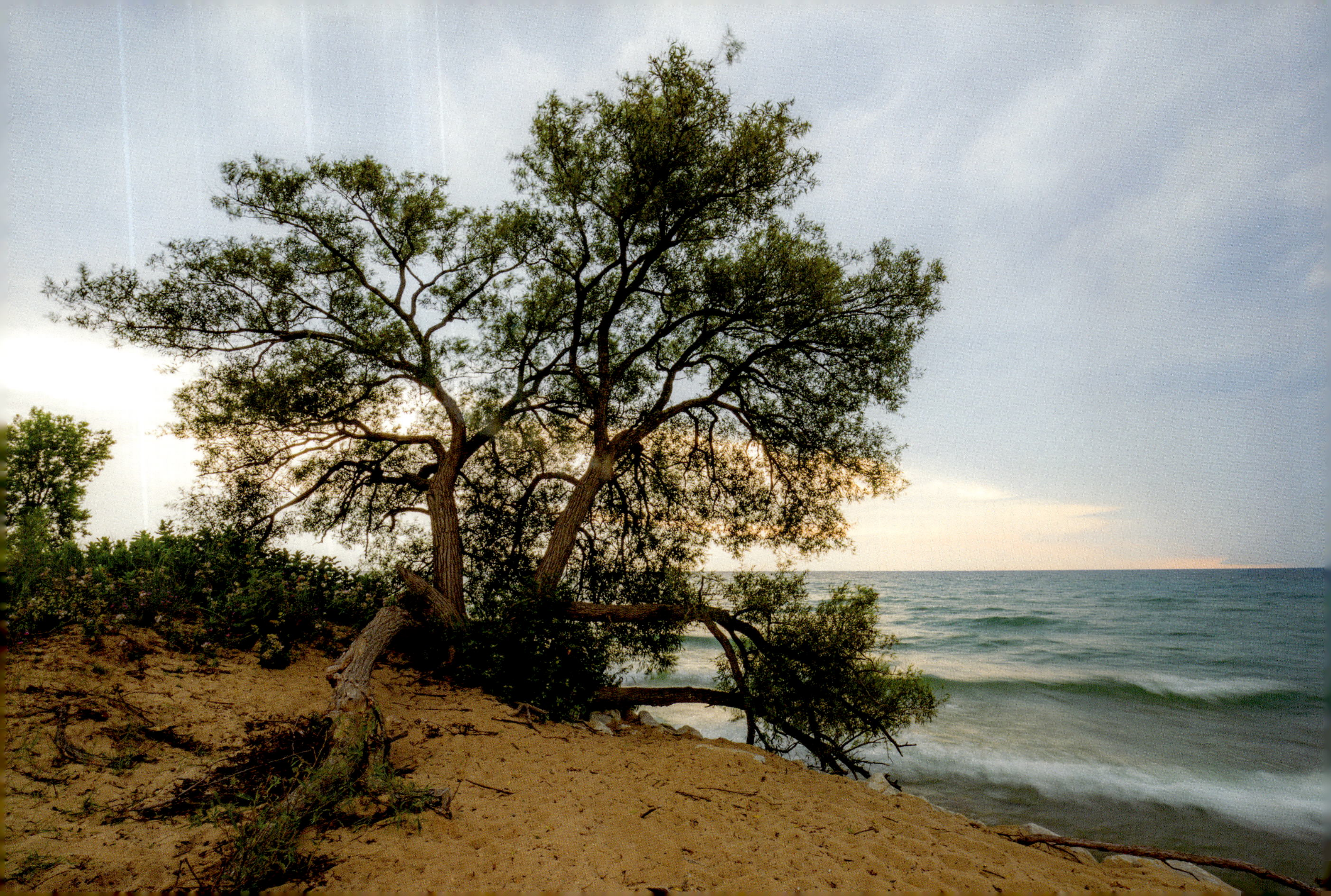

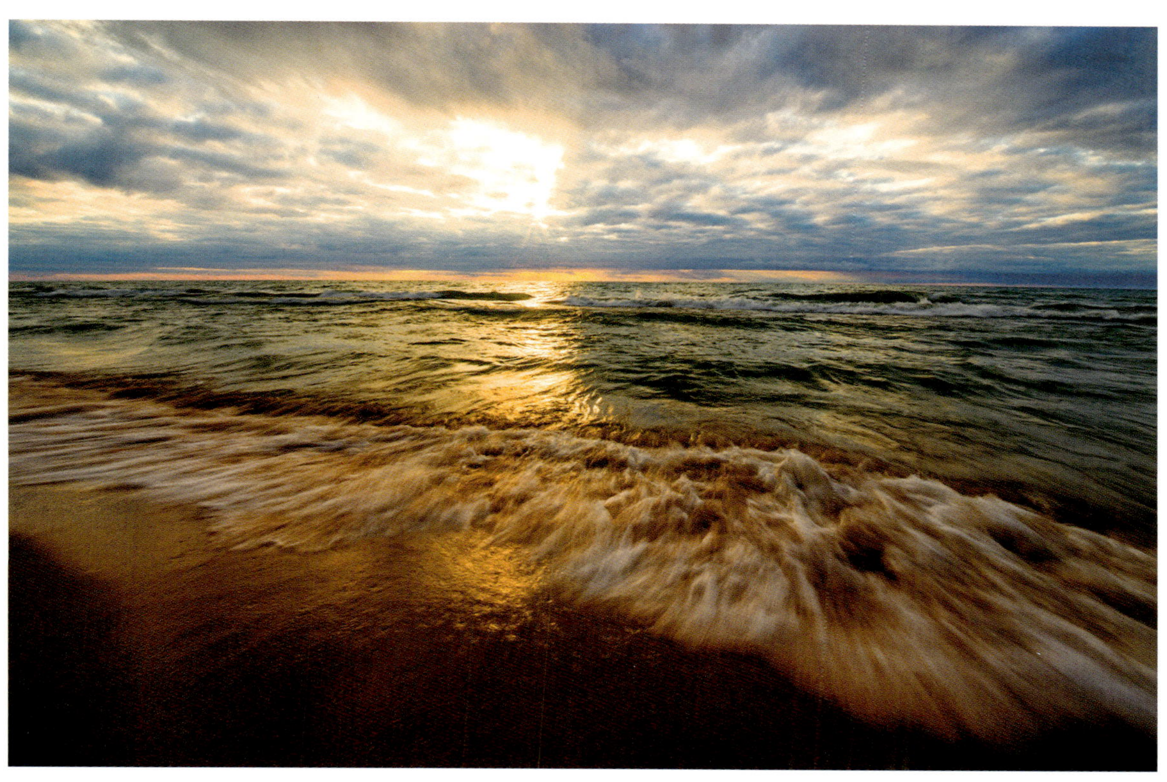

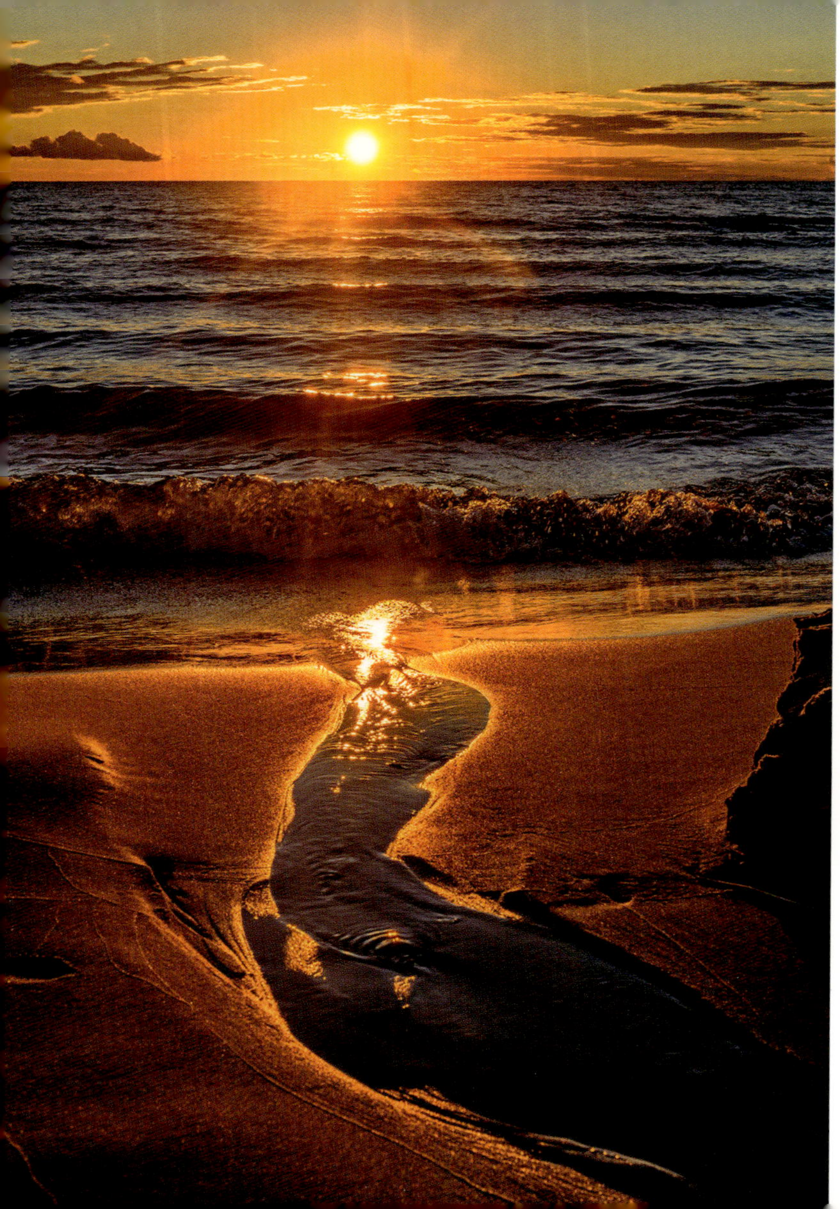

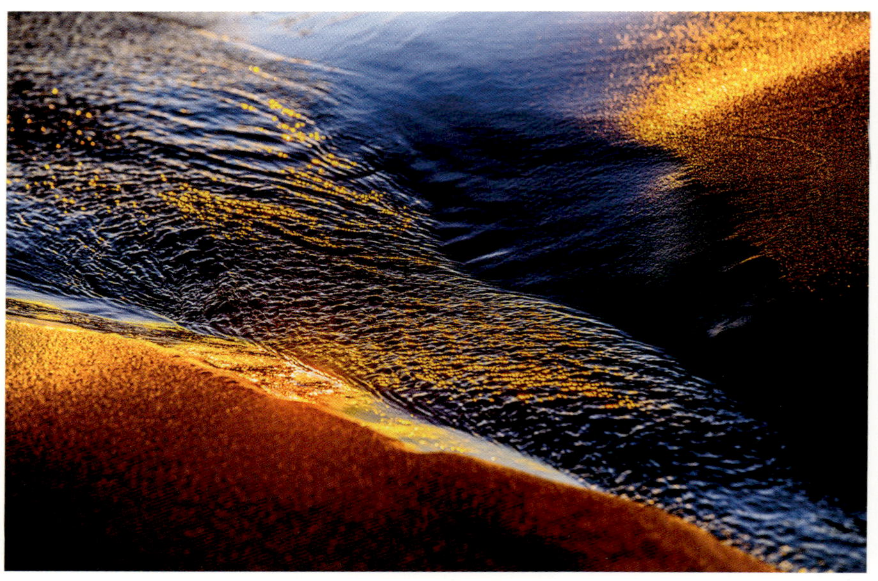

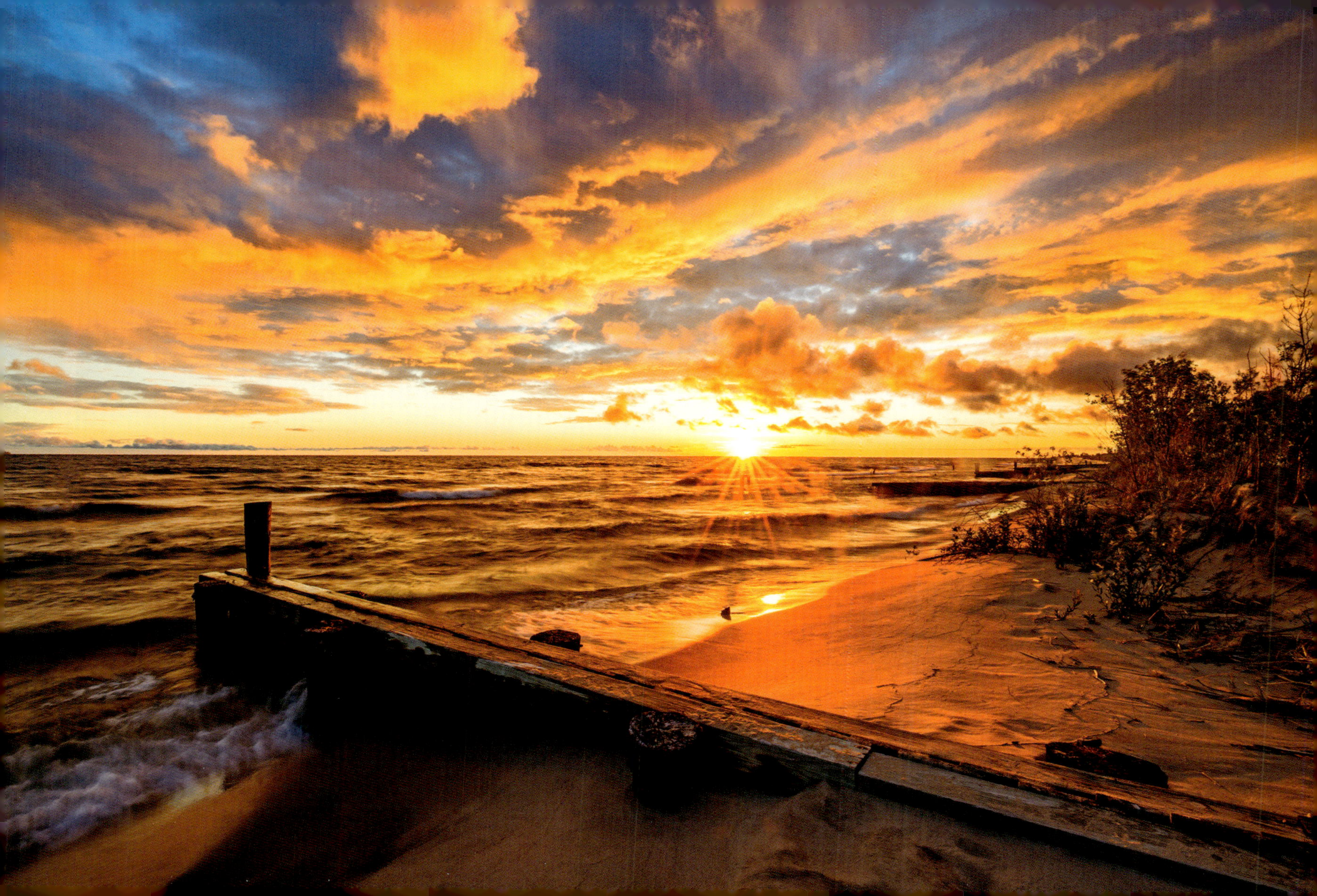

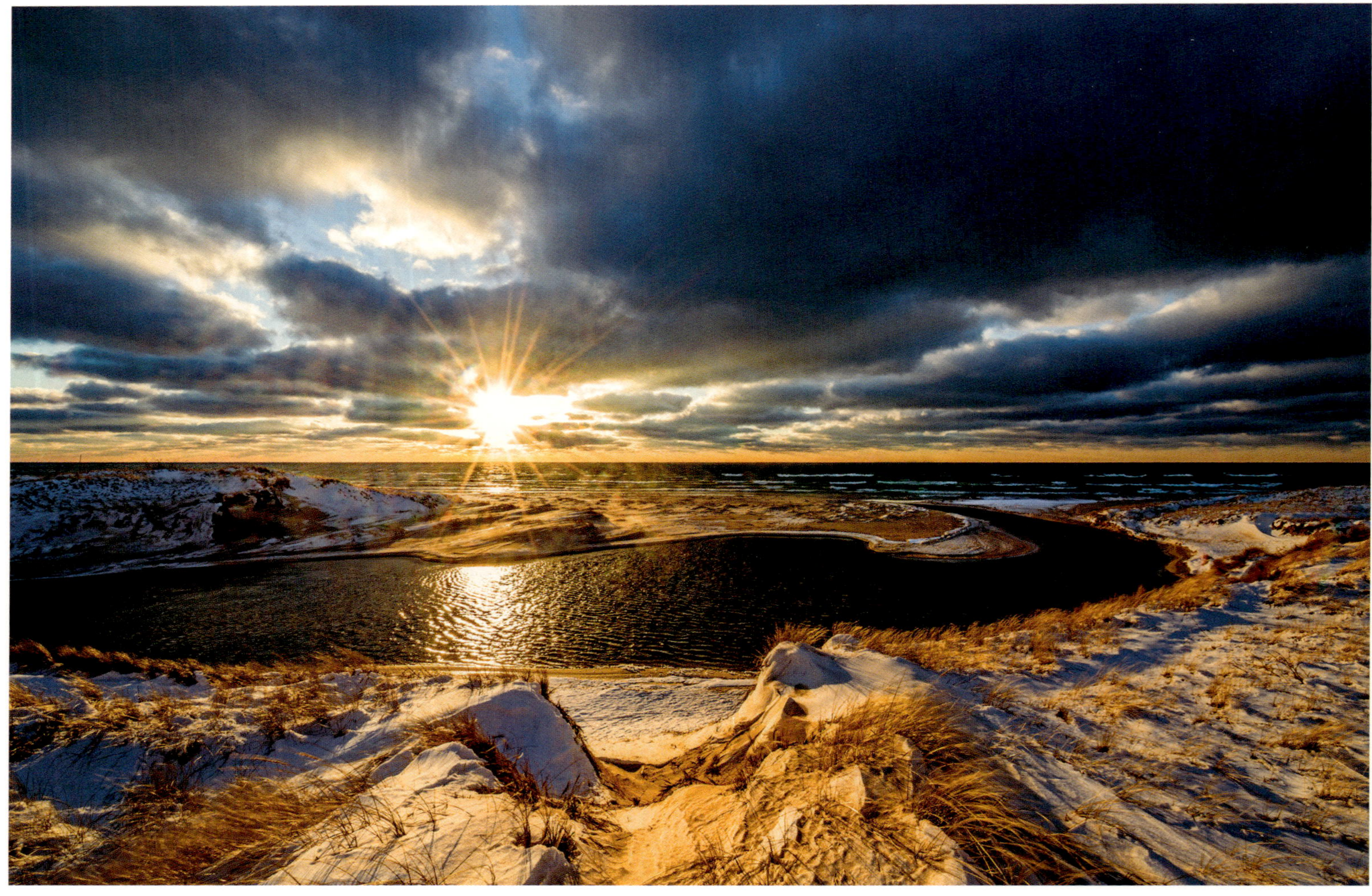

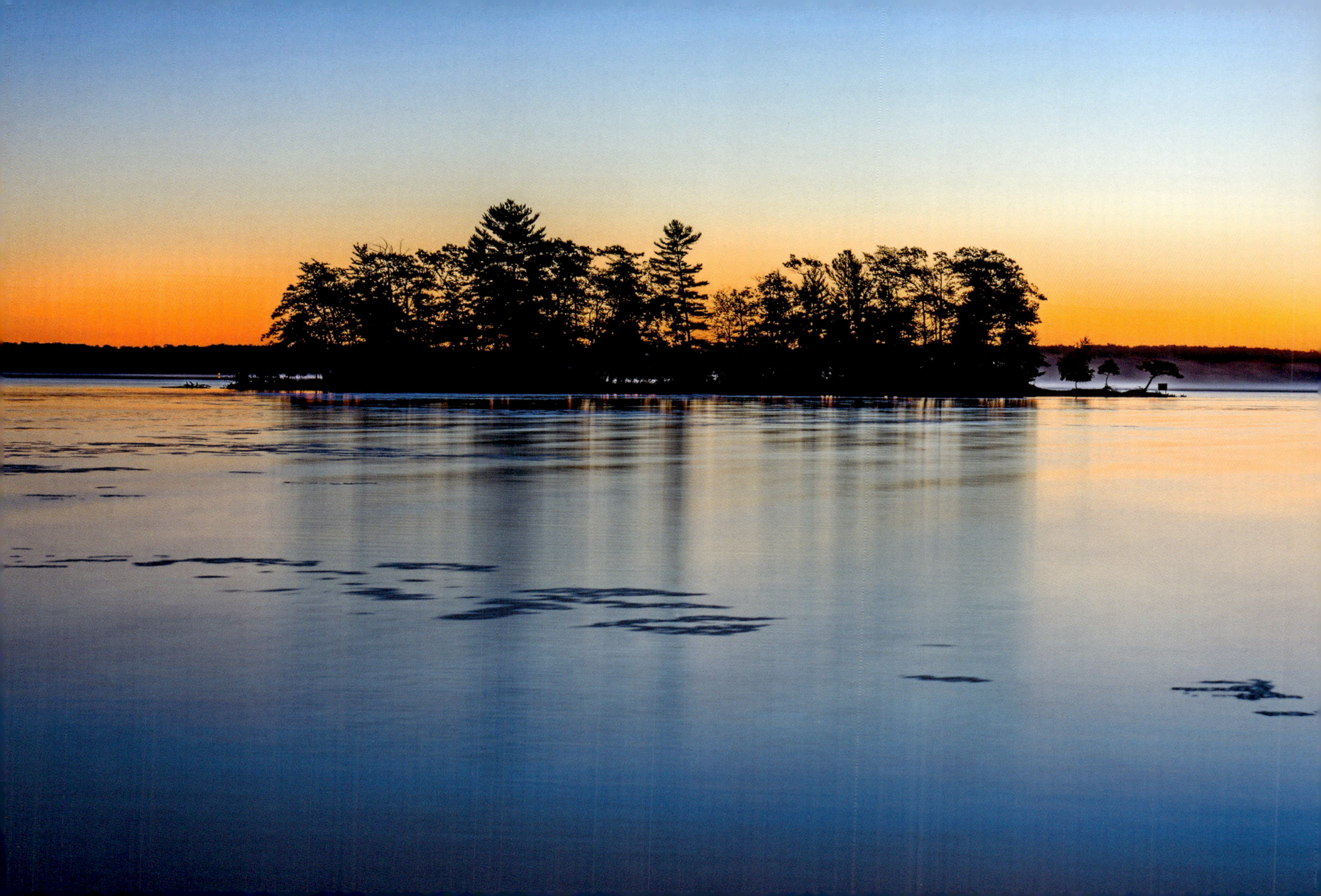

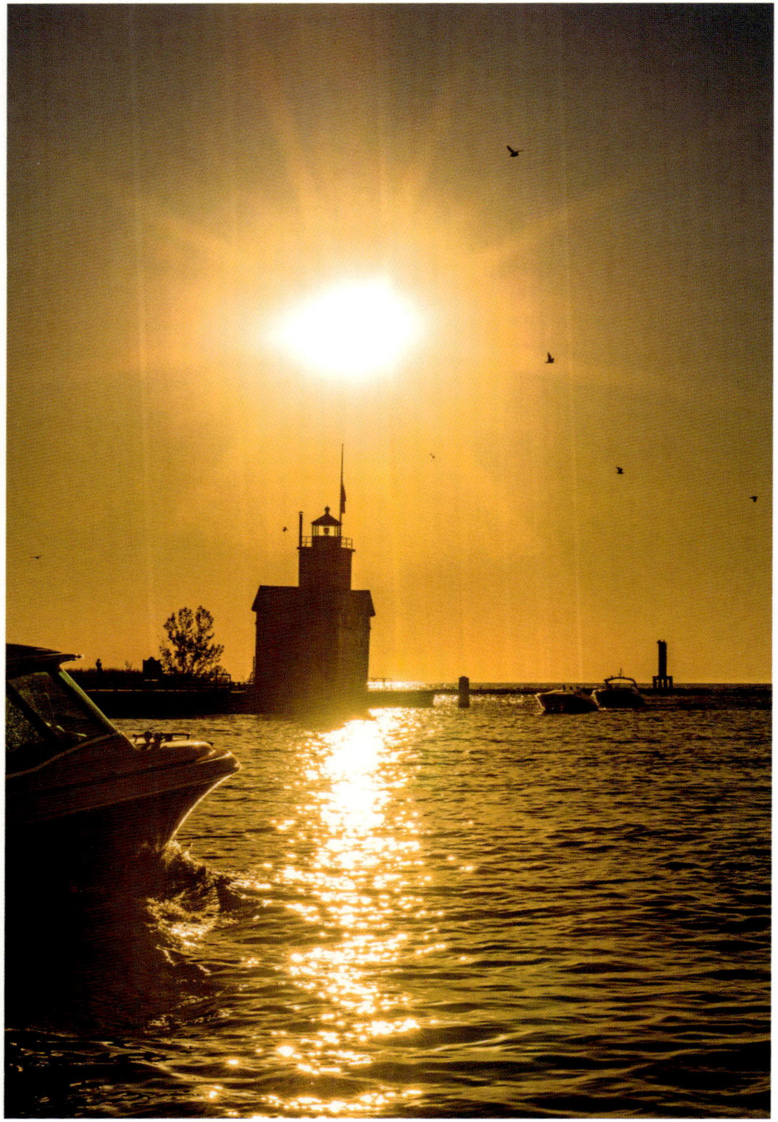

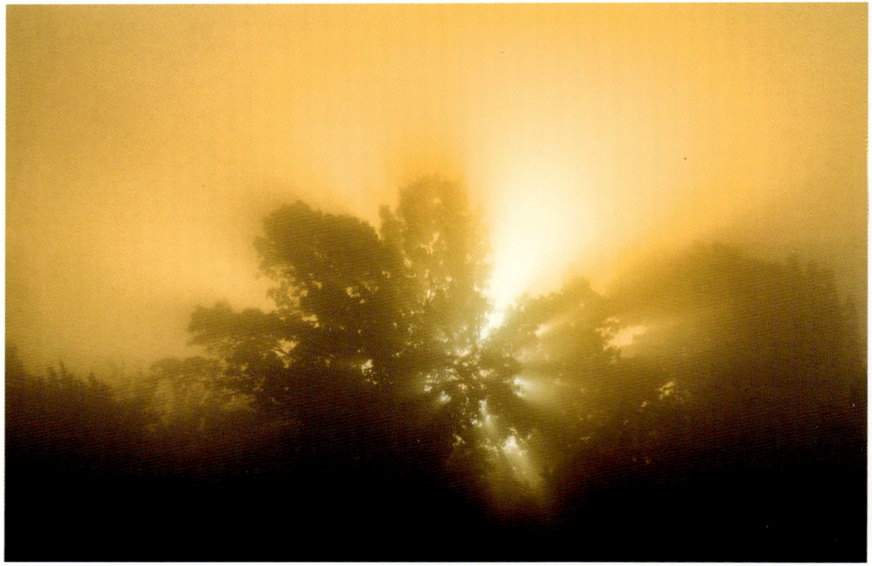

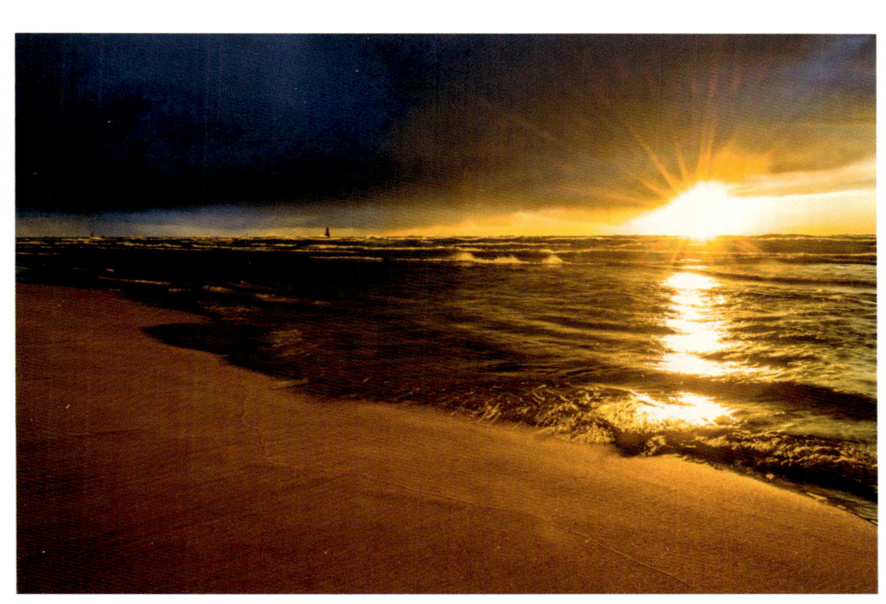

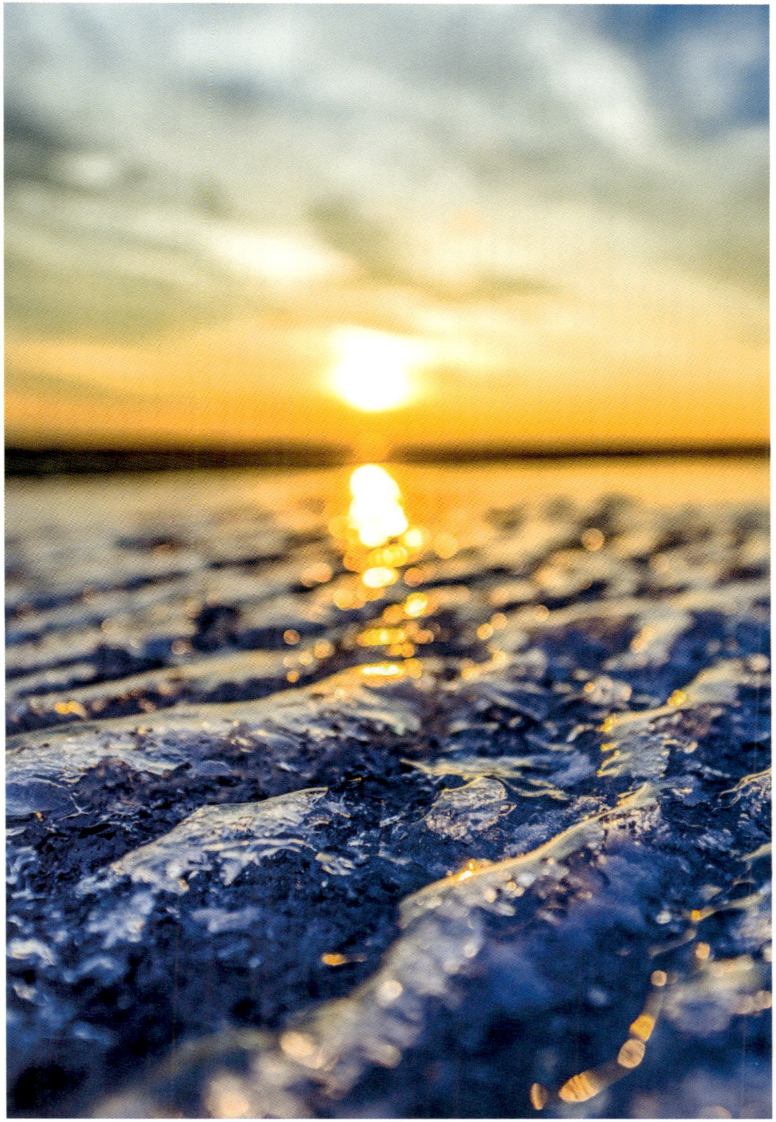

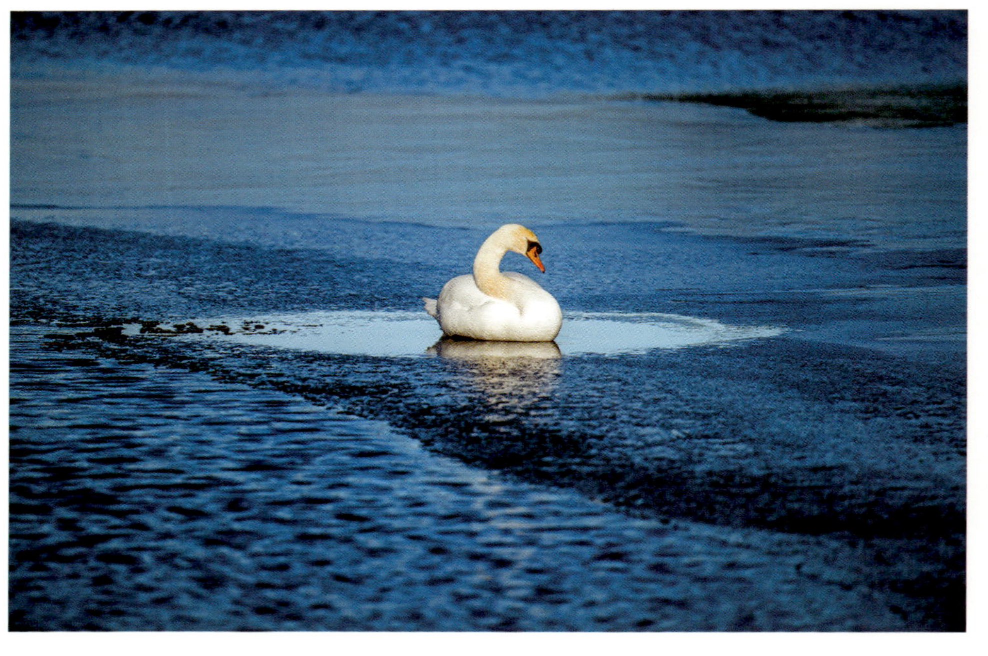

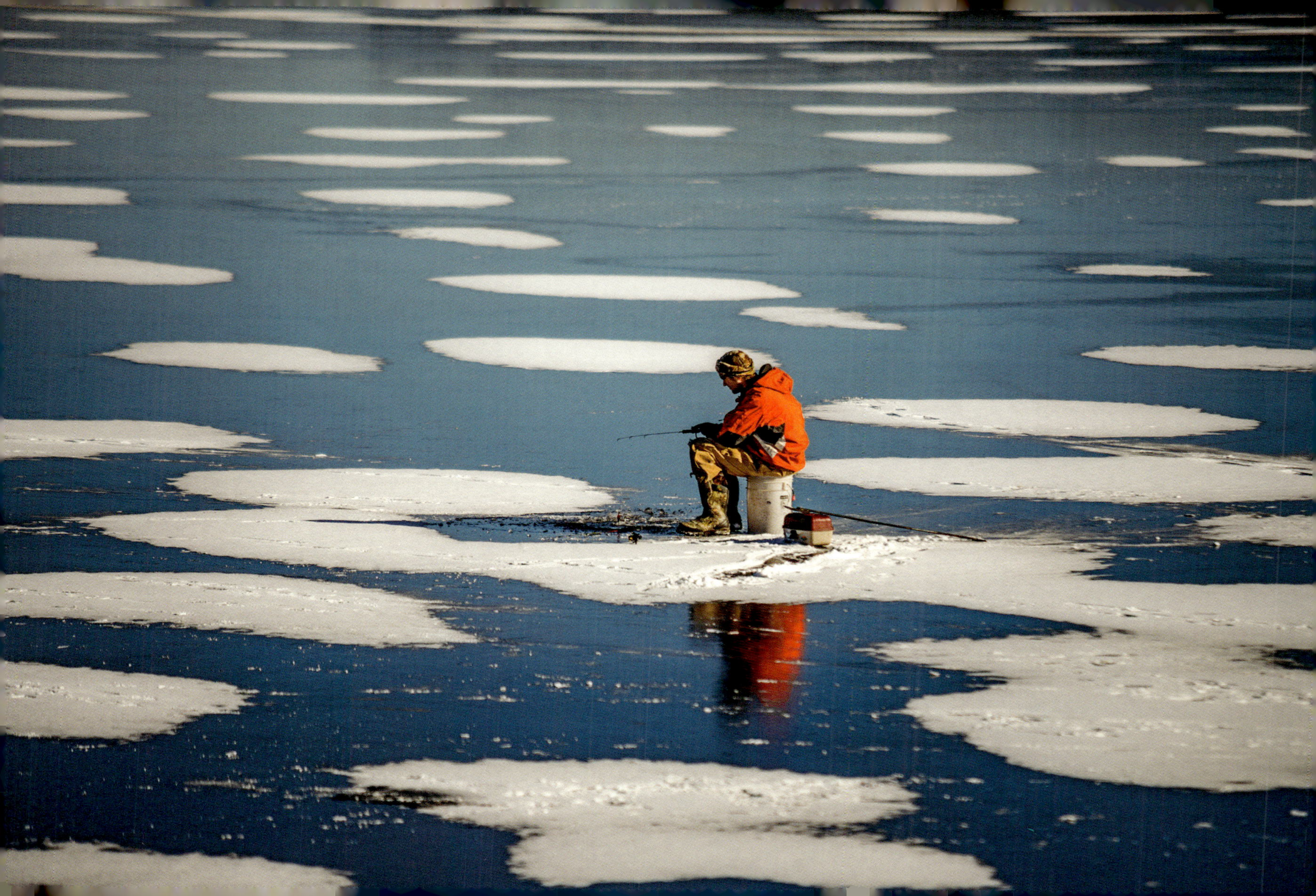

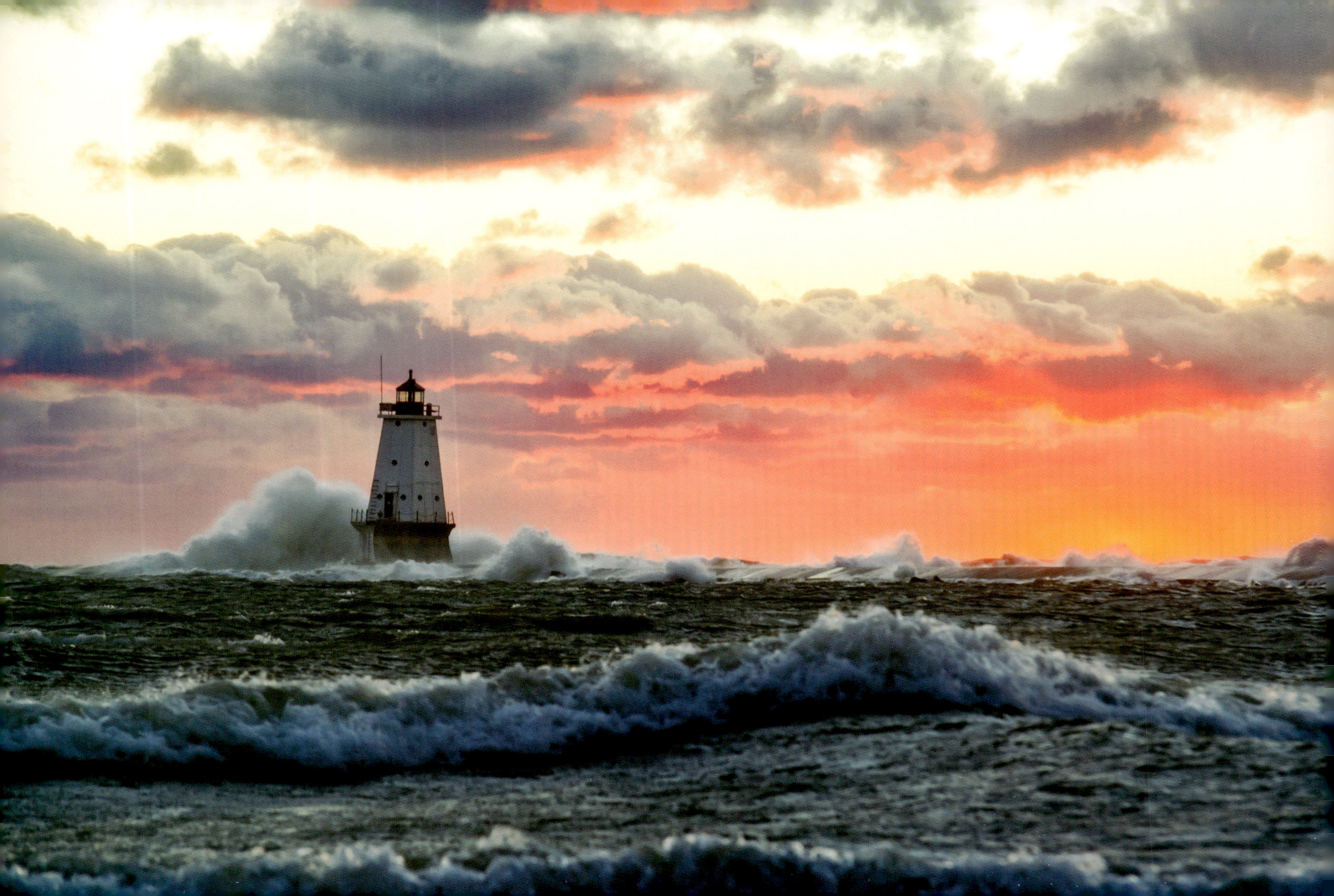

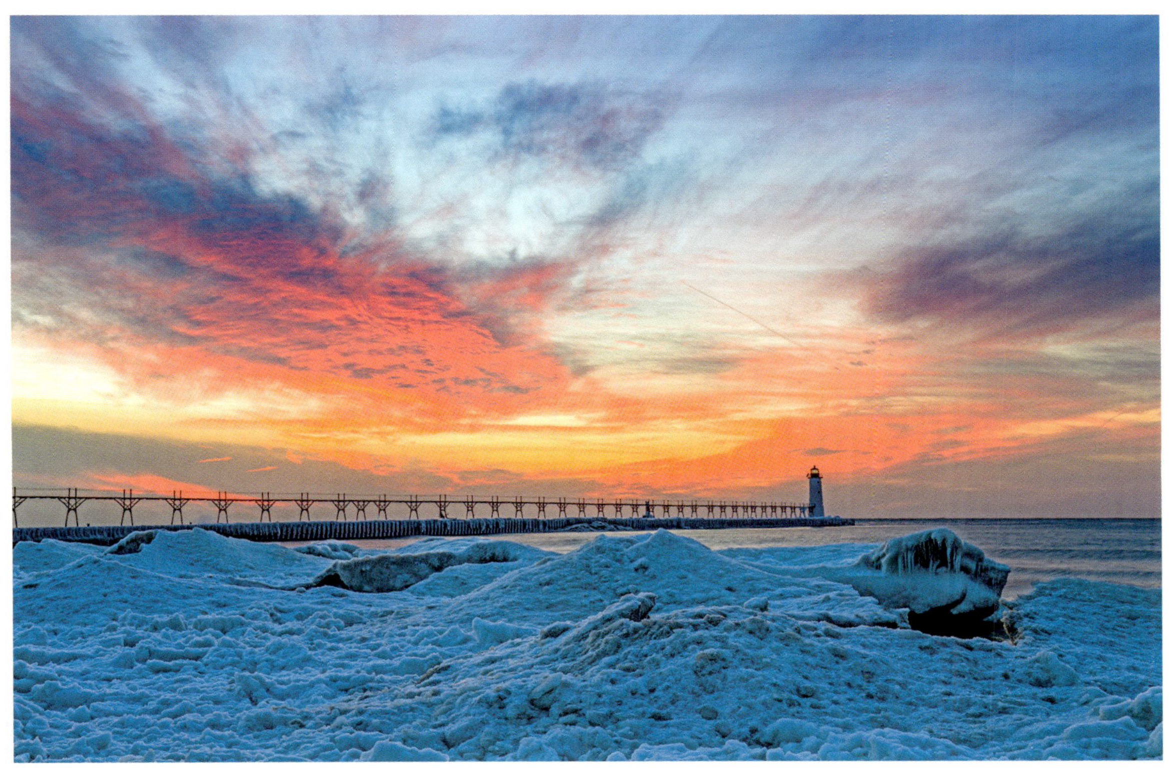

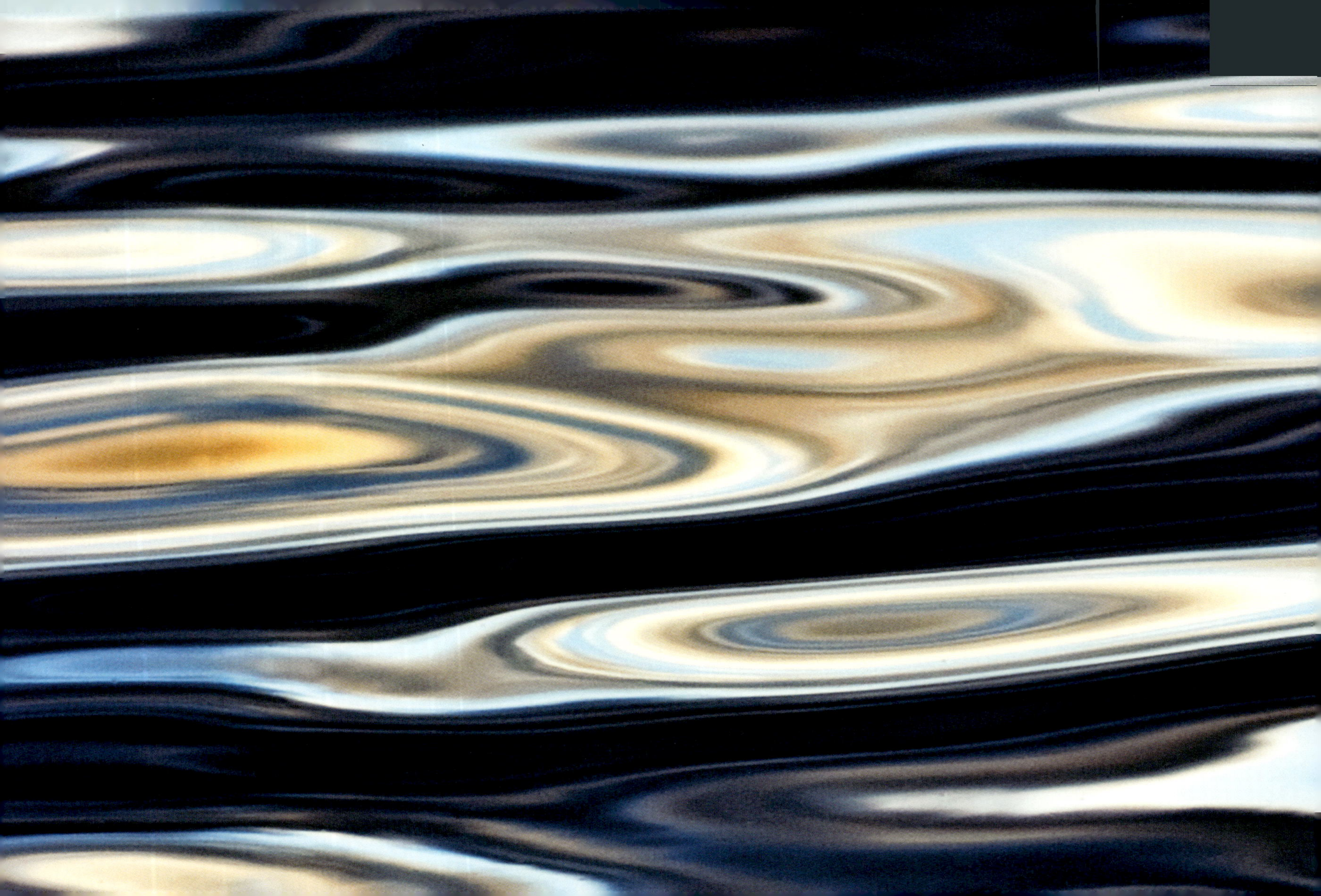

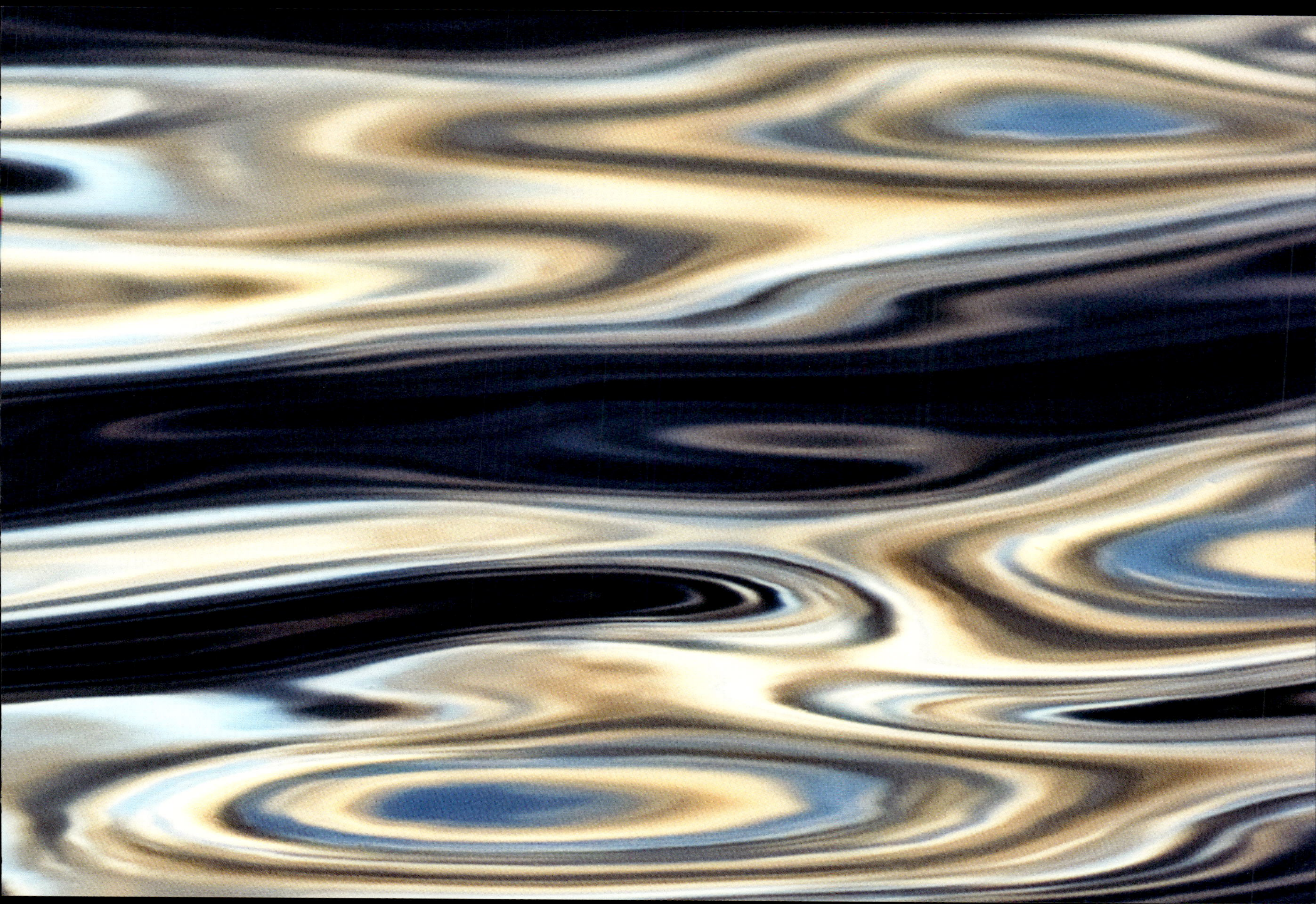

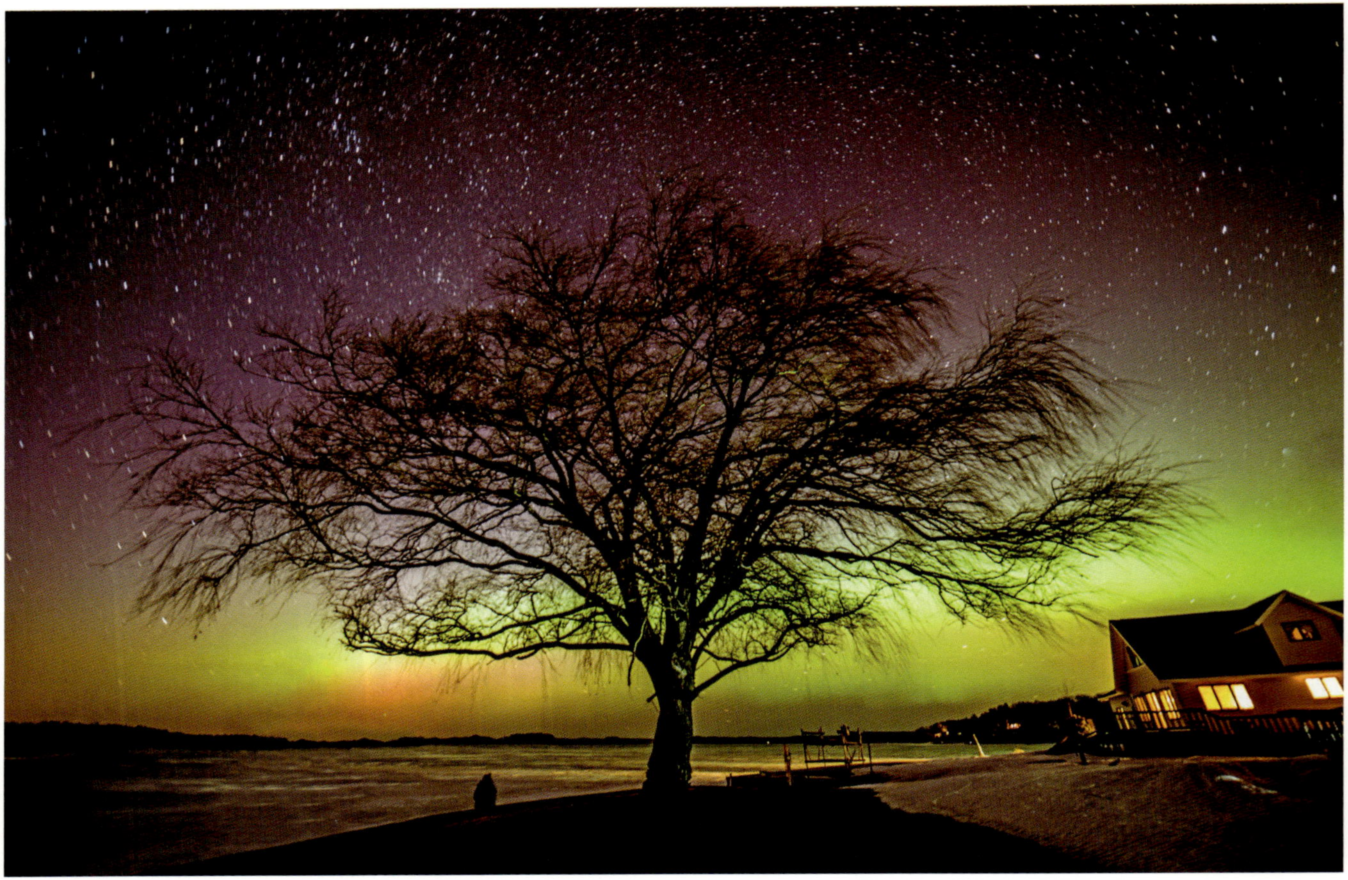

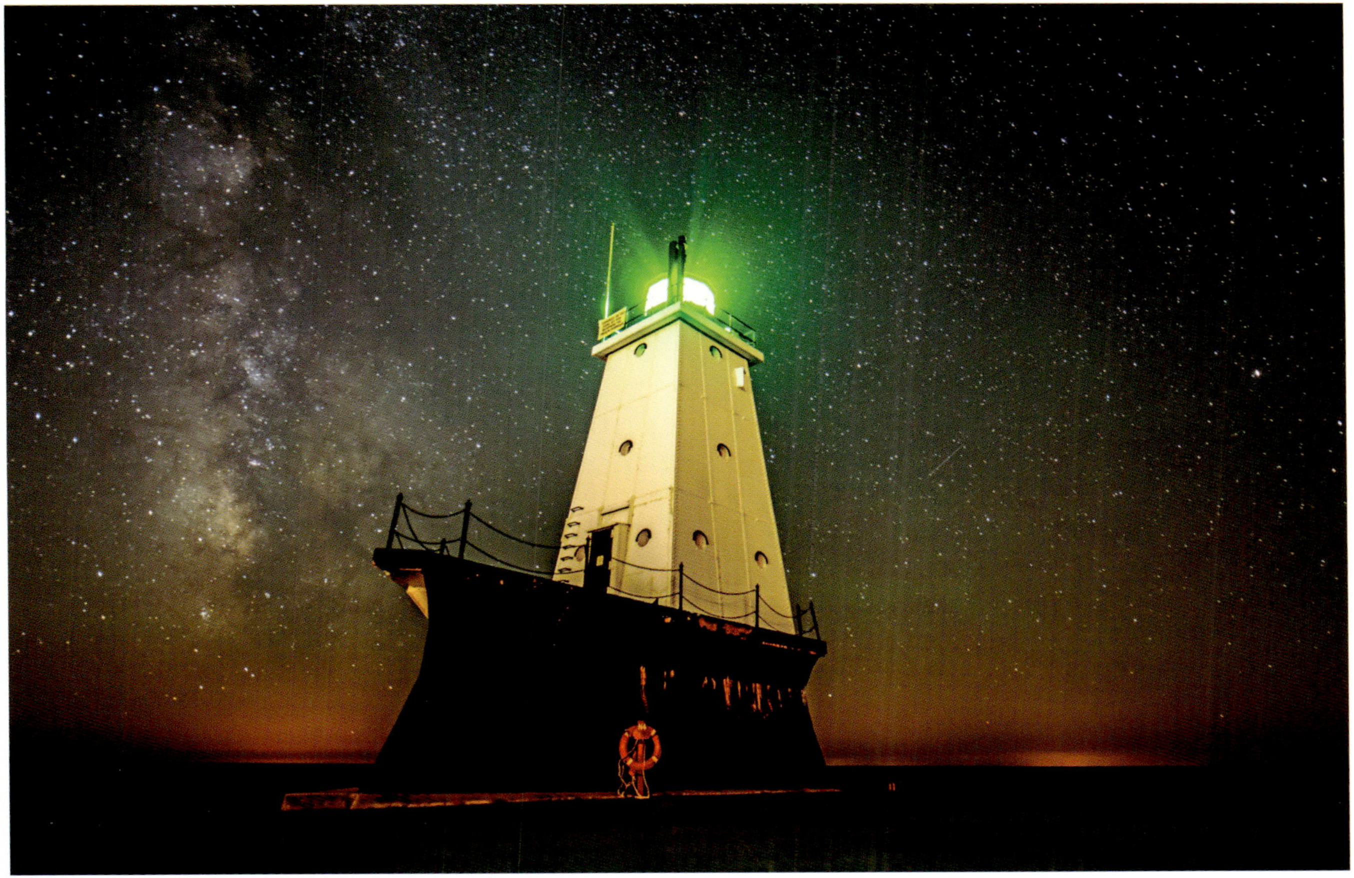

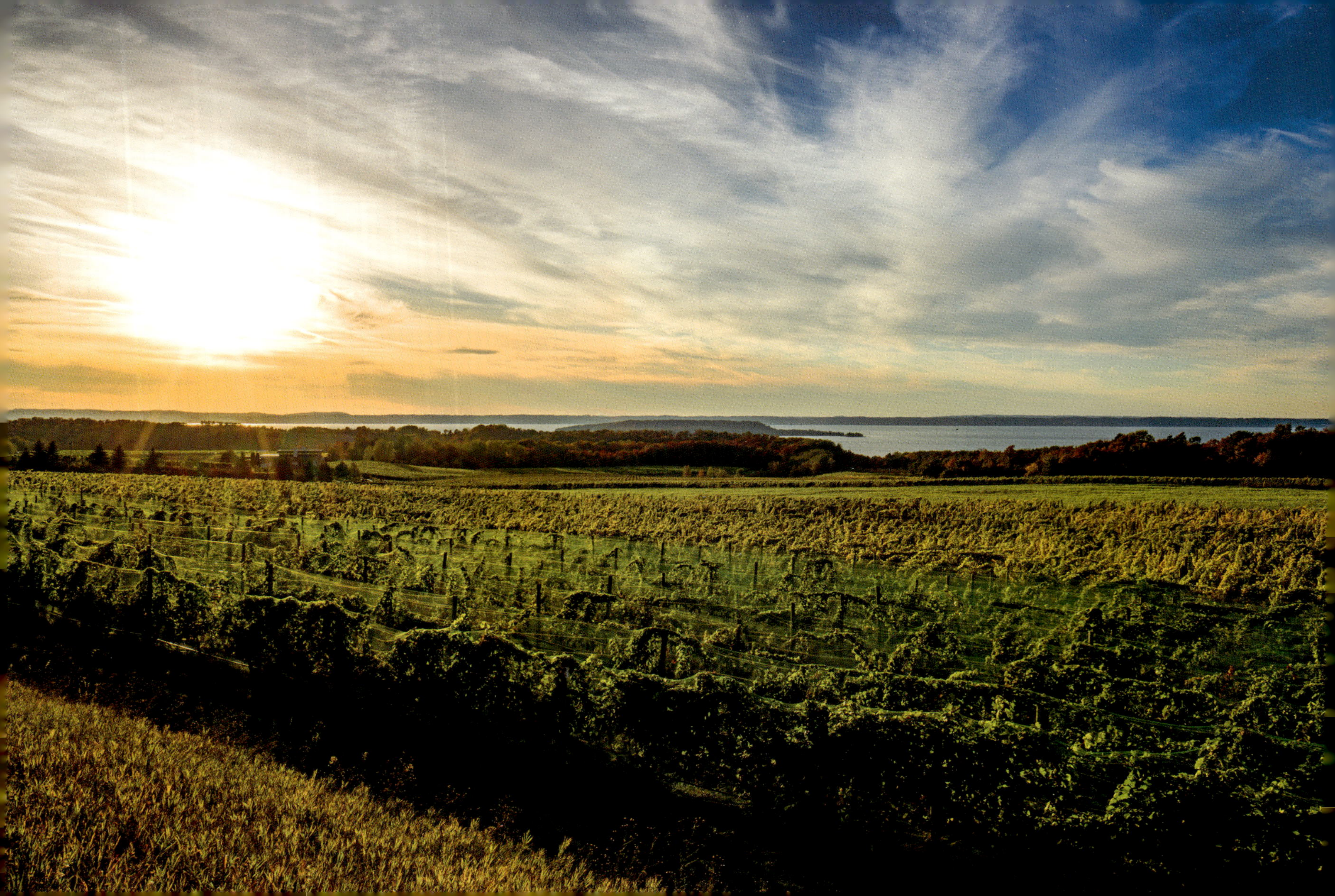

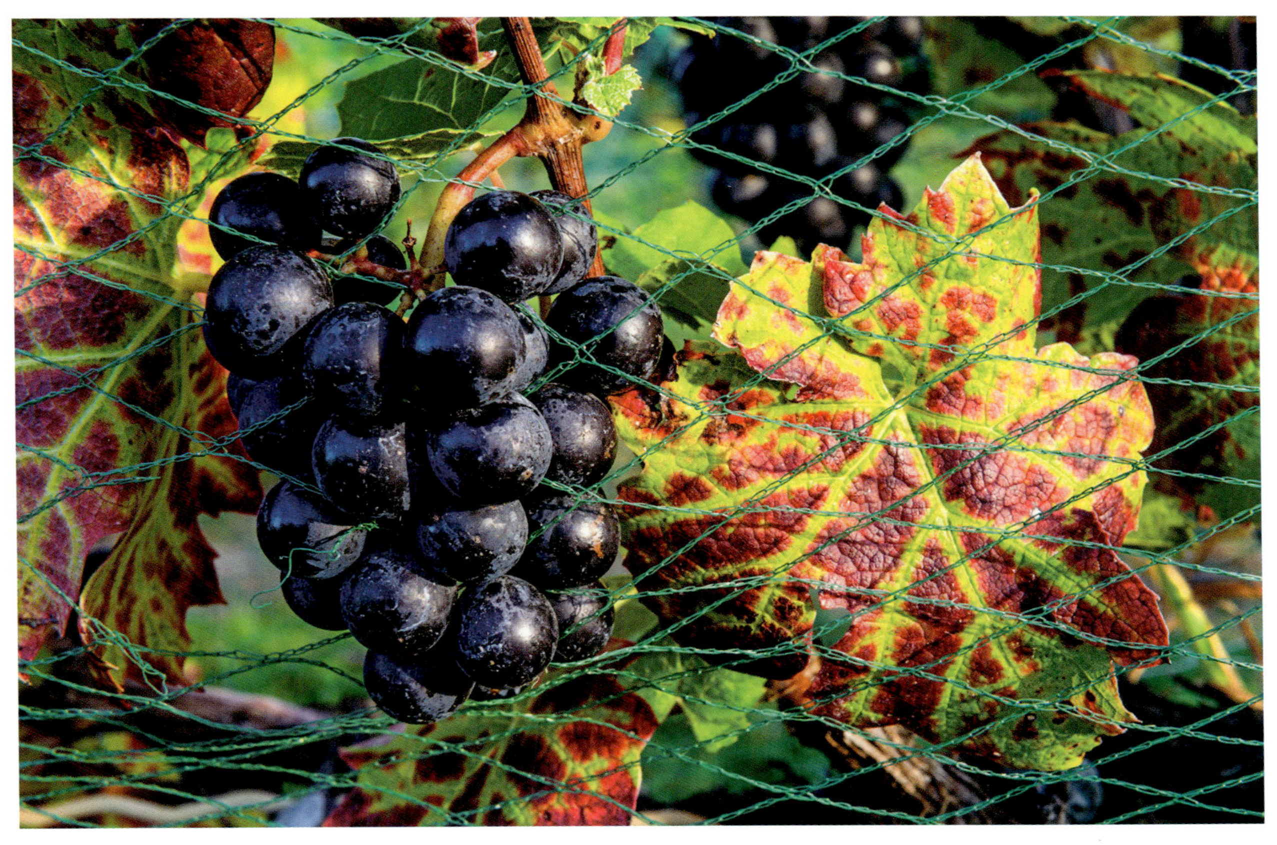

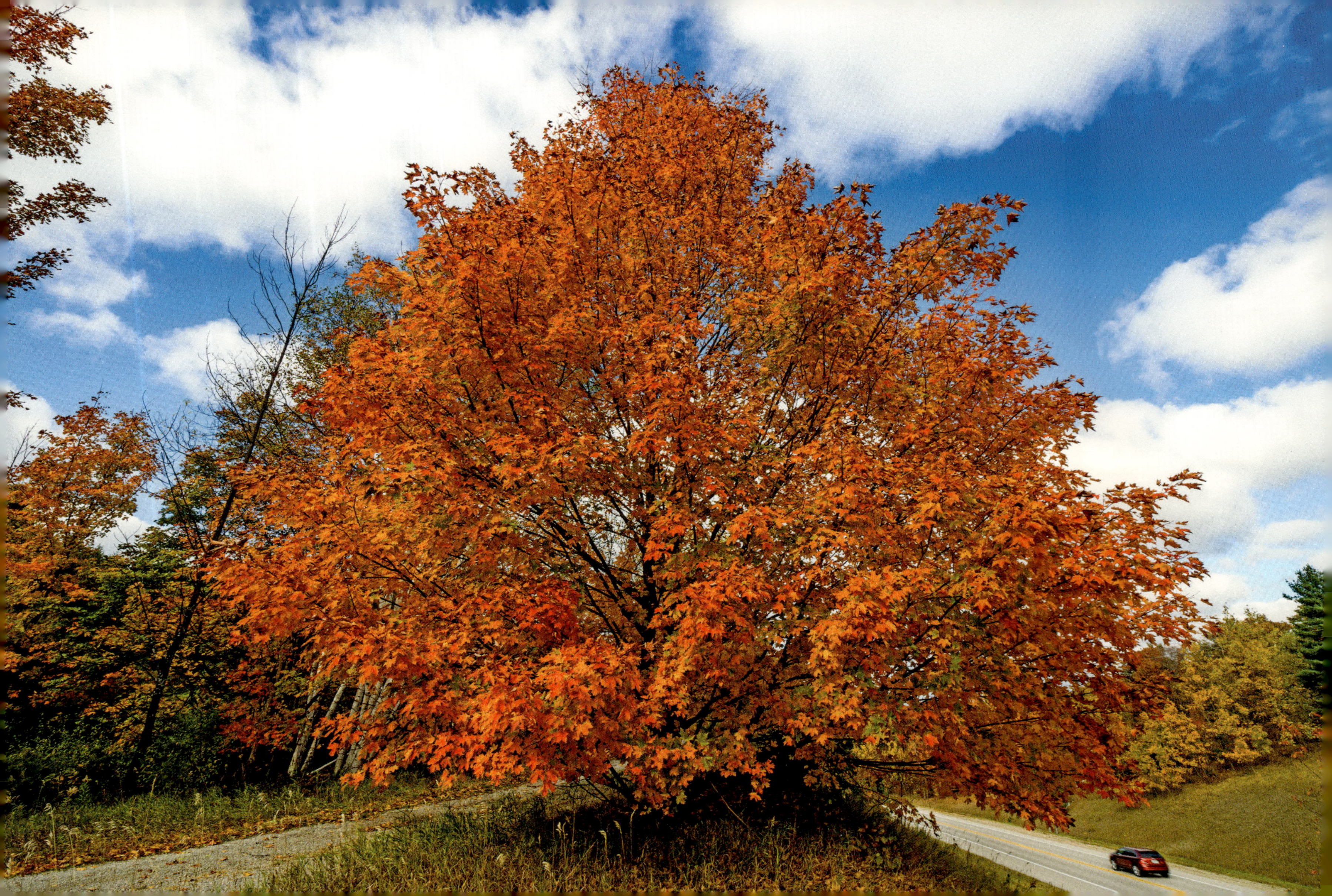

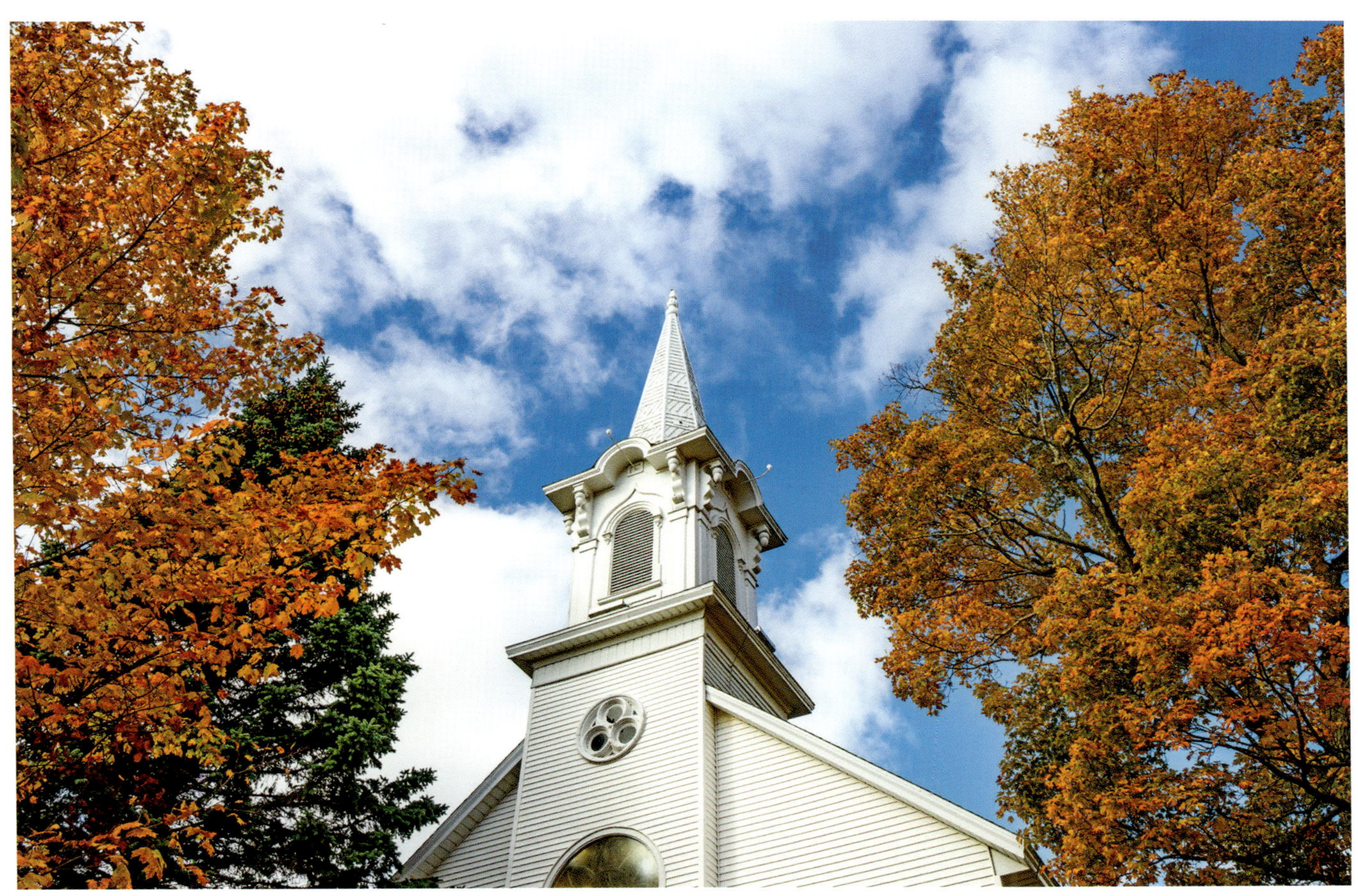

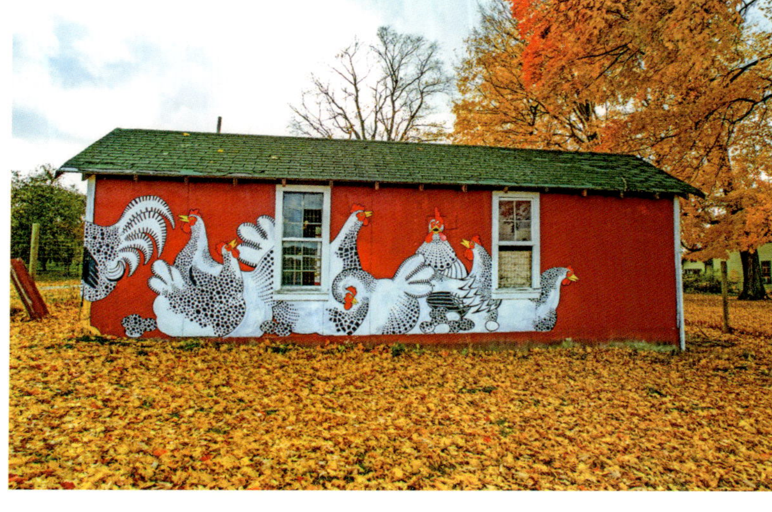

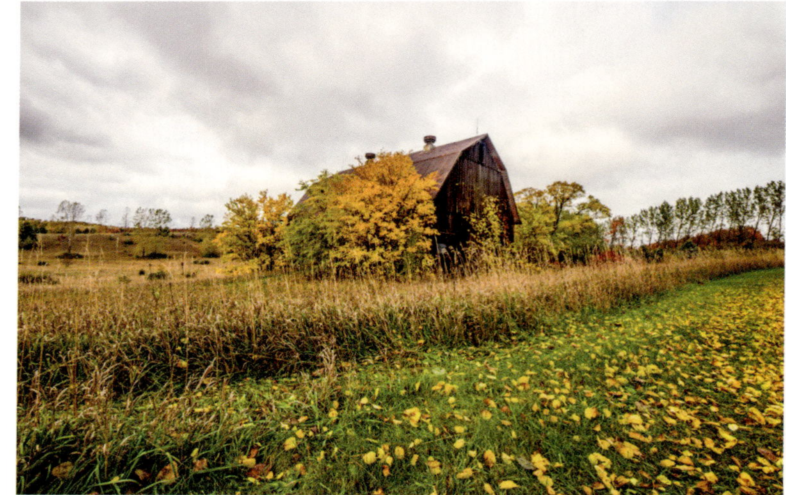

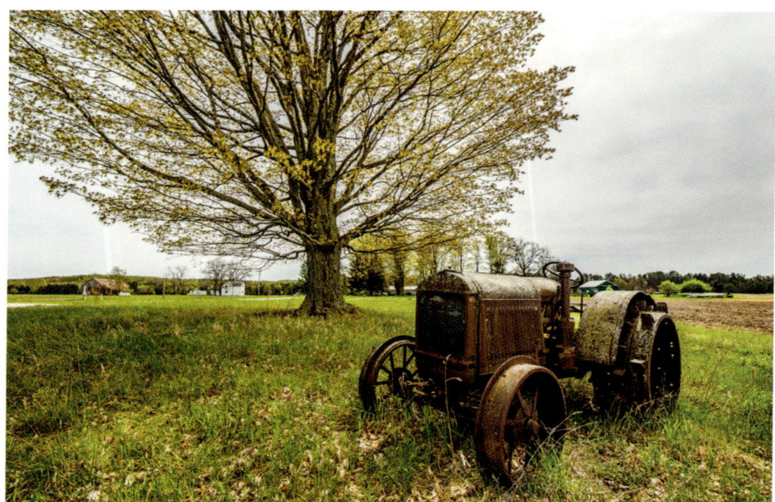

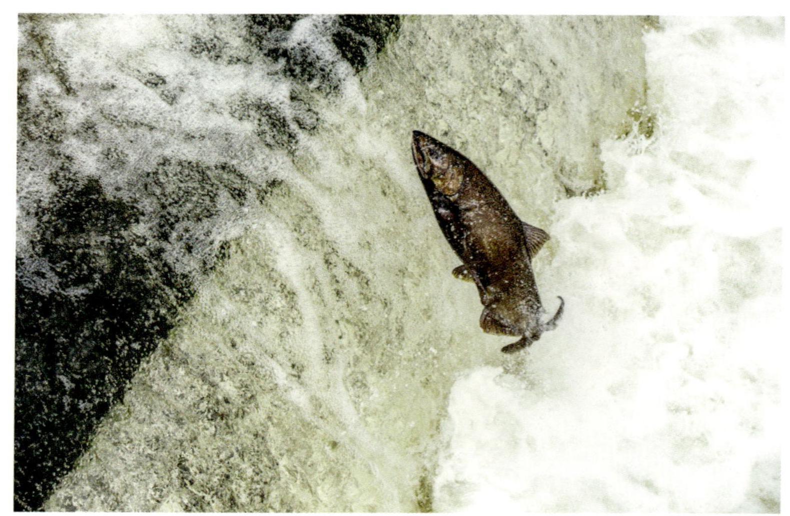

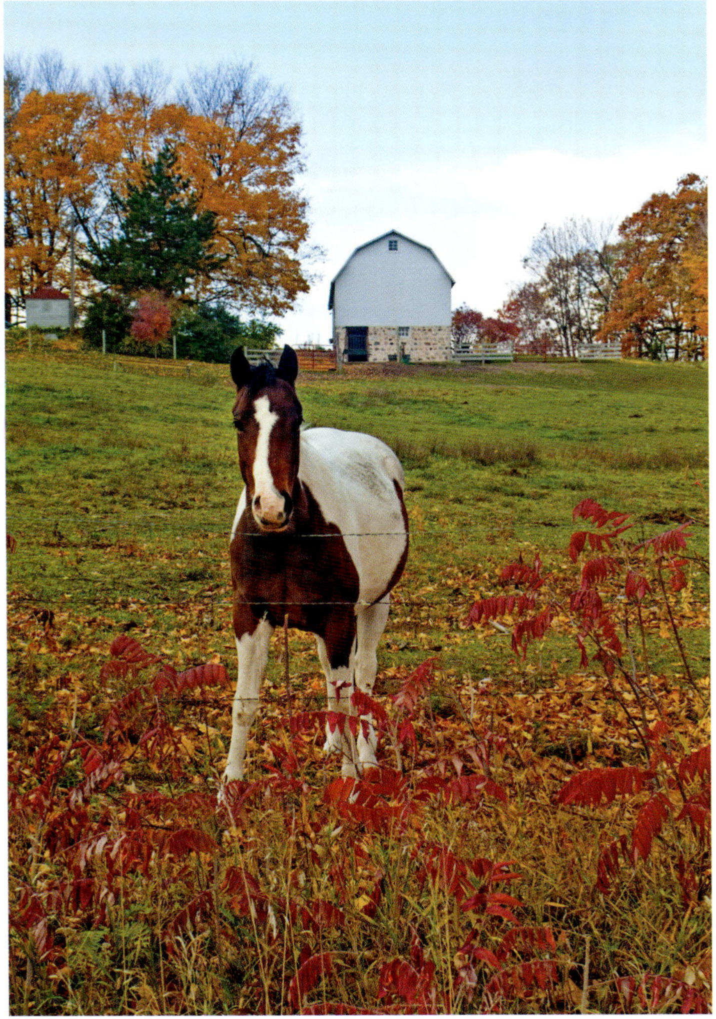

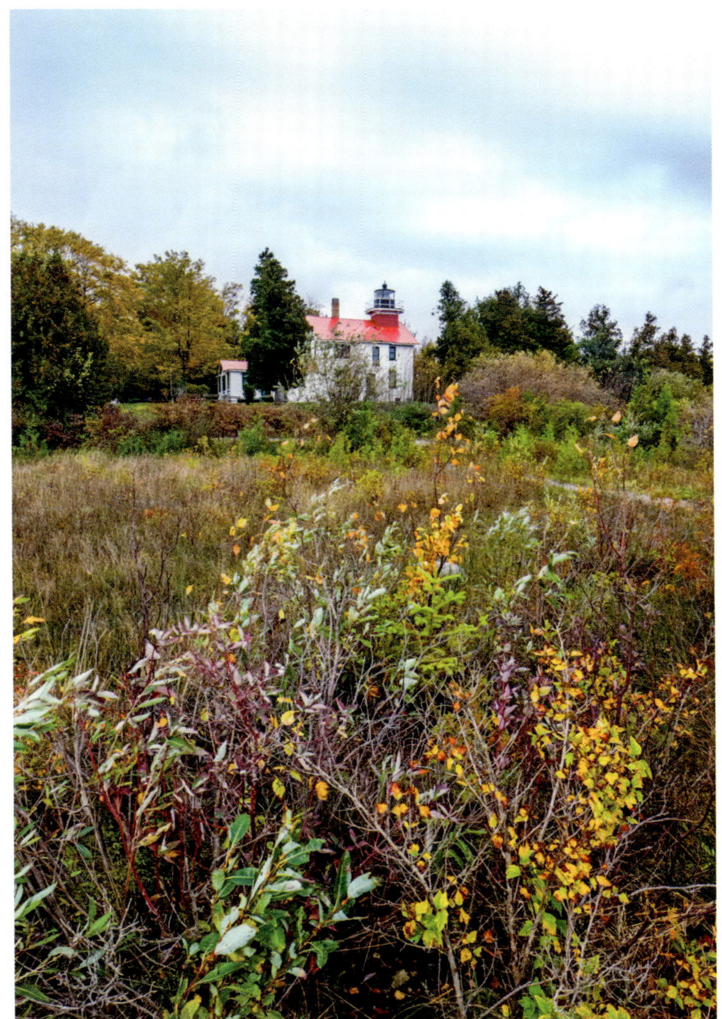

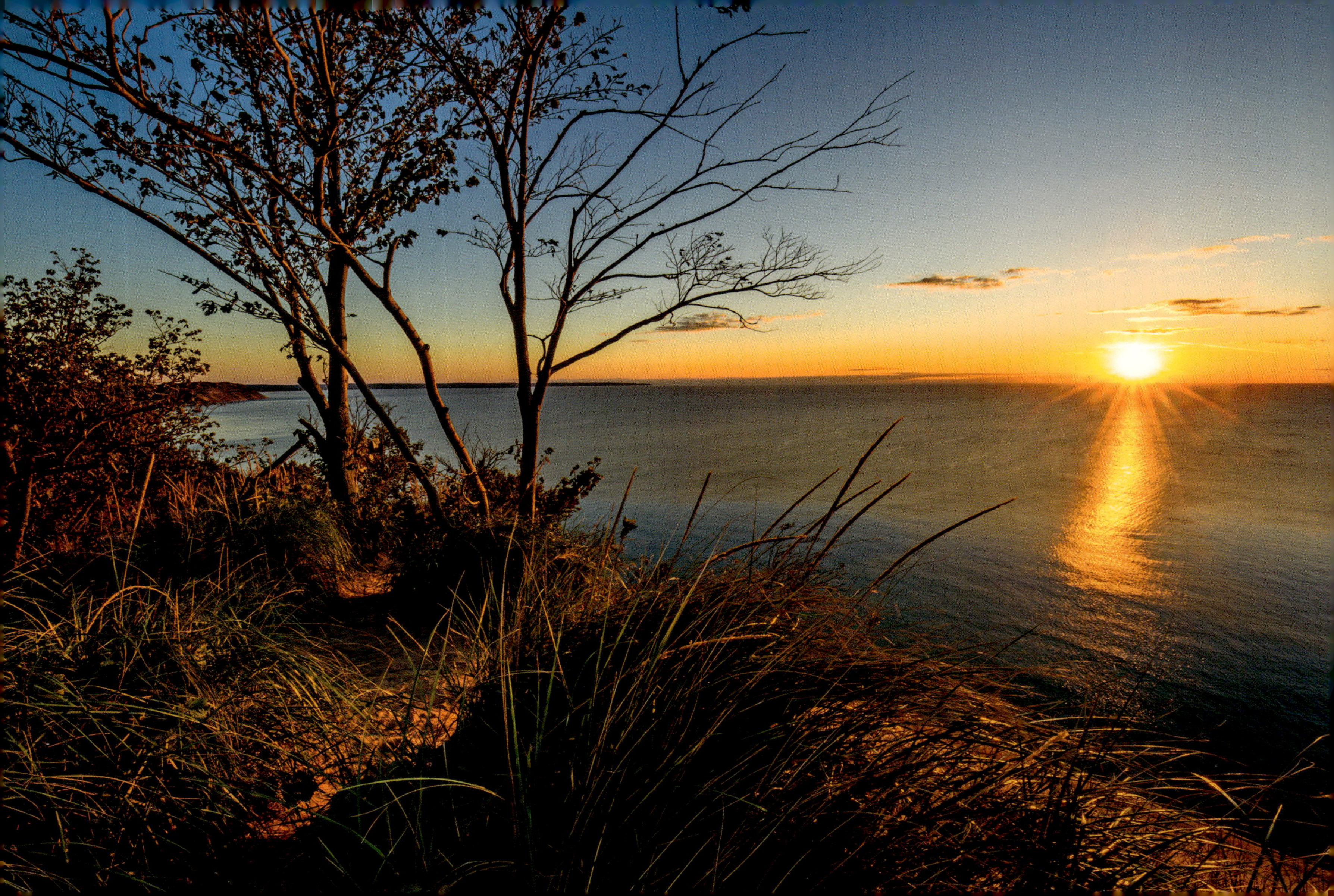

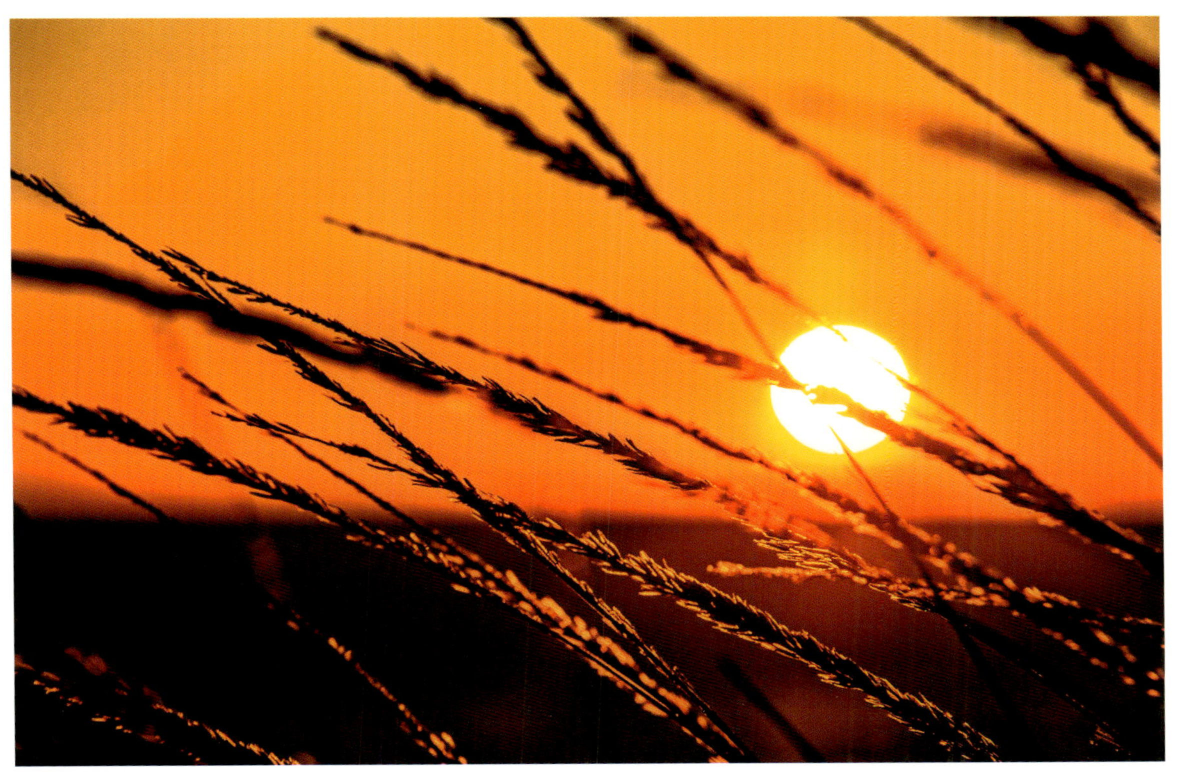

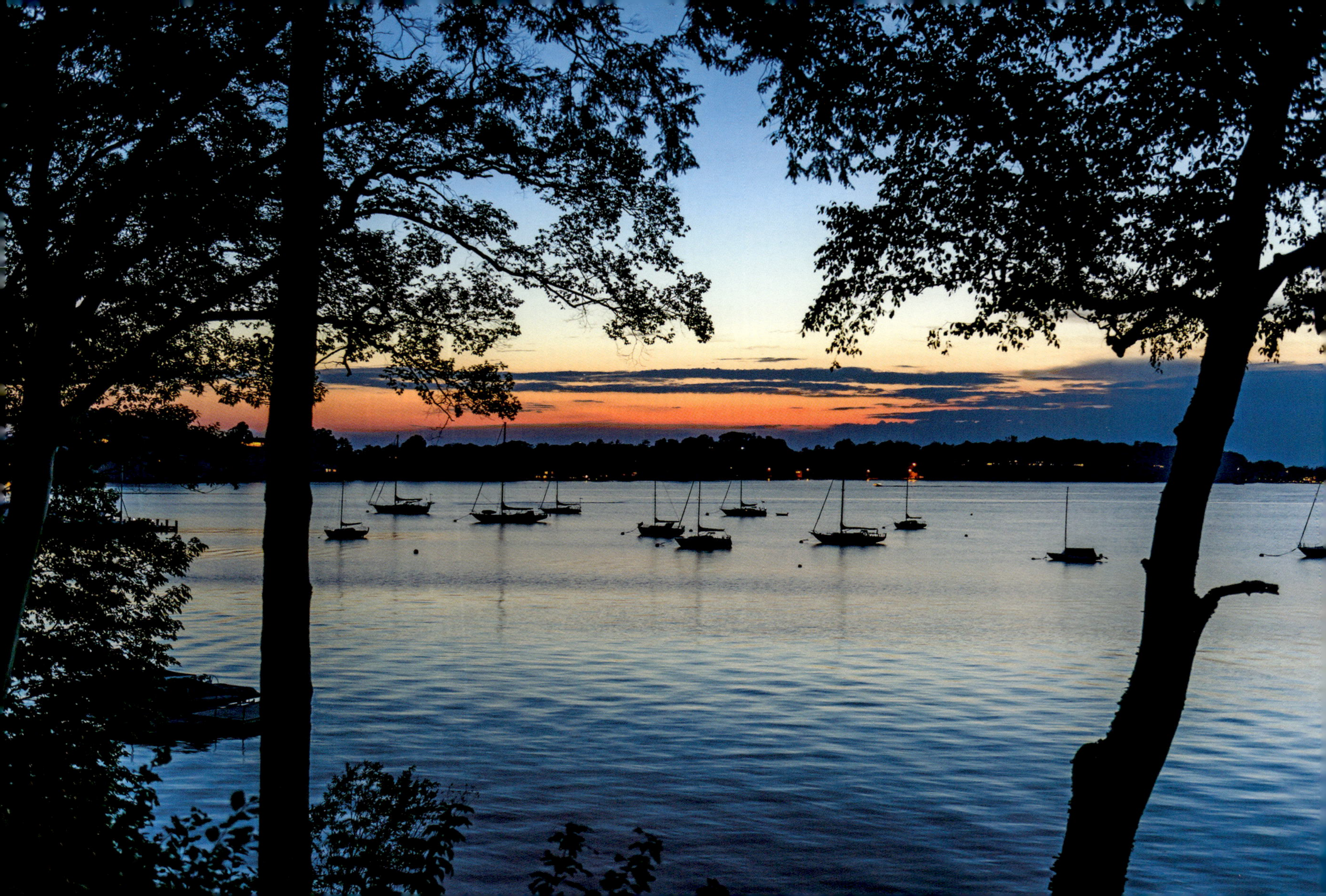

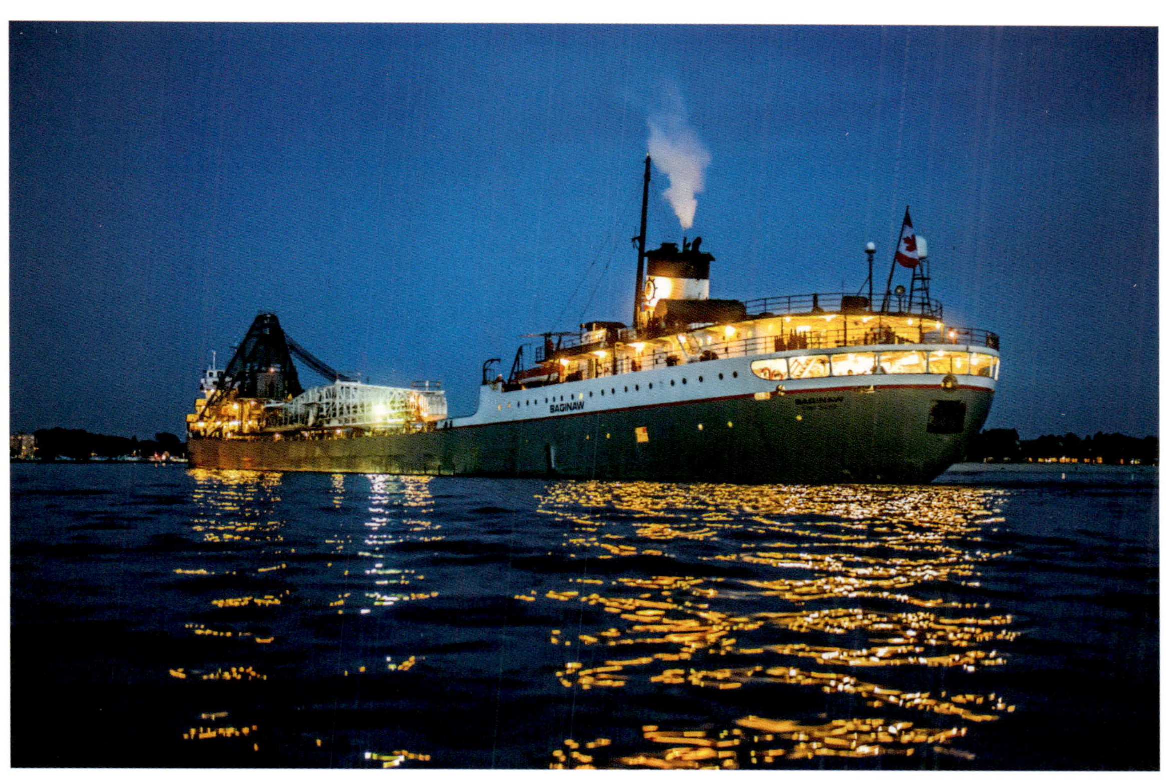
SAGINAW

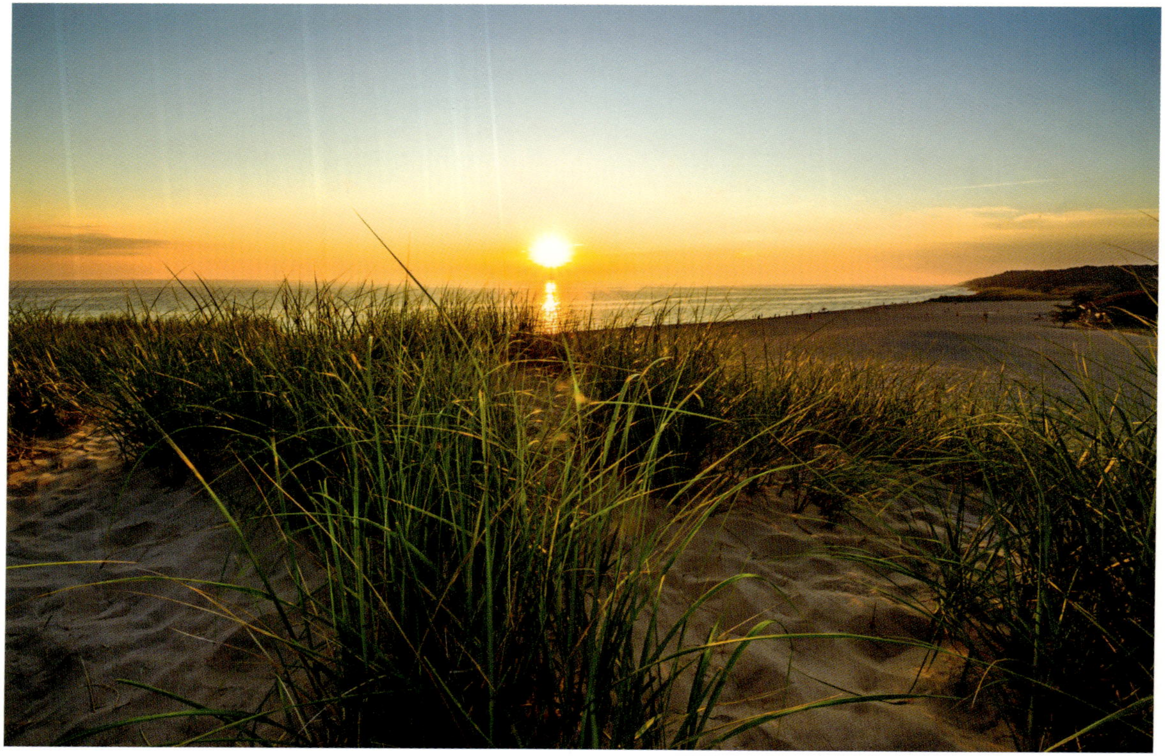

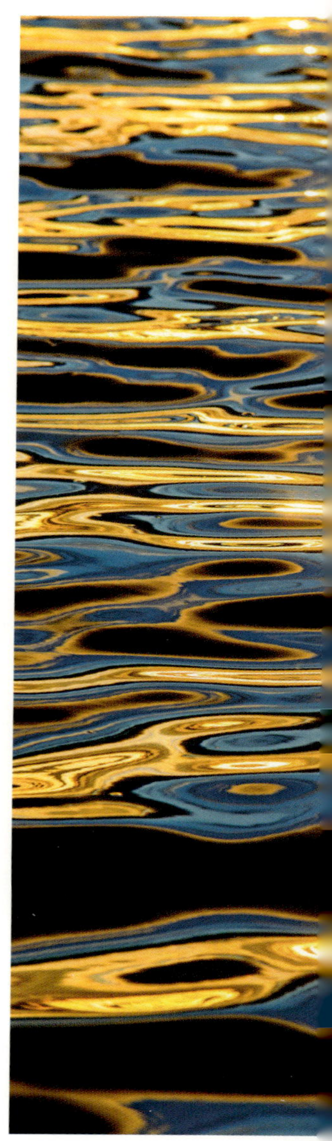

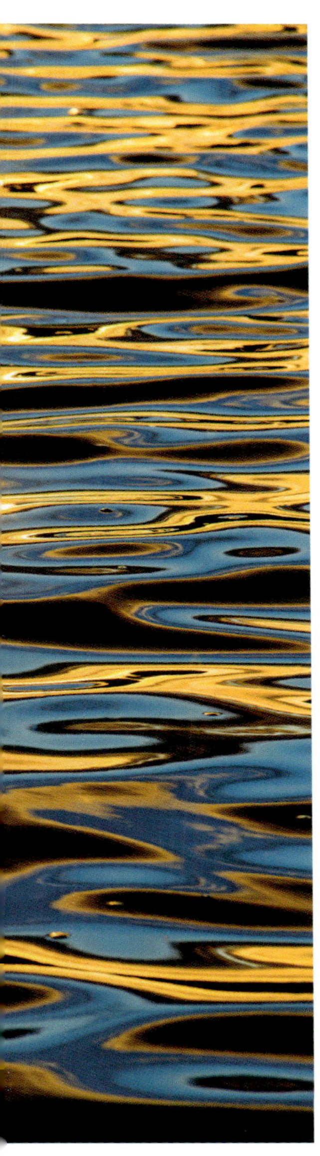

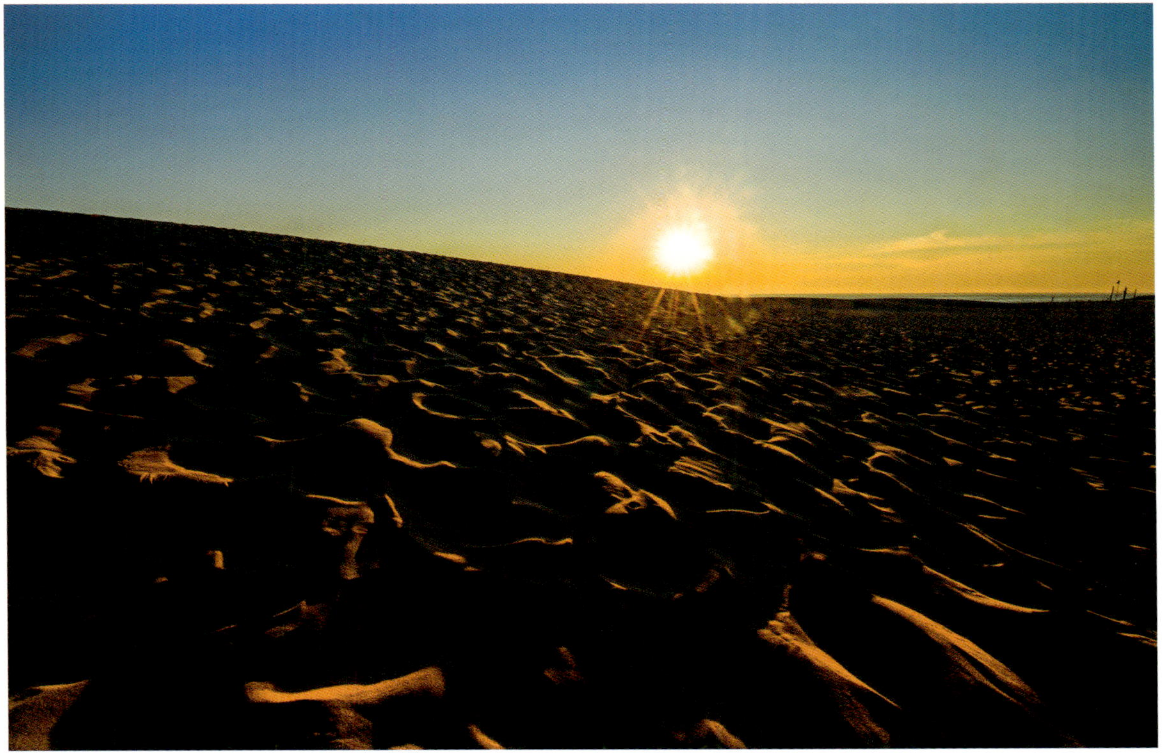

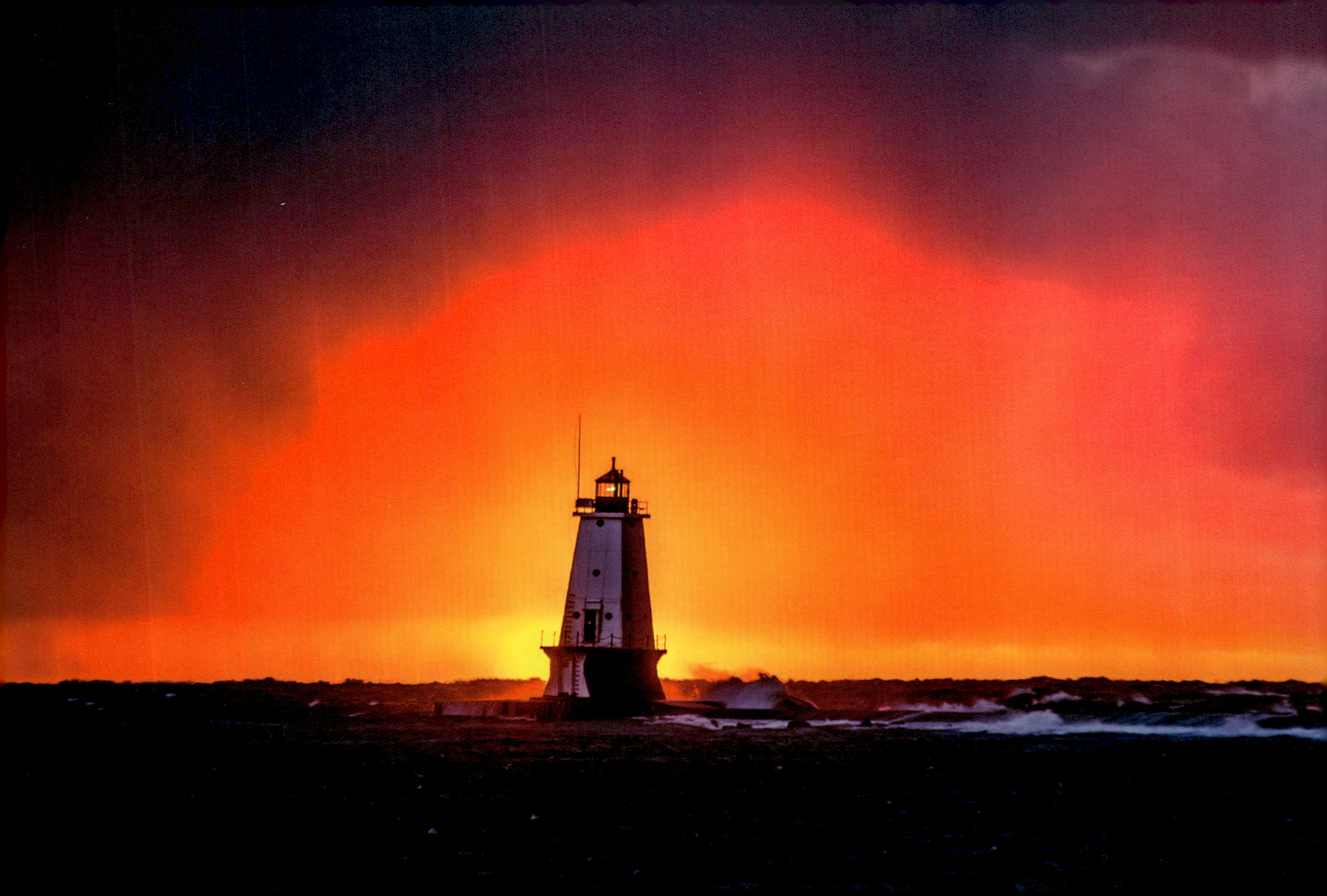

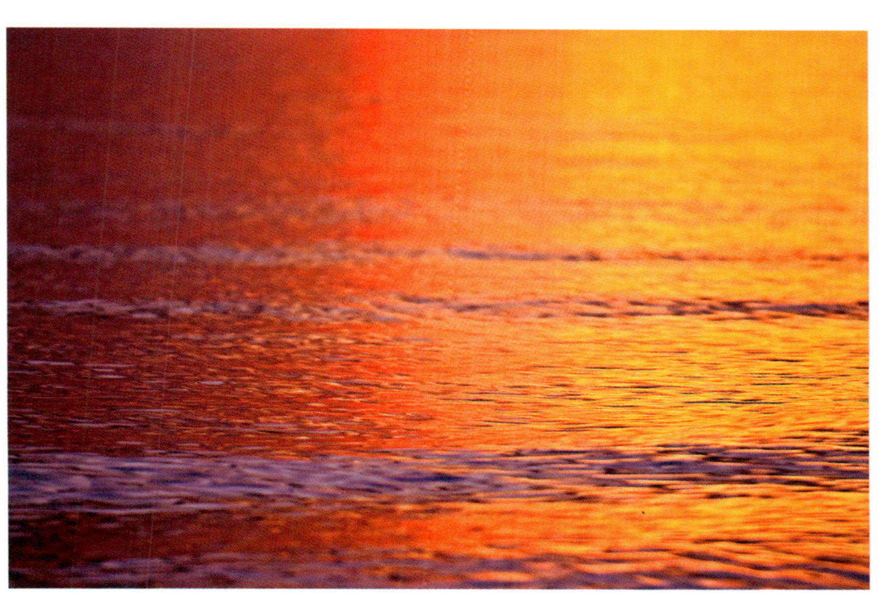

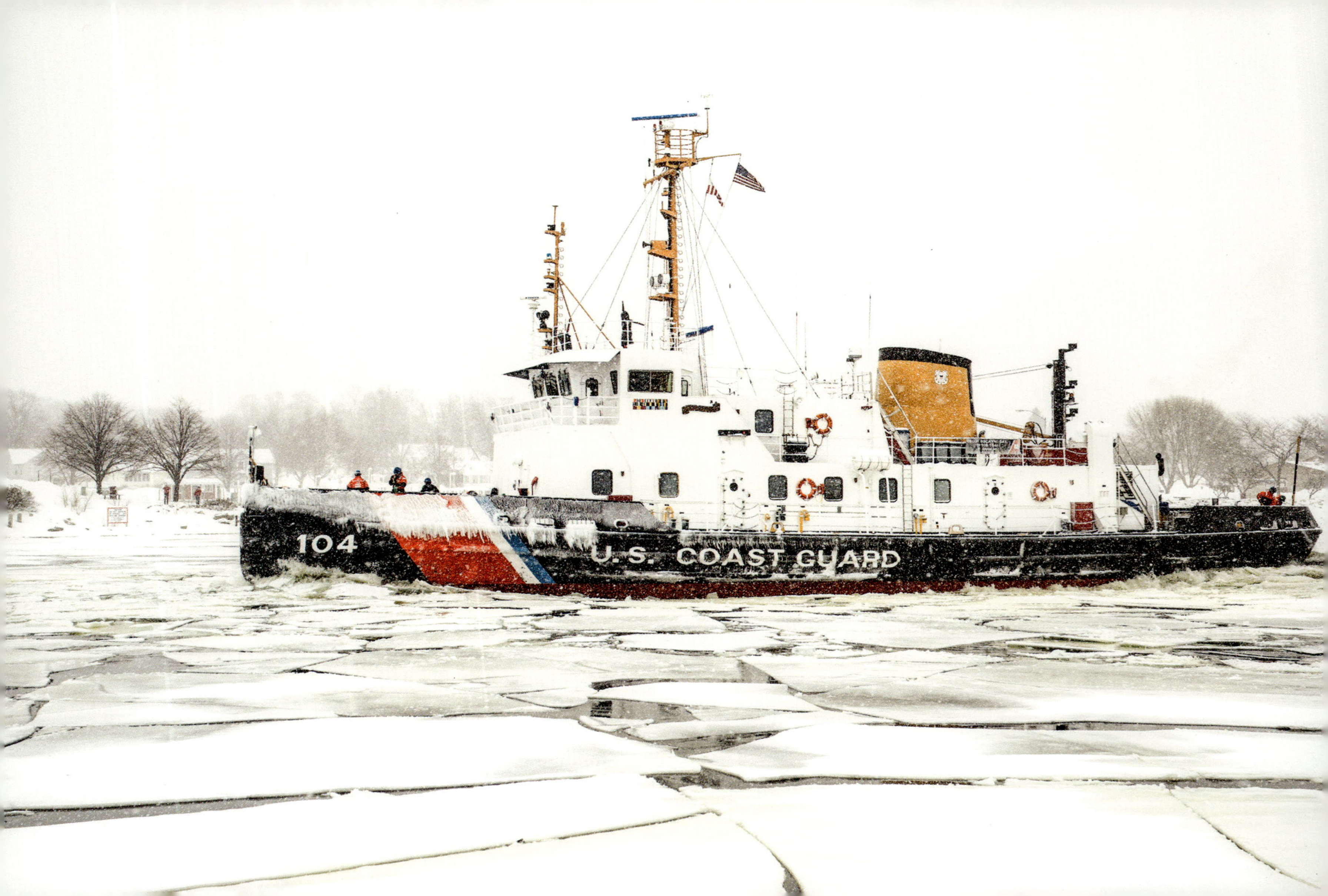
104
U.S. COAST GUARD

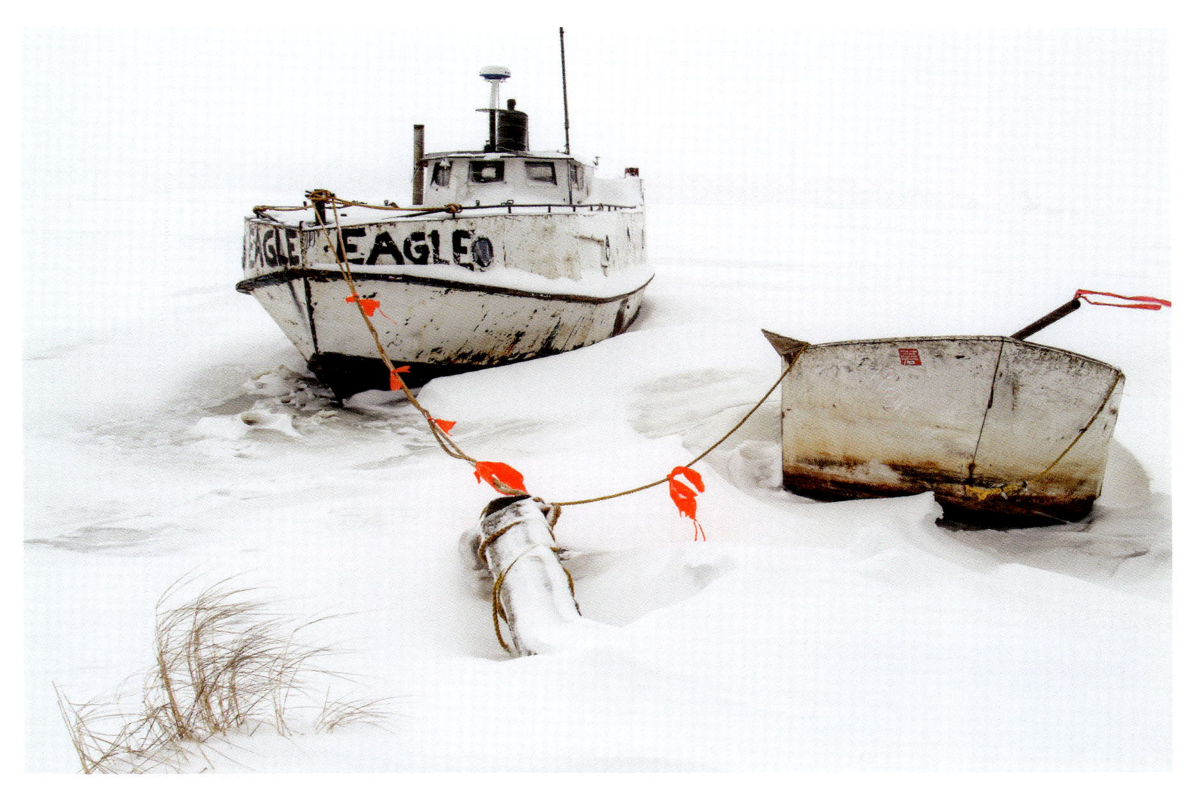
EAGLE

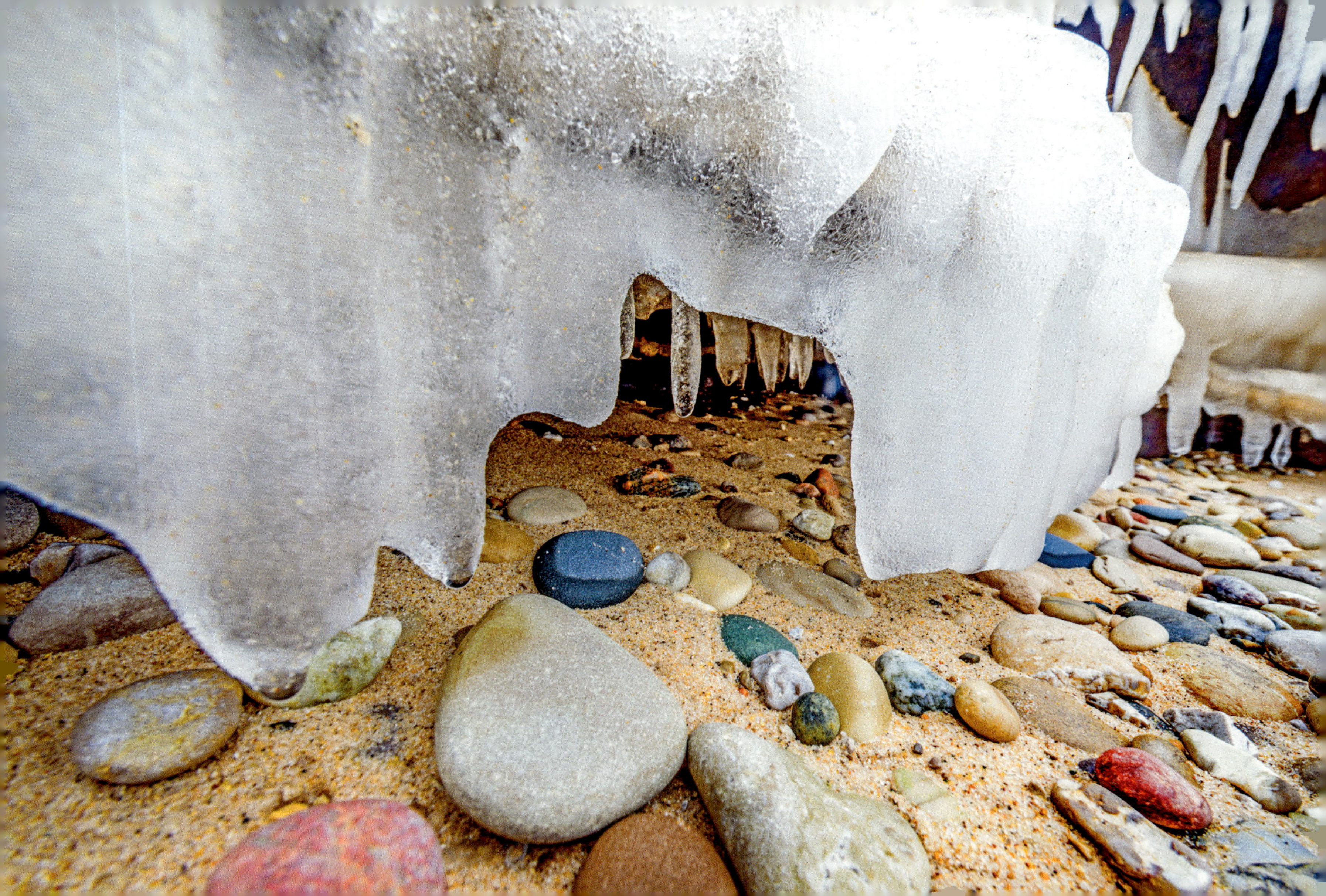

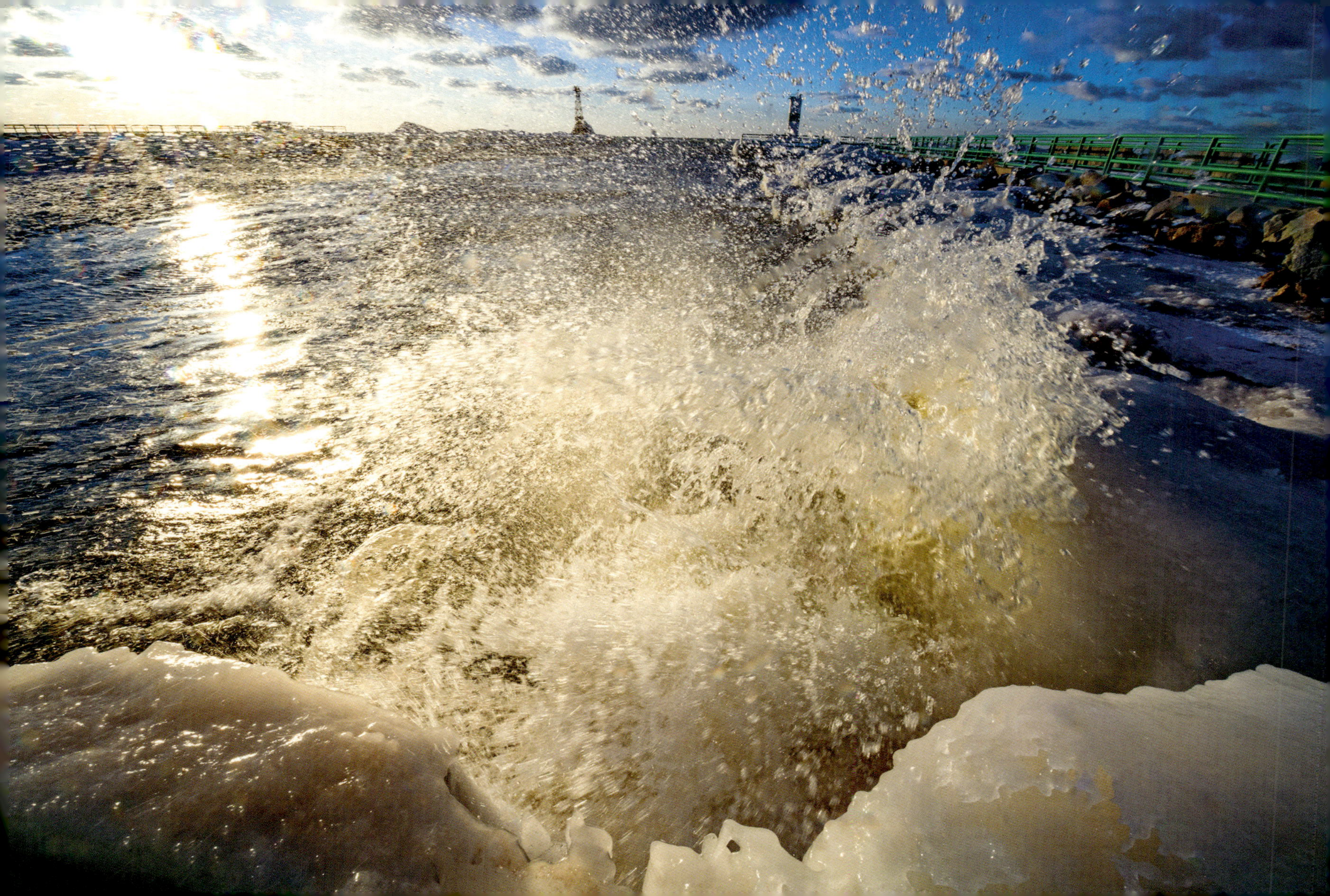

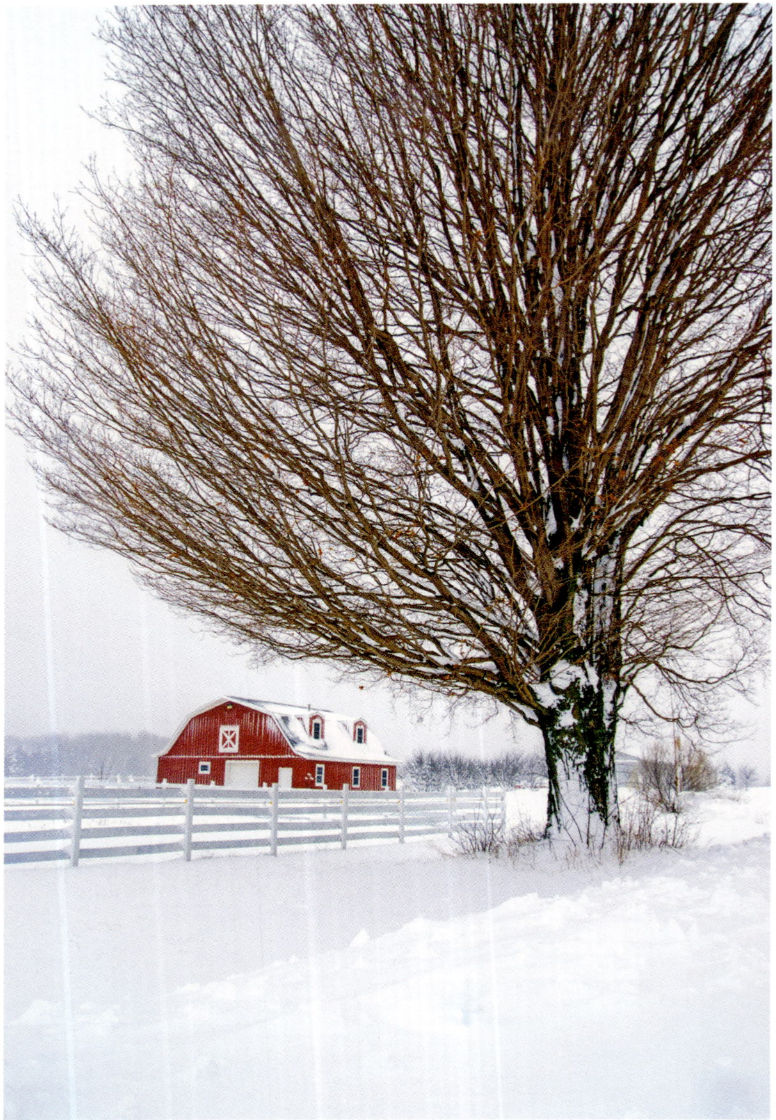

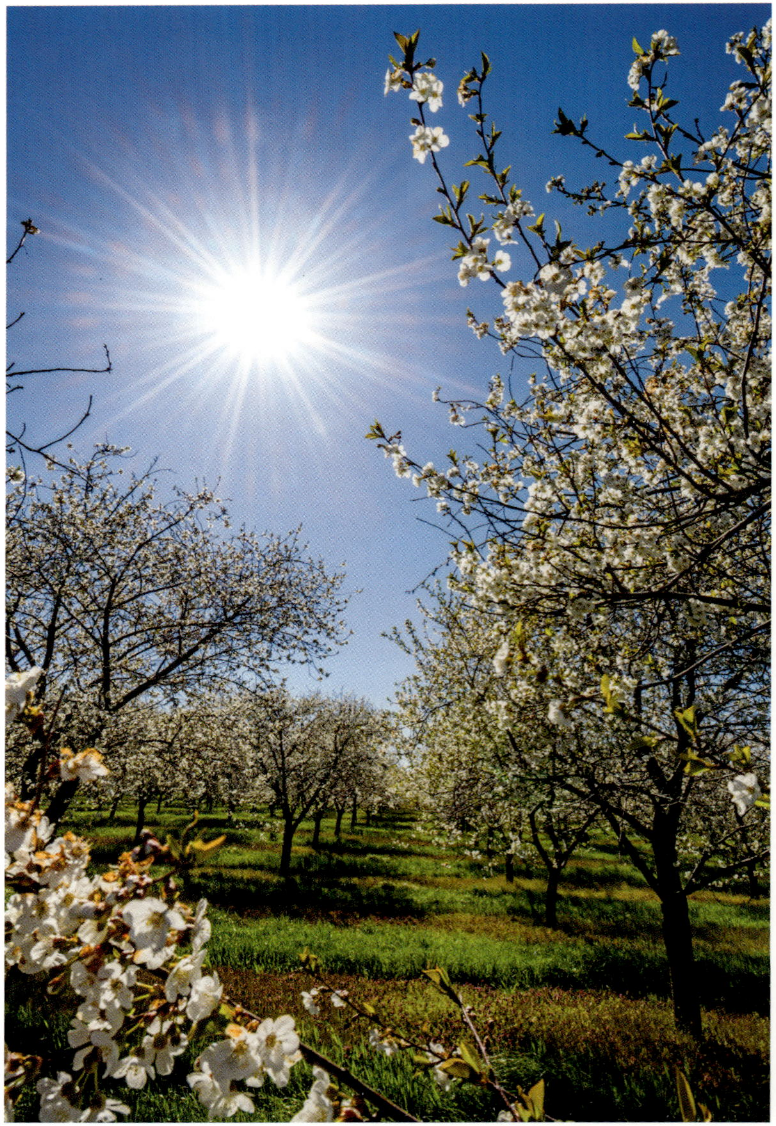

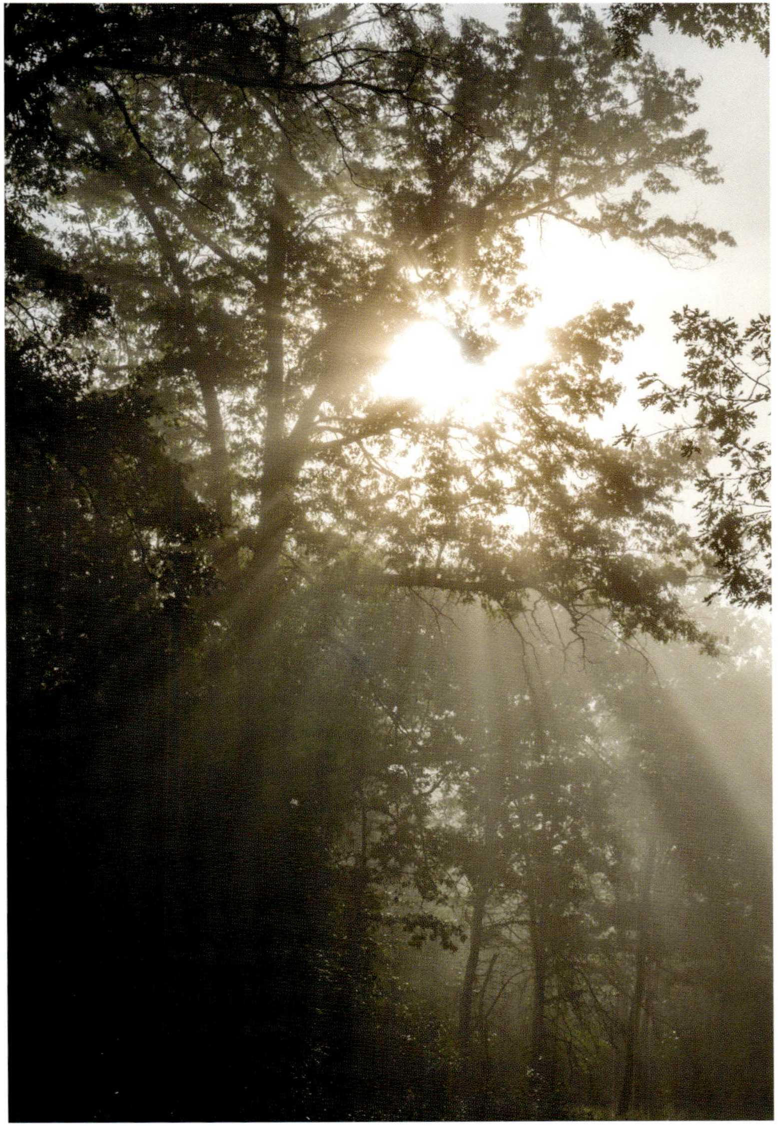

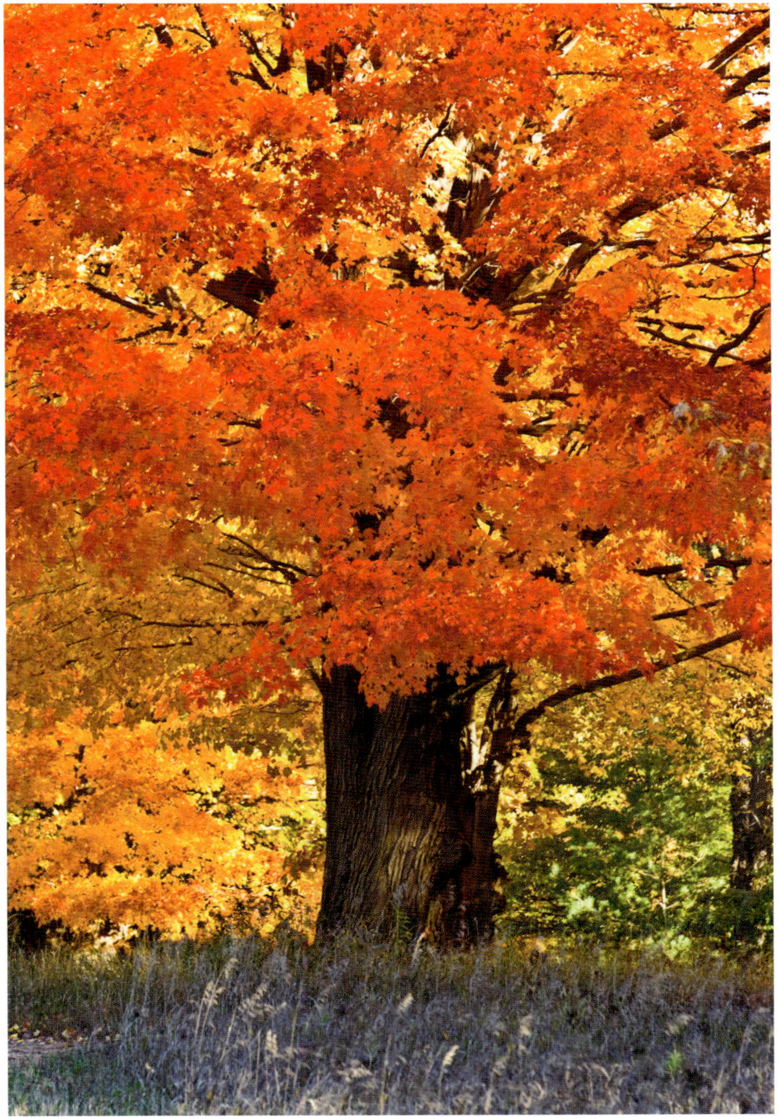

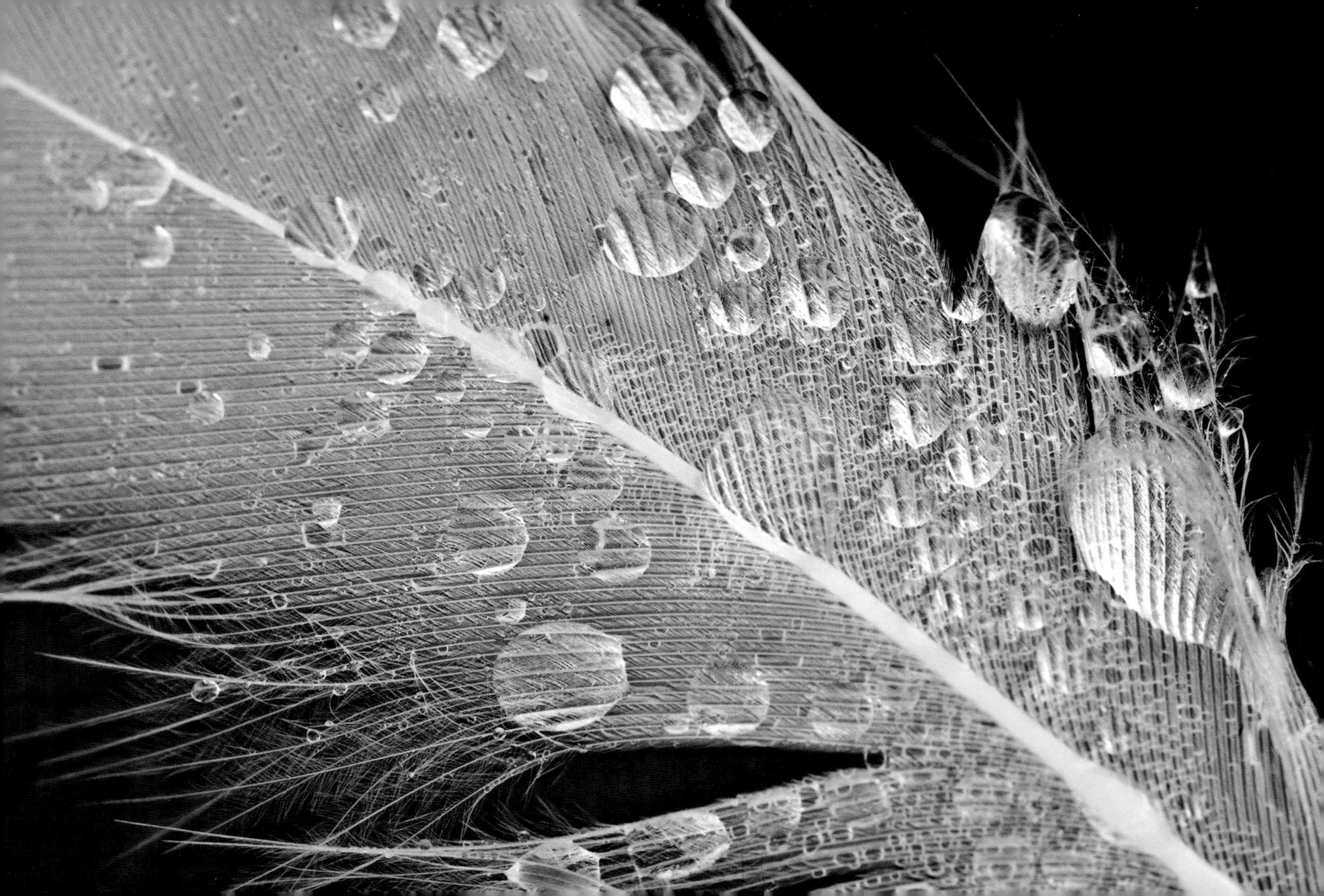

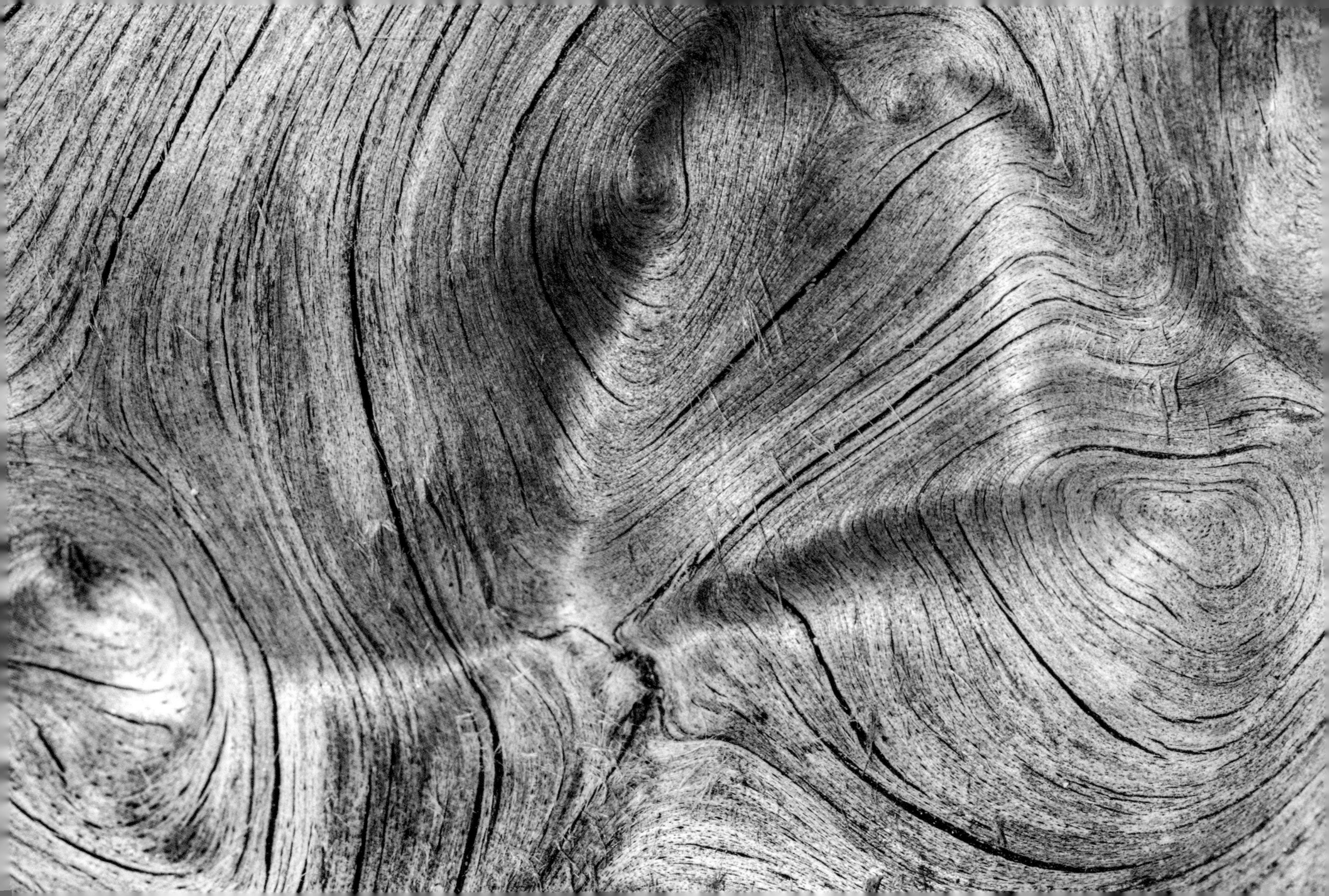

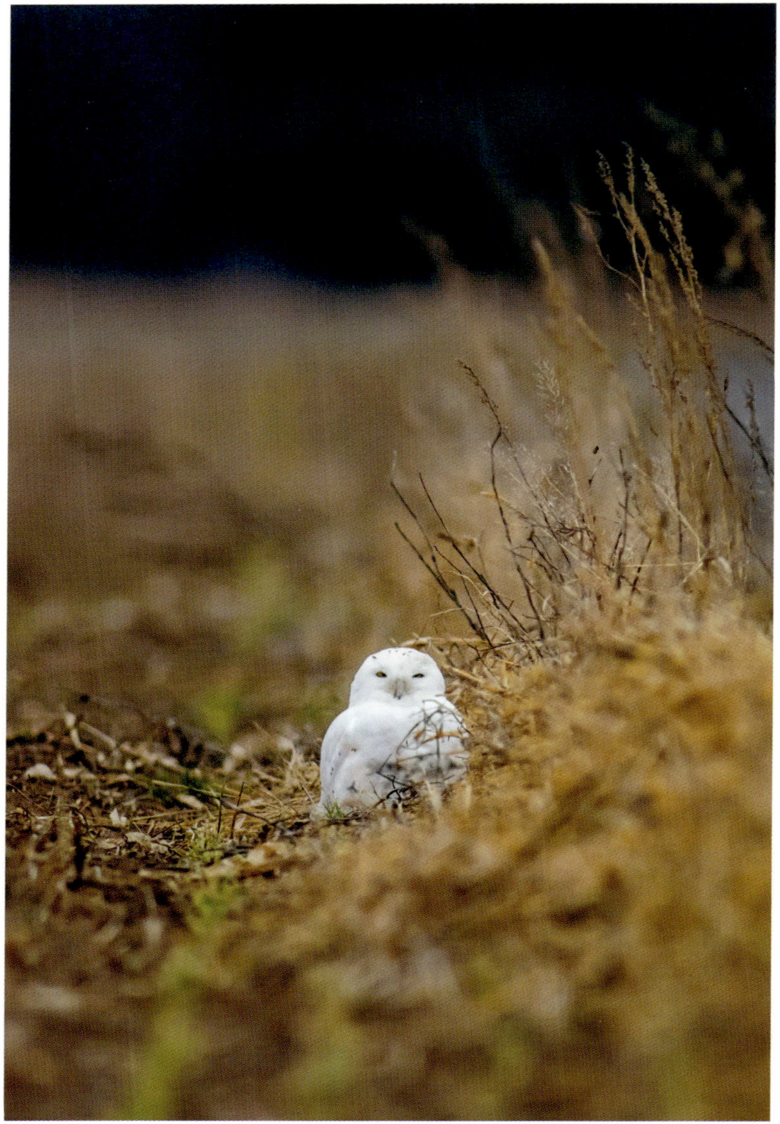

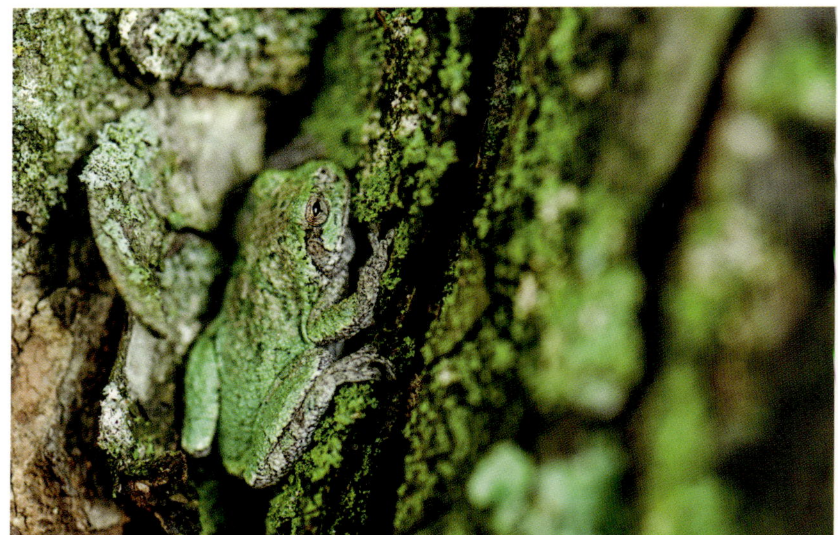

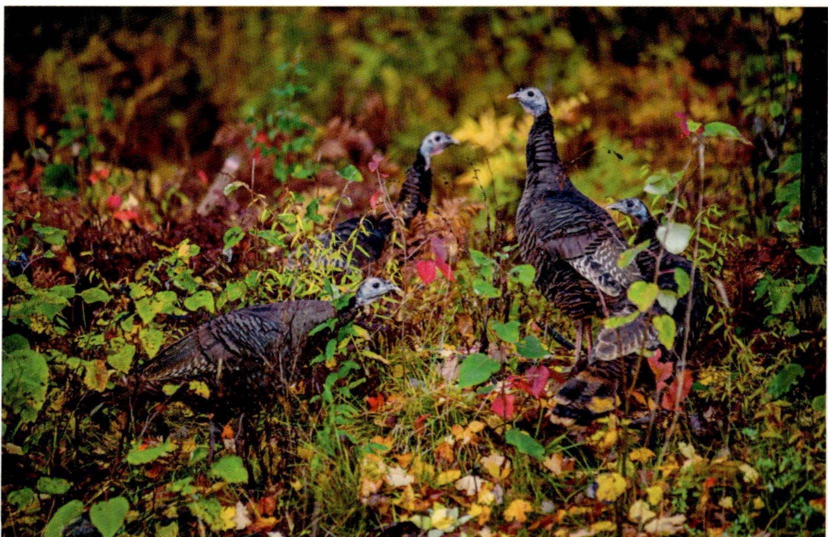

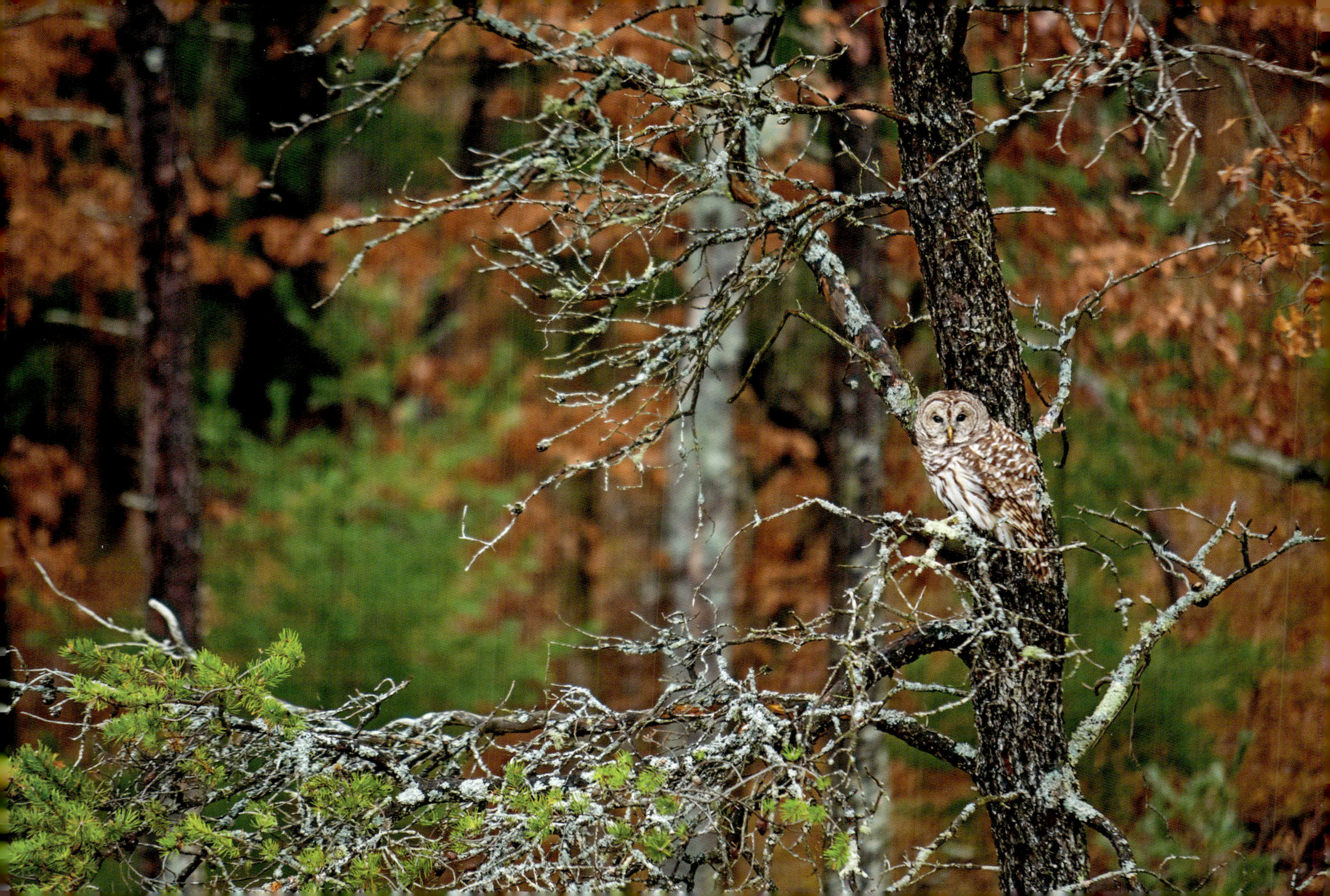

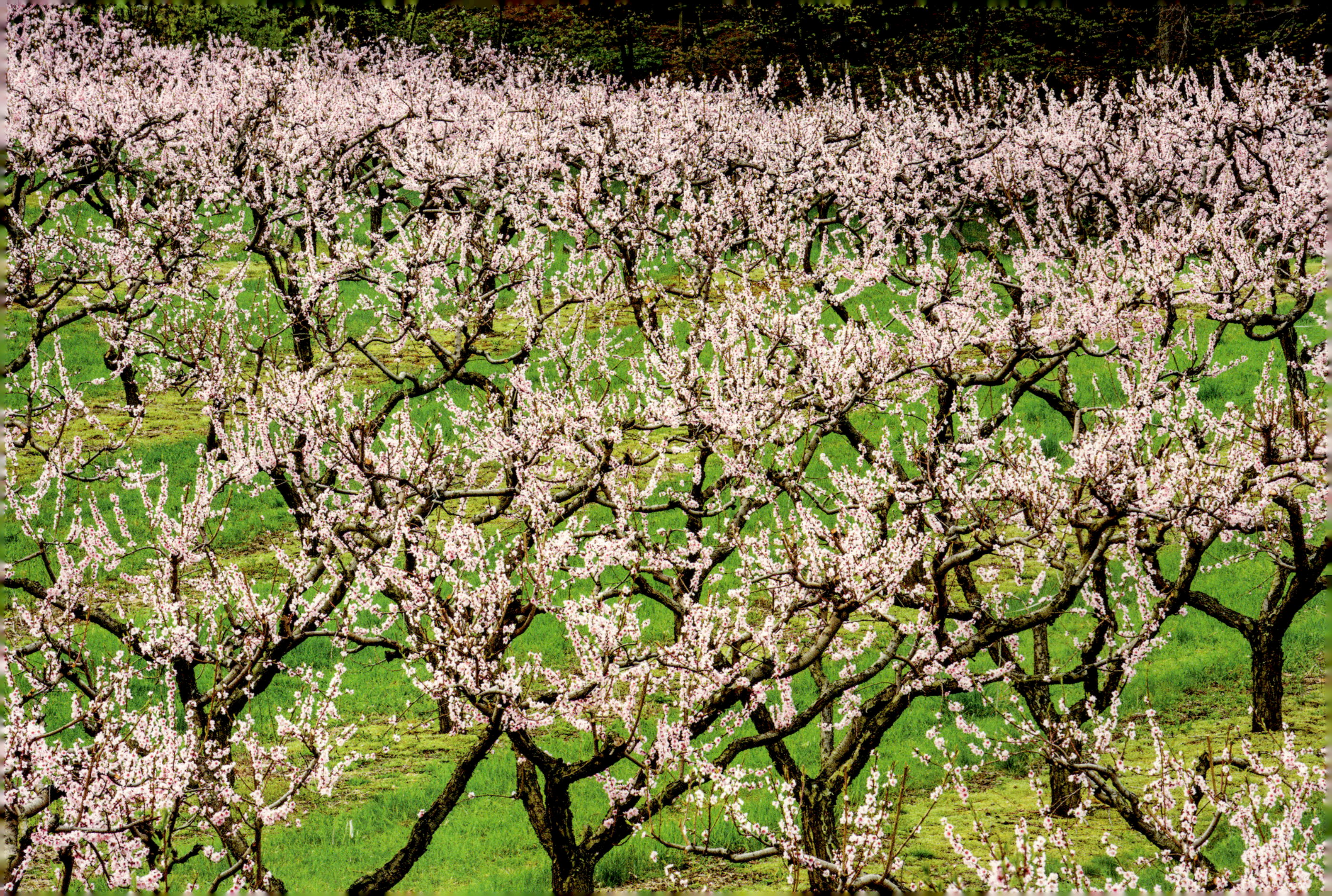

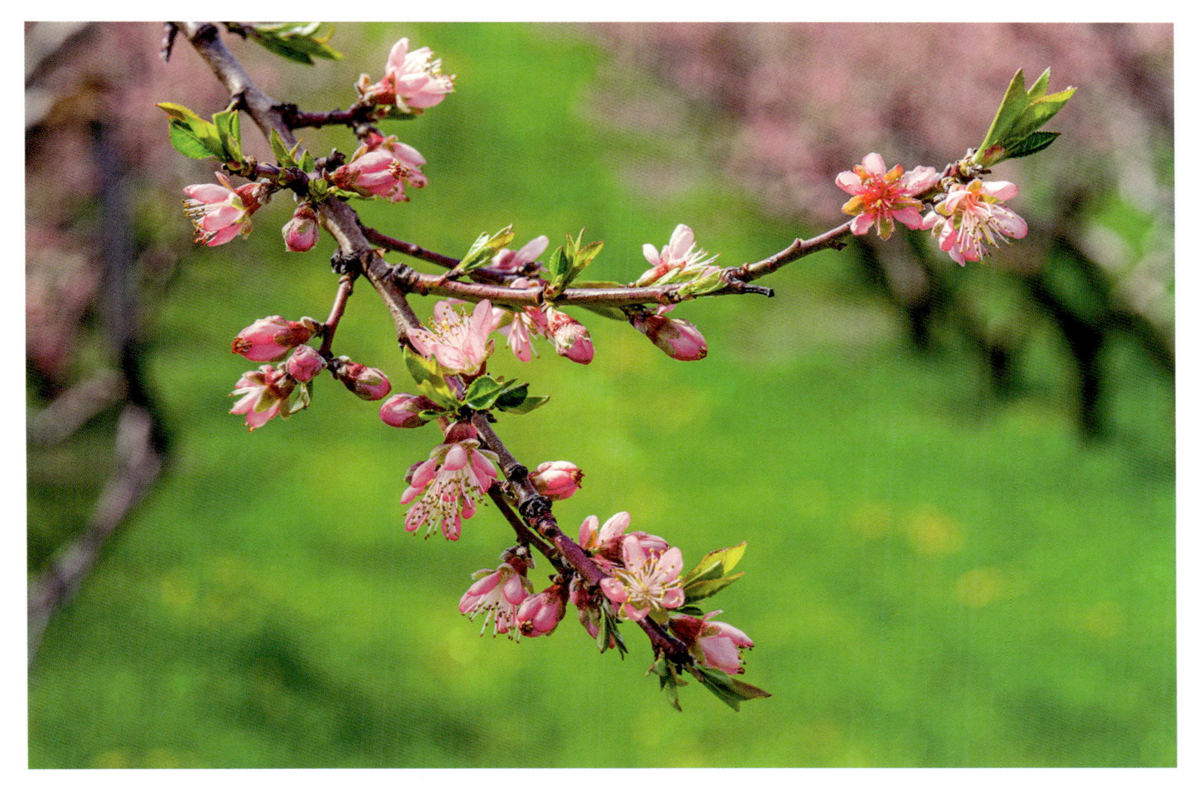

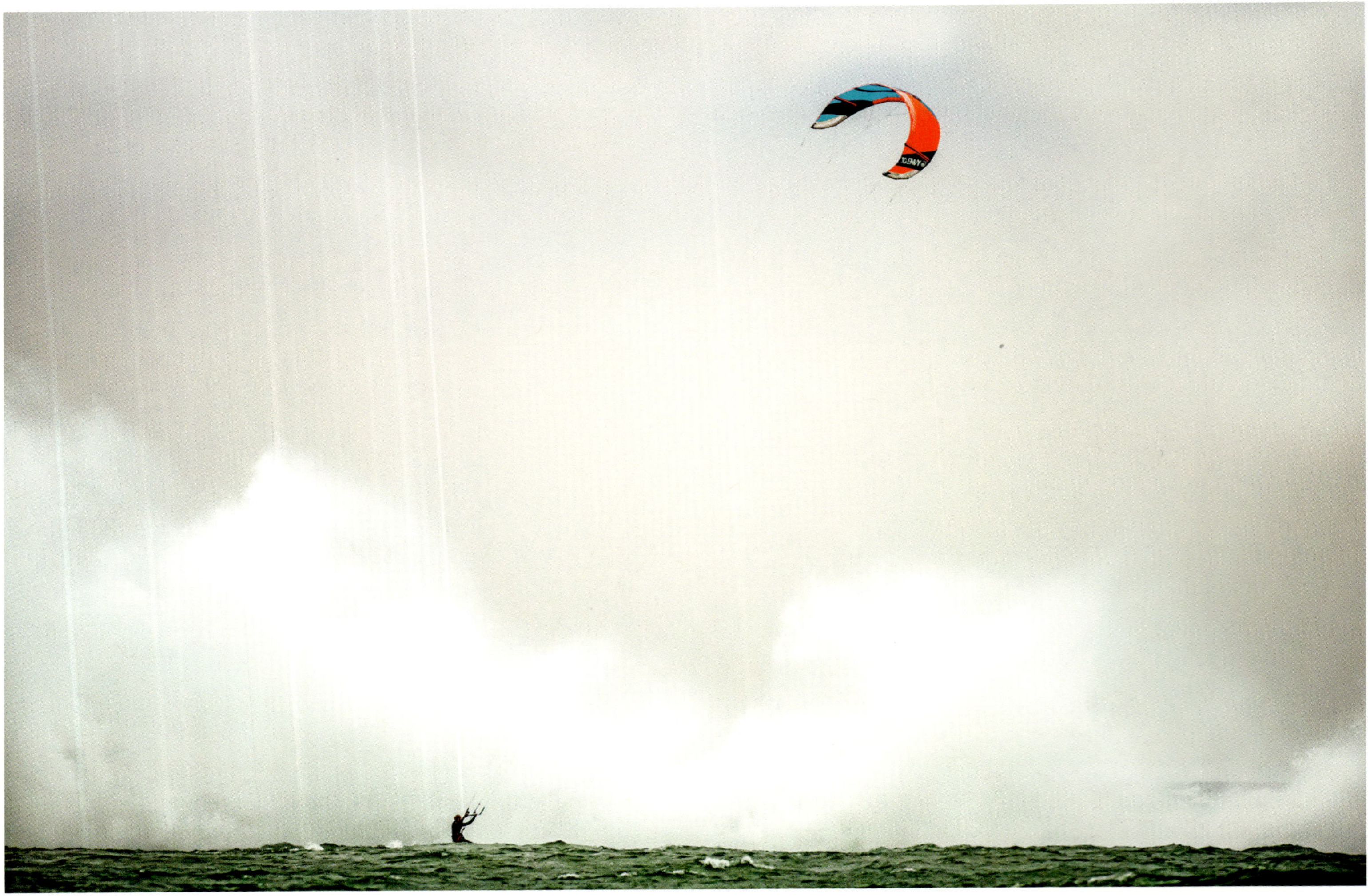

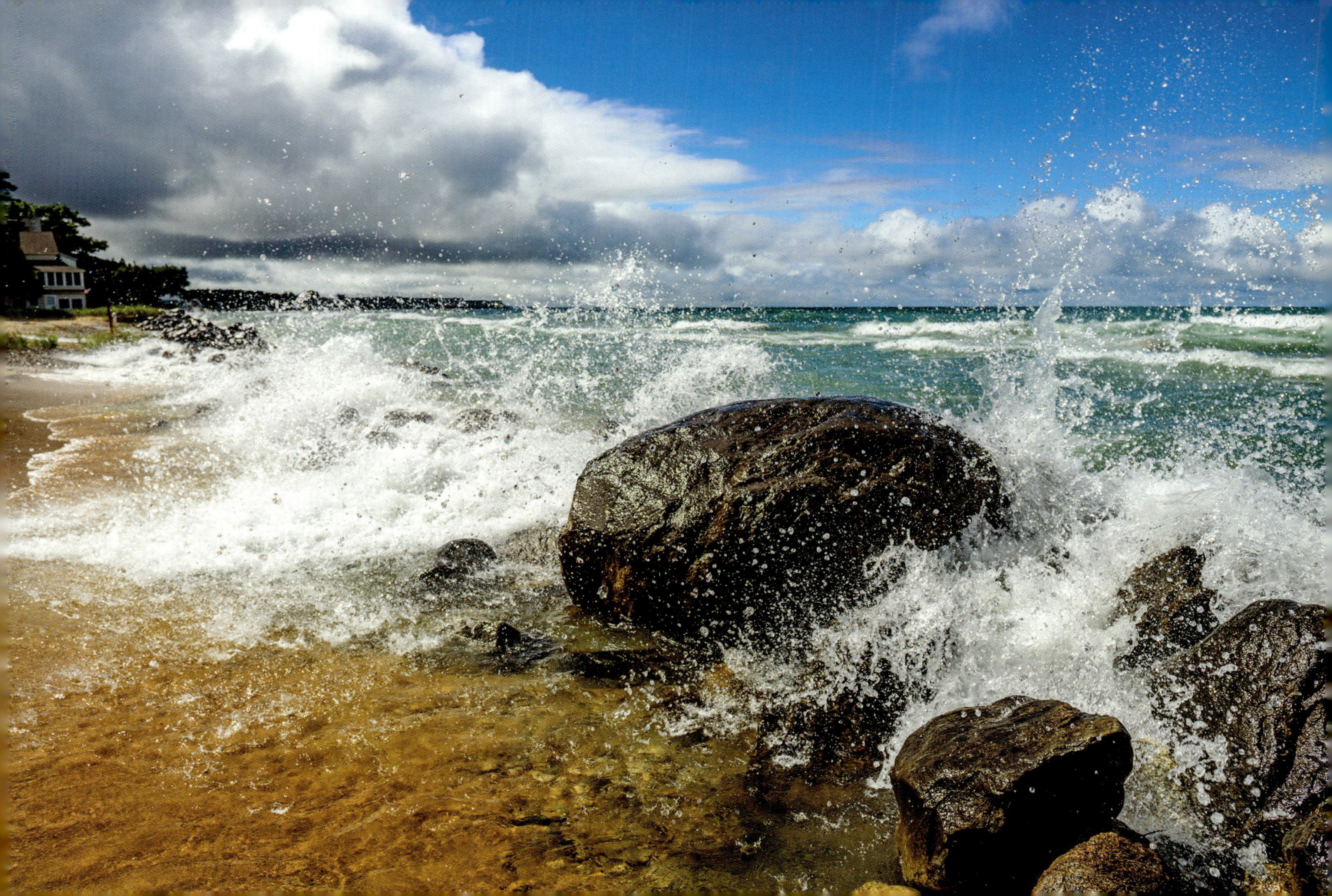

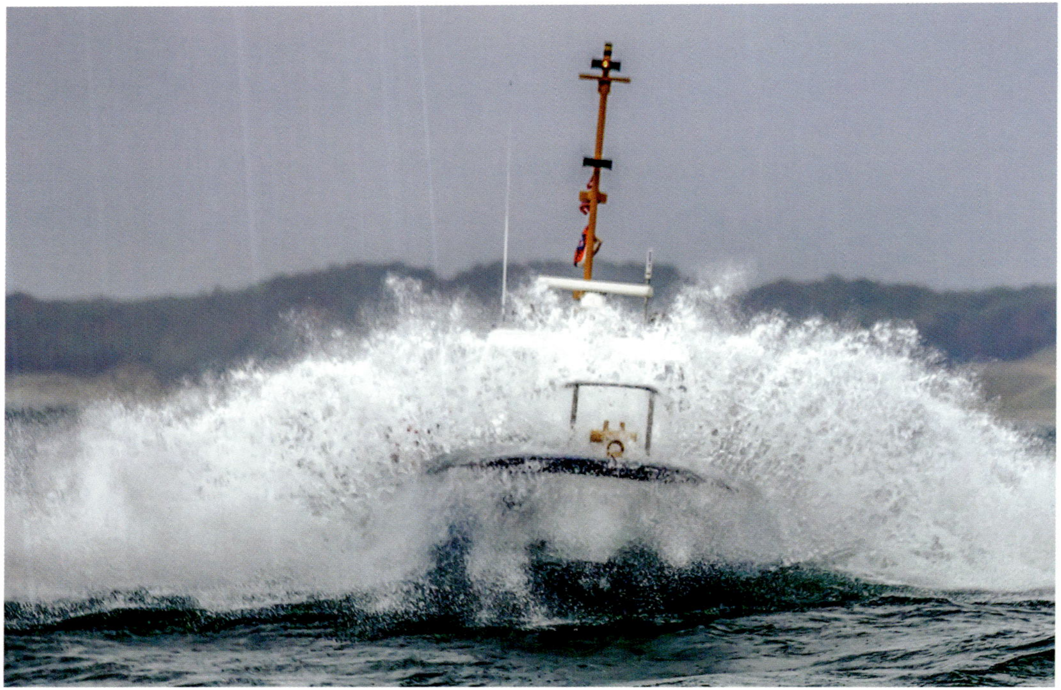

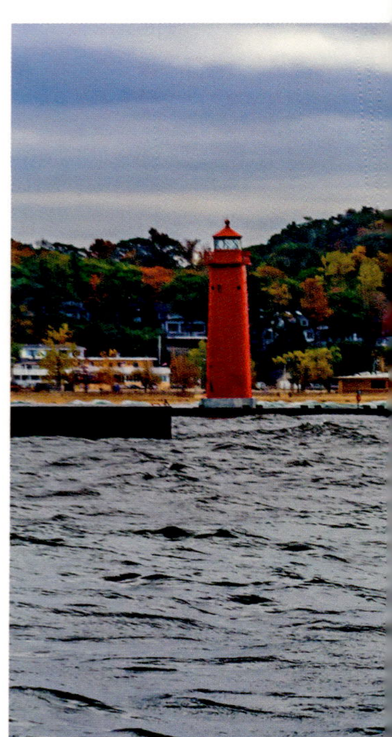

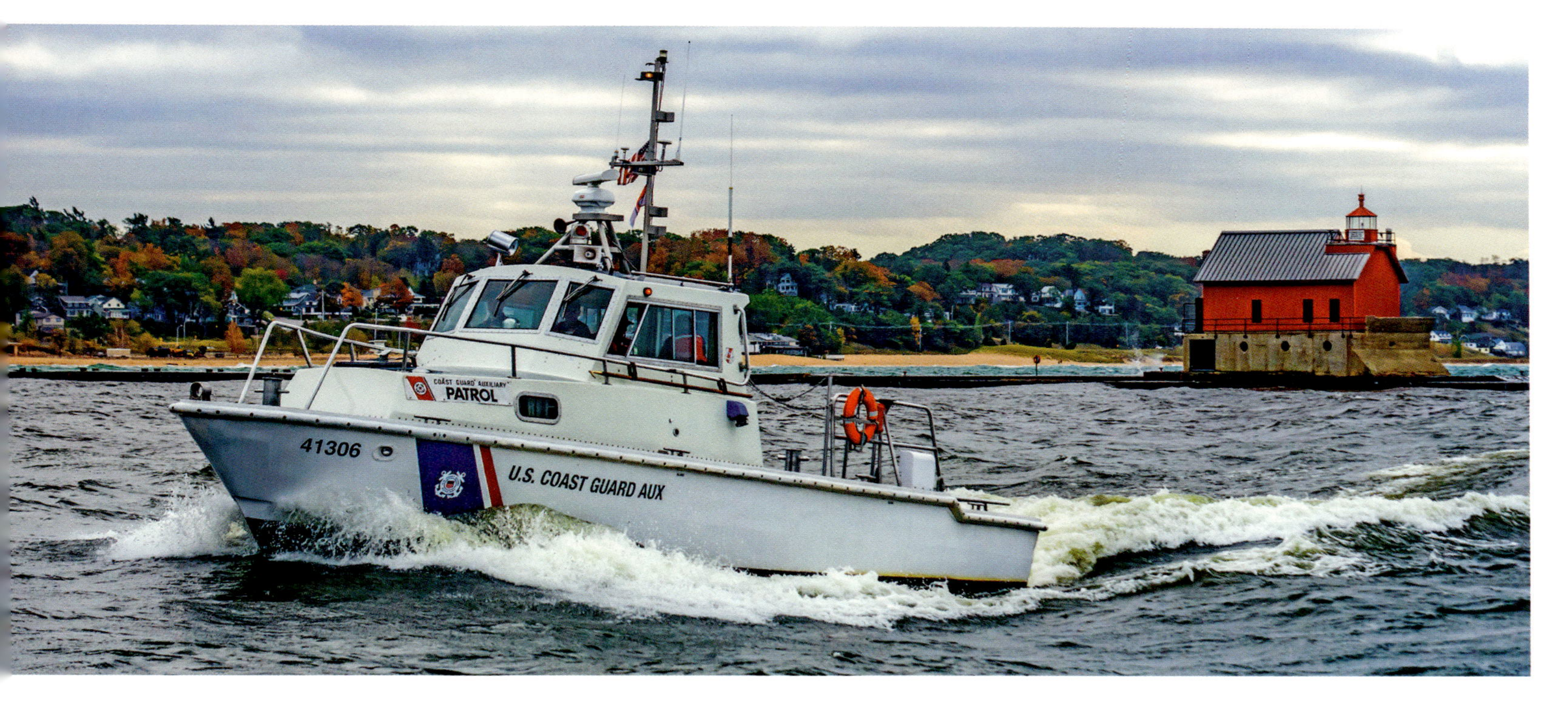
COAST GUARD AUXILIARY
PATROL
41306
U.S. COAST GUARD AUX

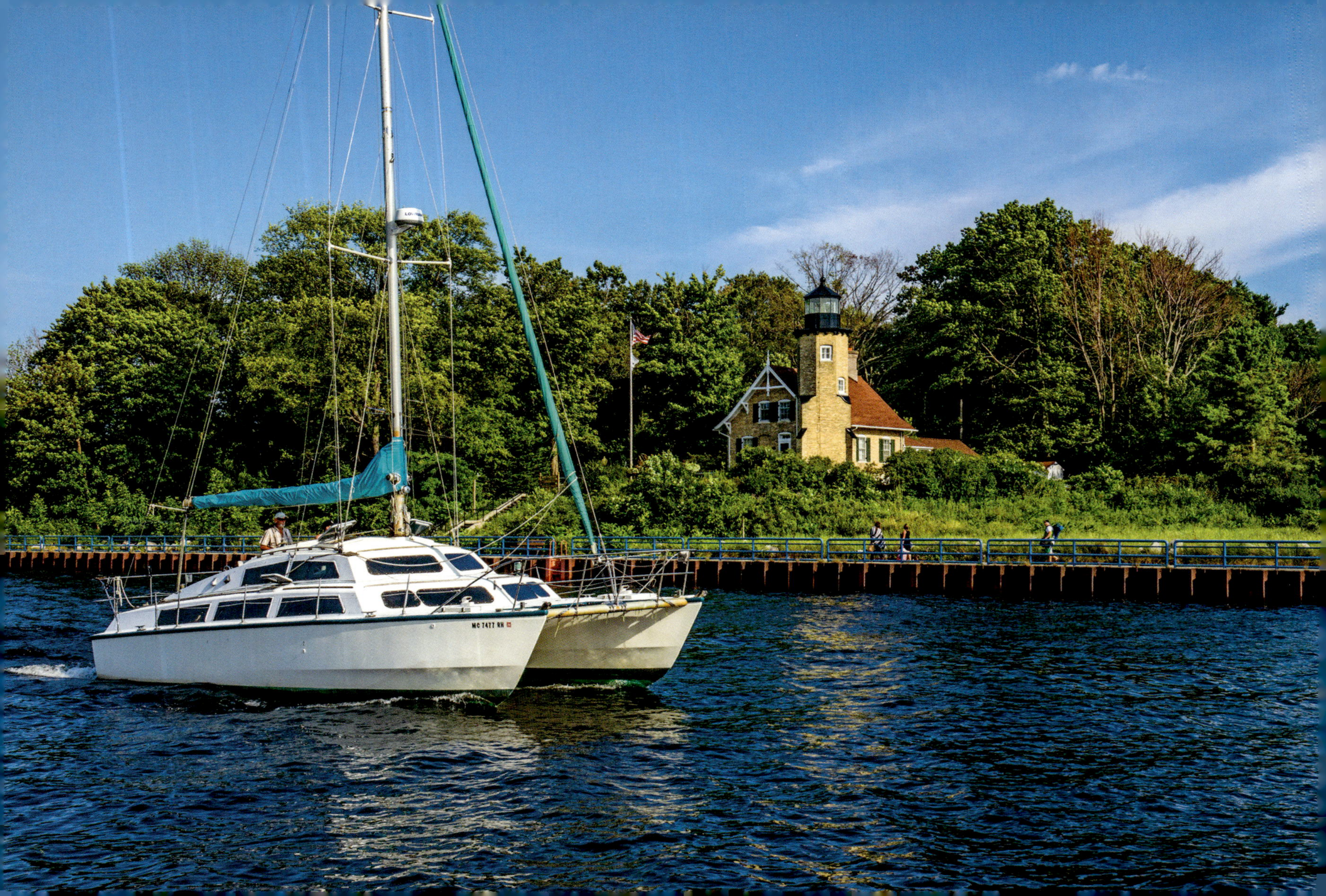
MC 7477 RH

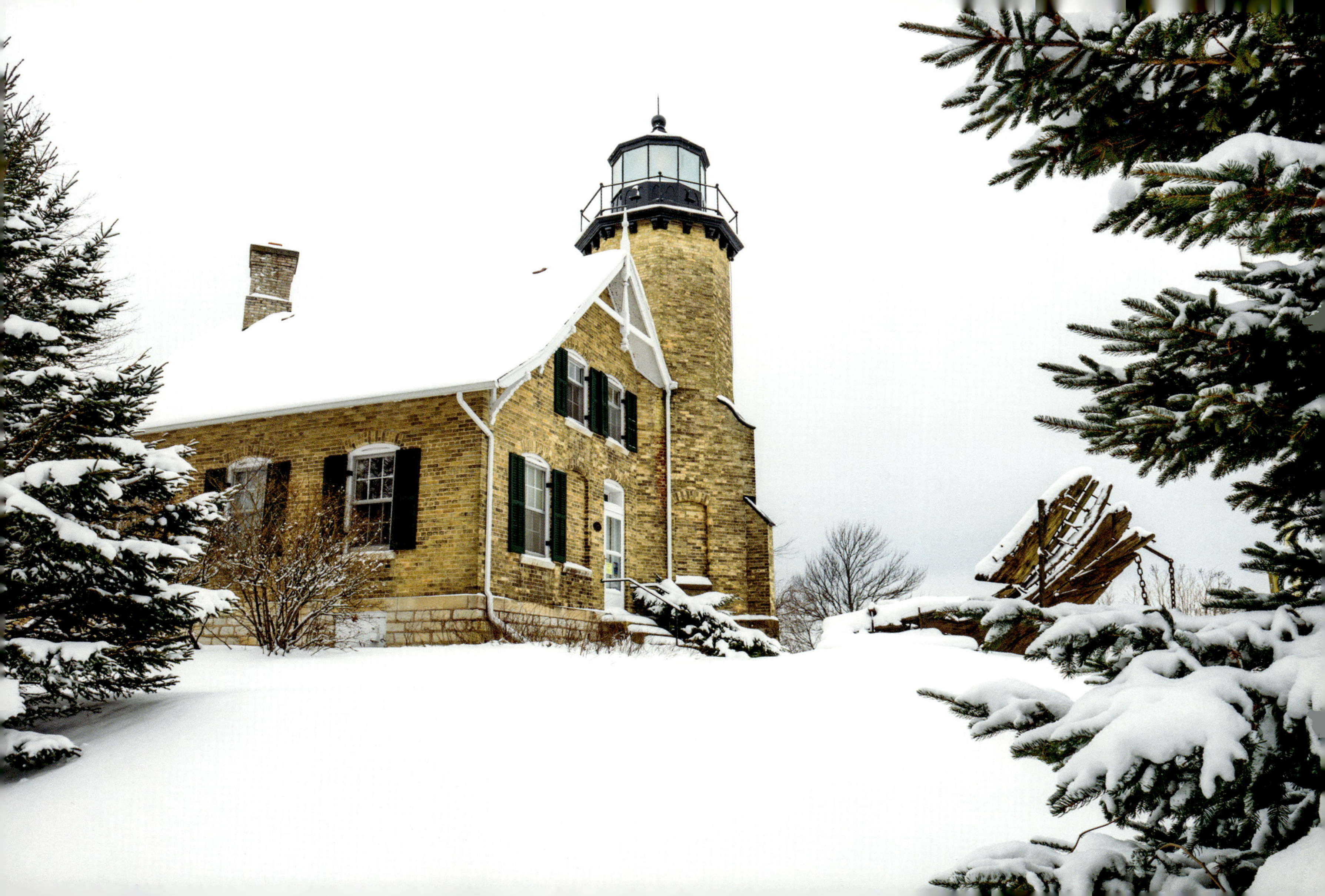

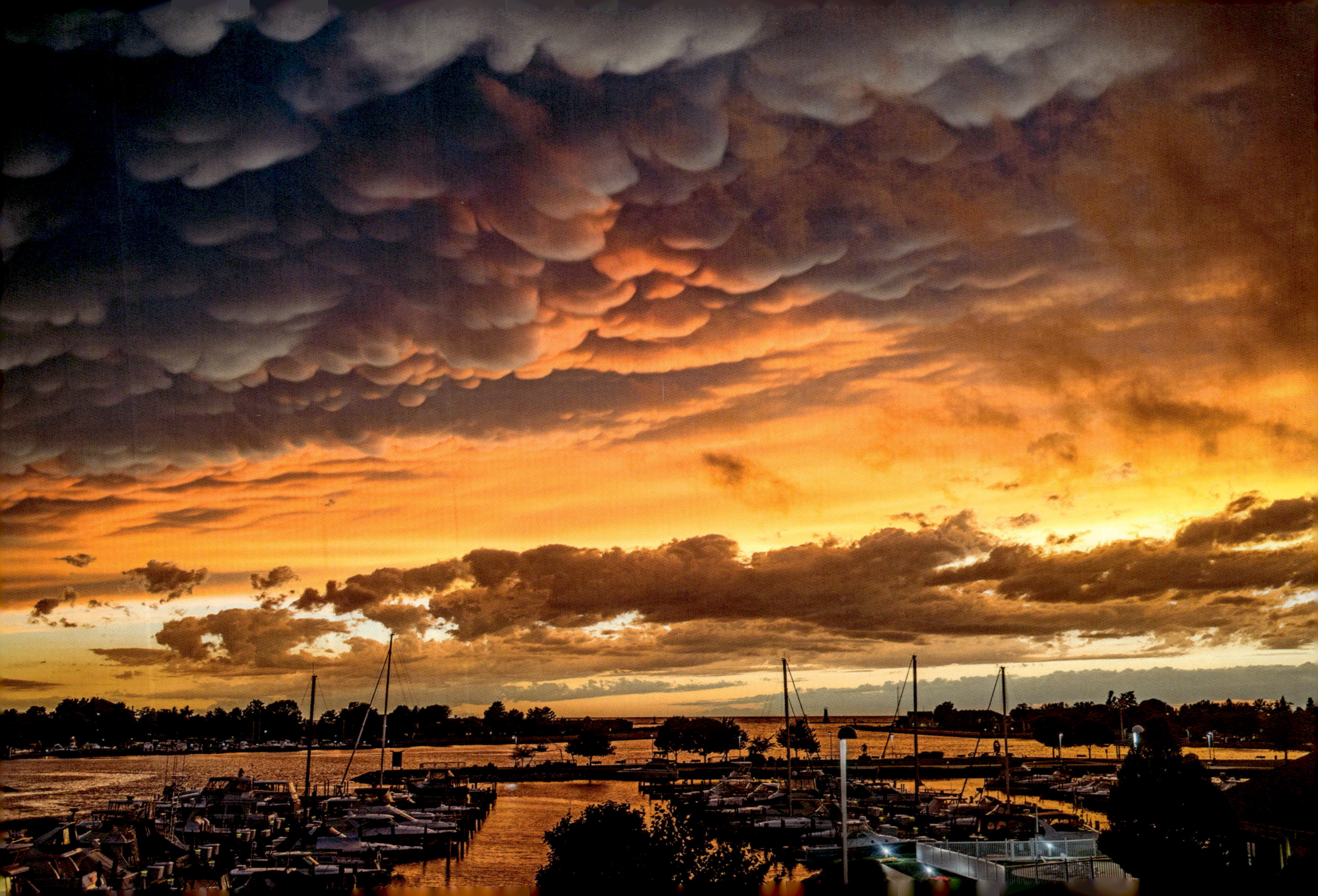

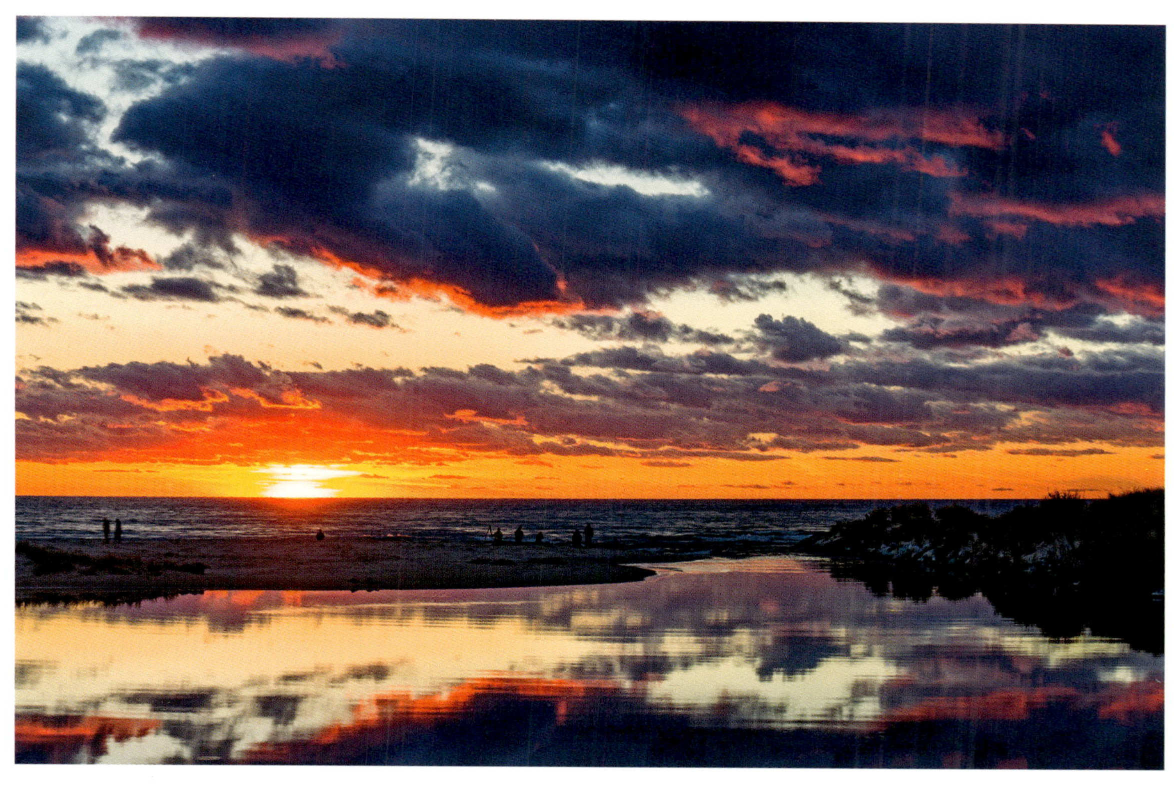

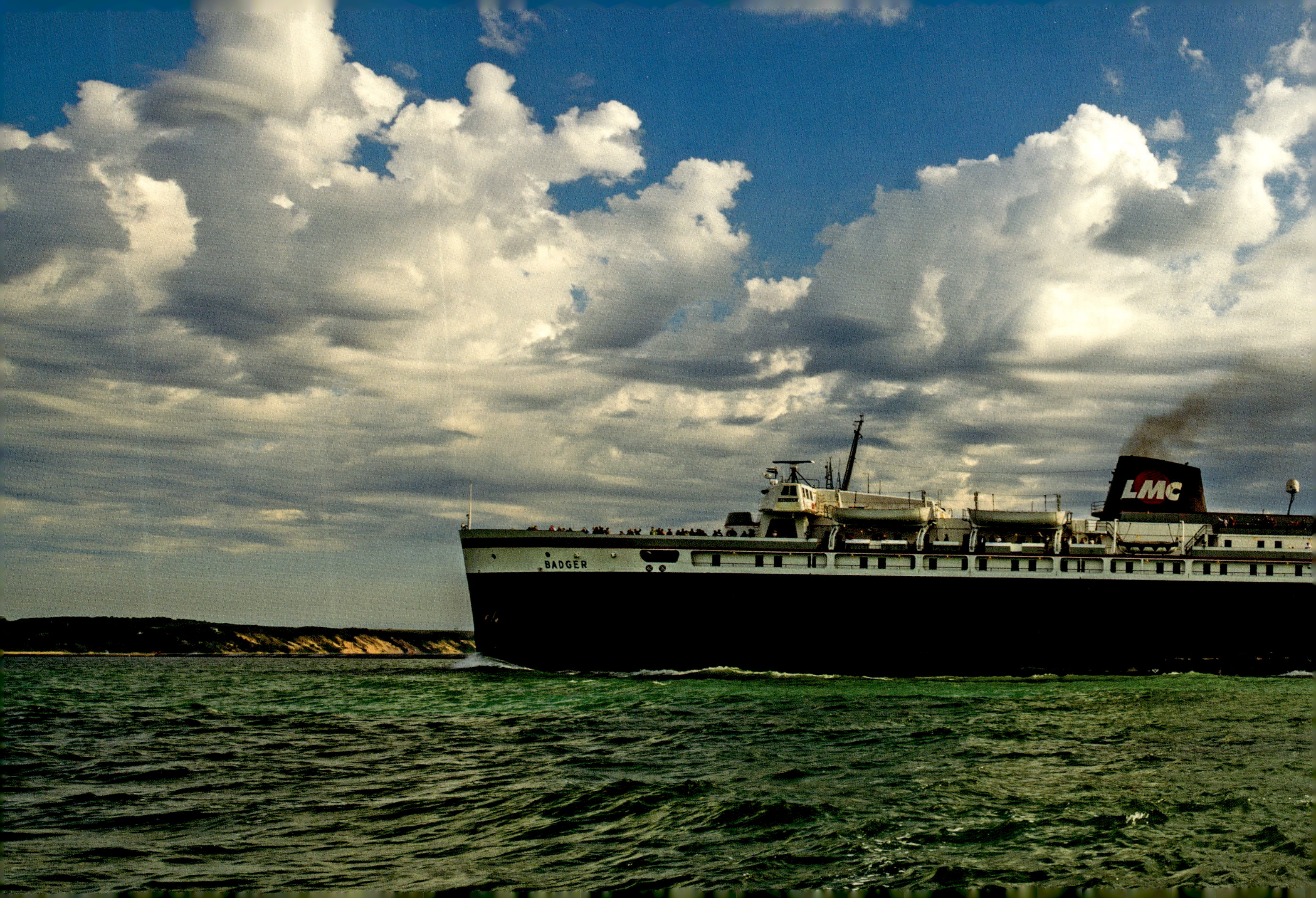
BADGER
LMC

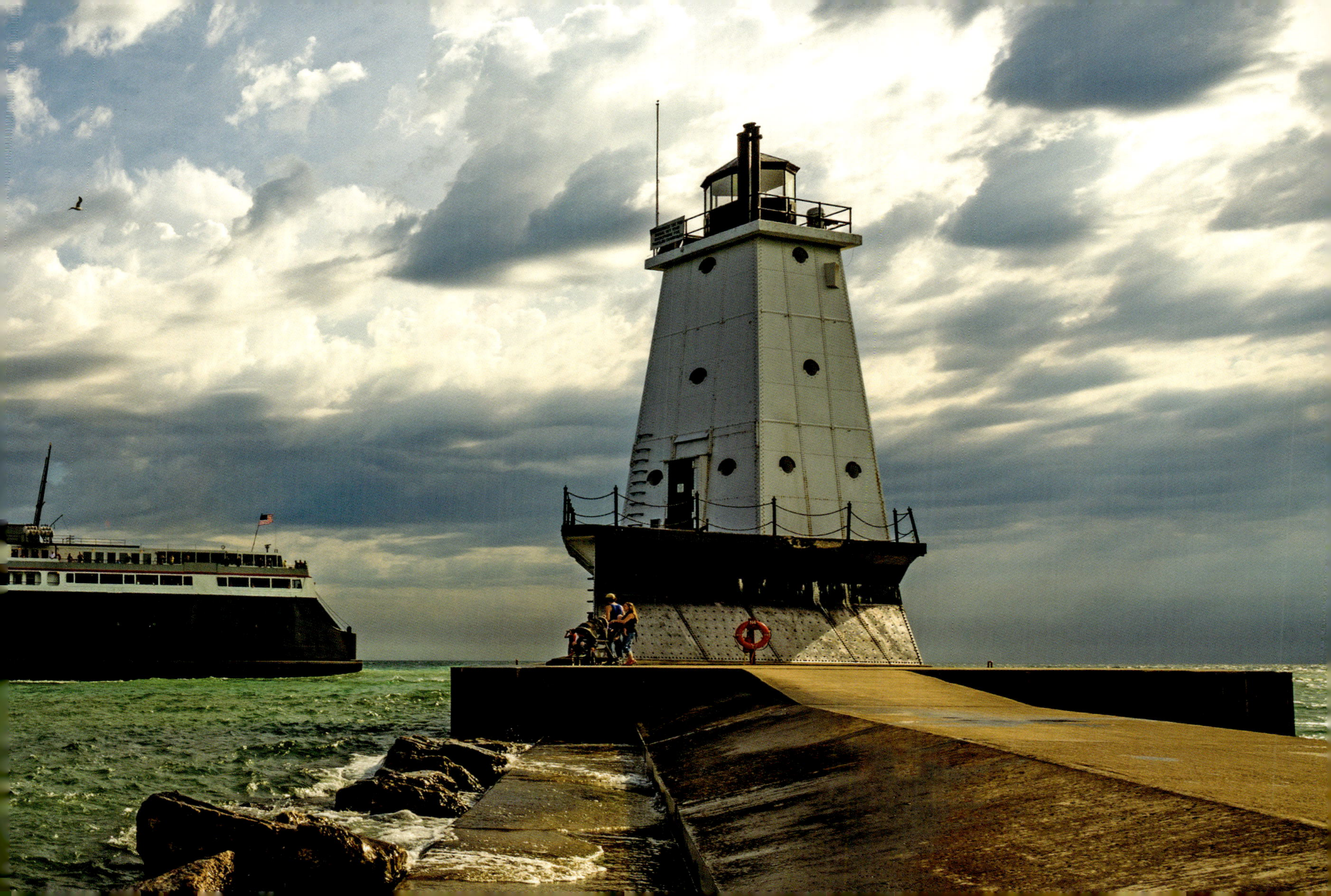

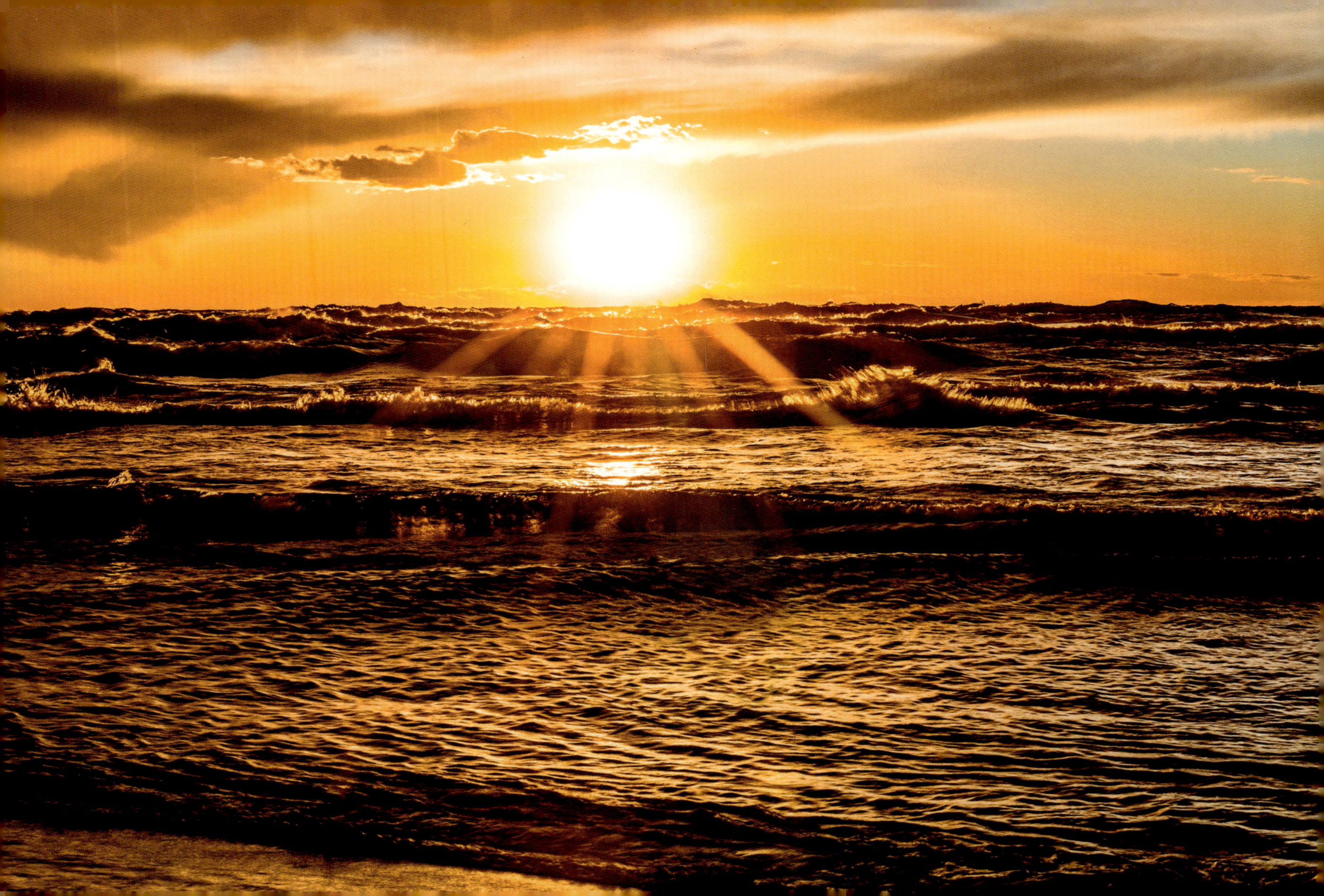

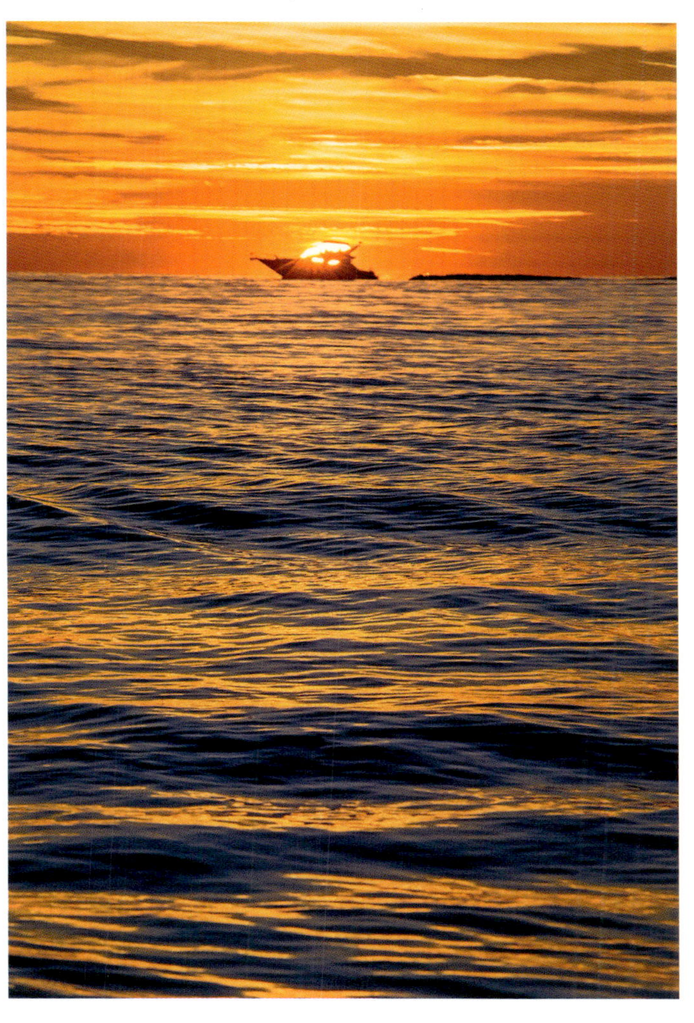

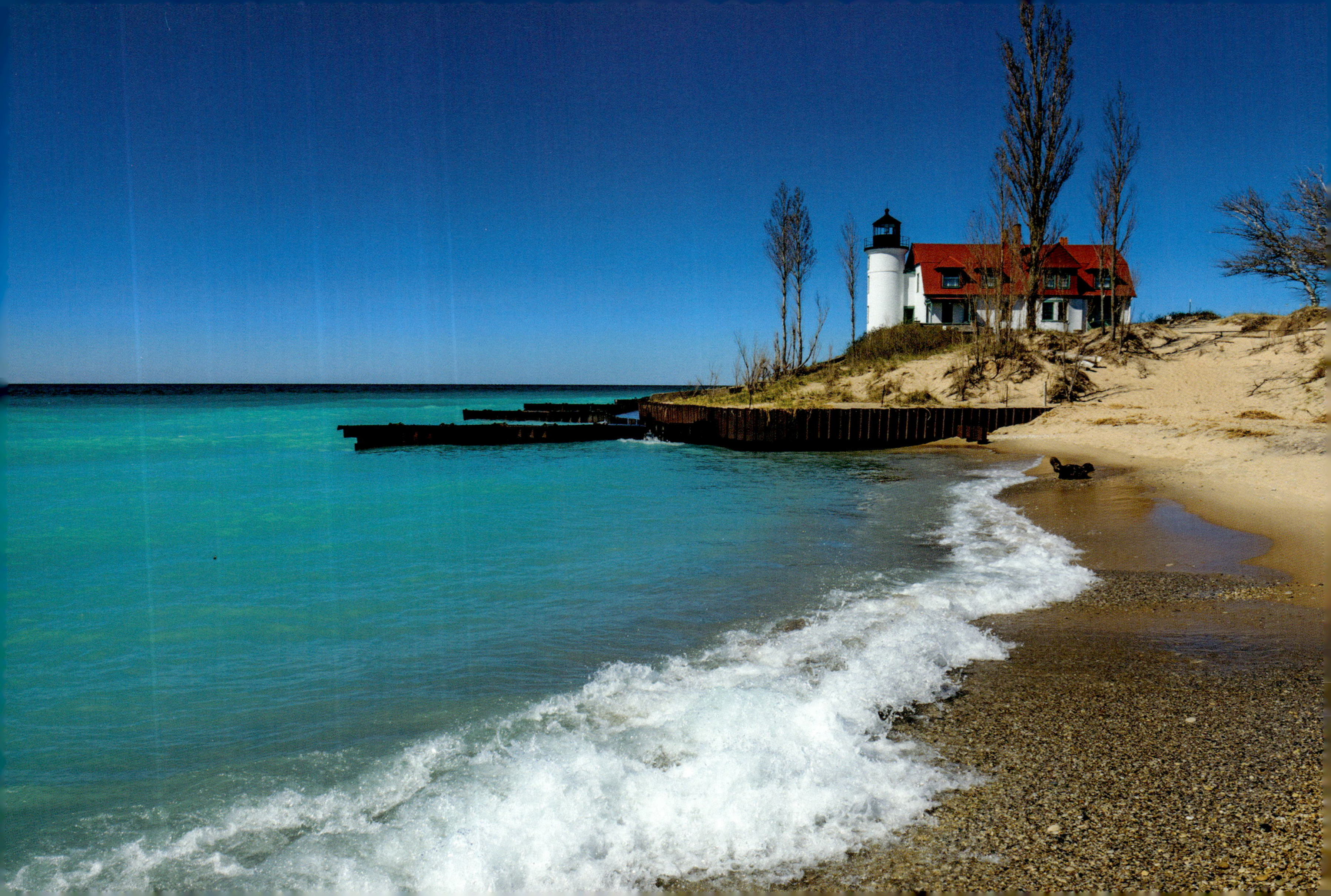

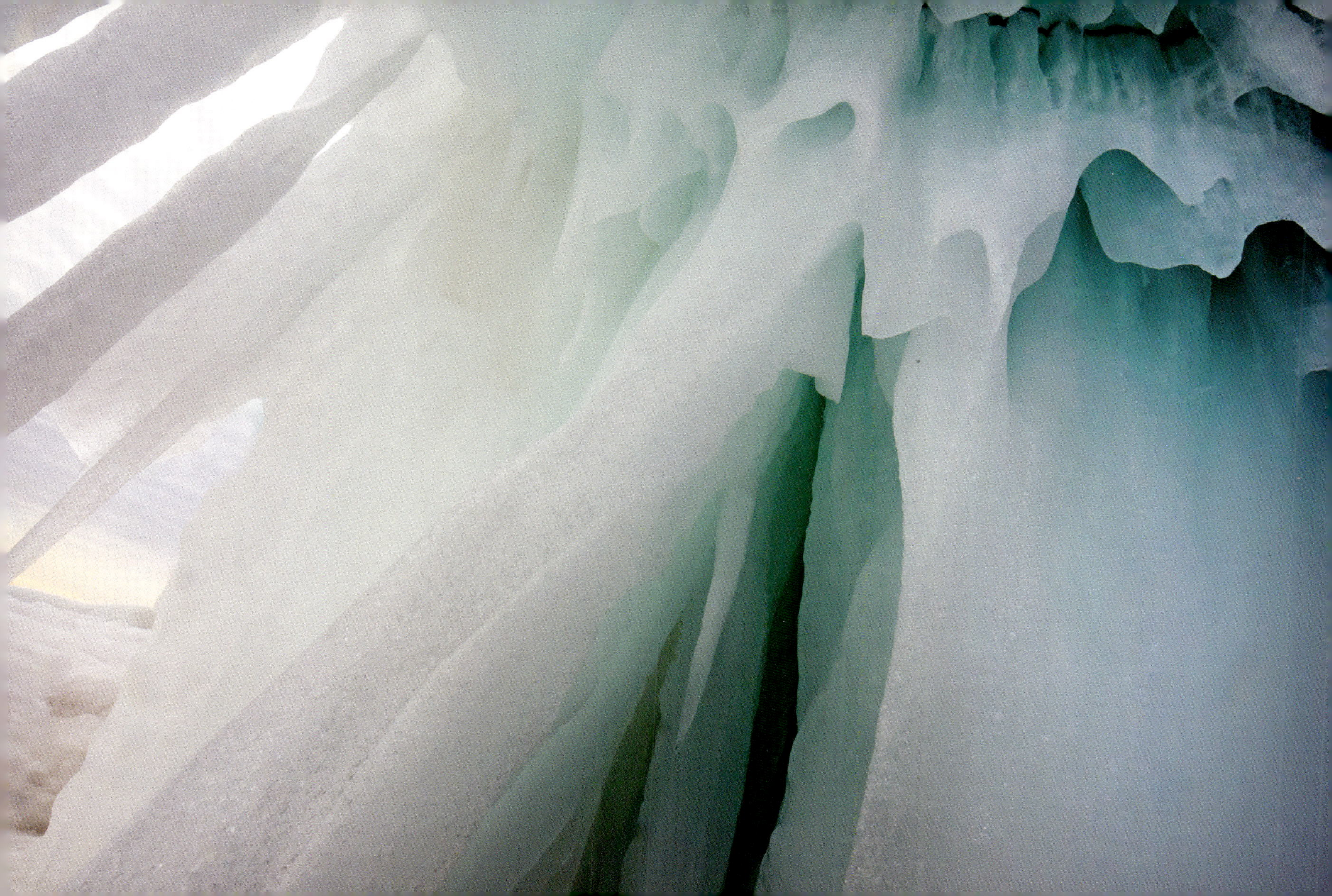

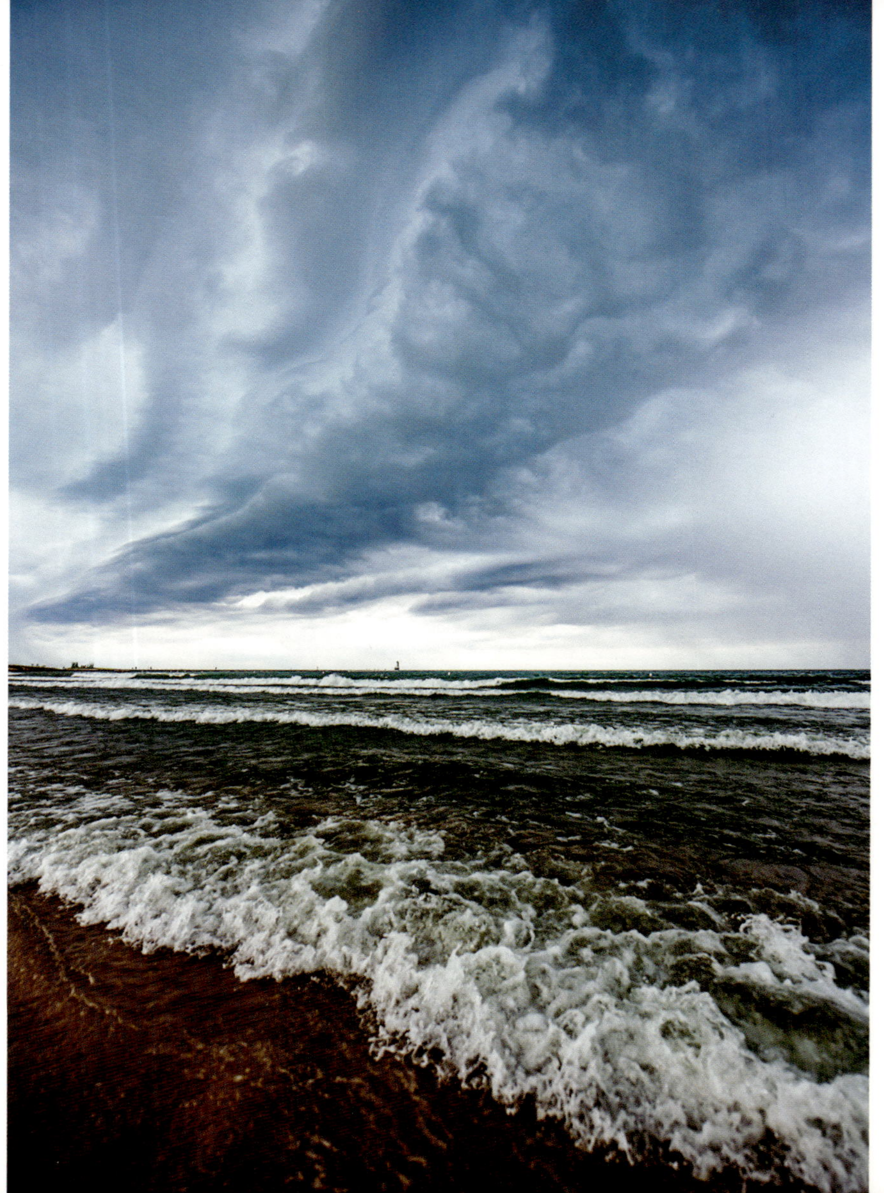

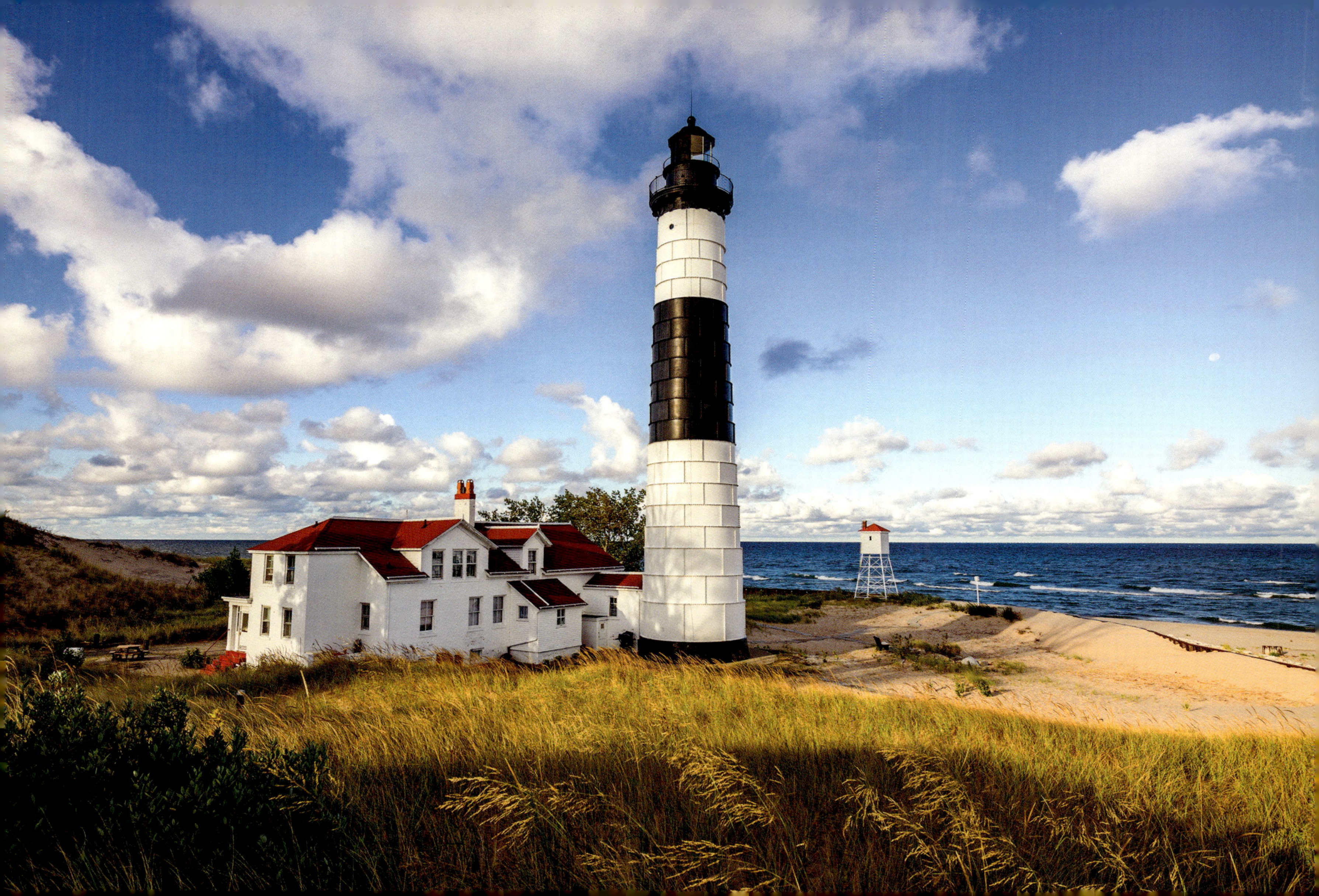

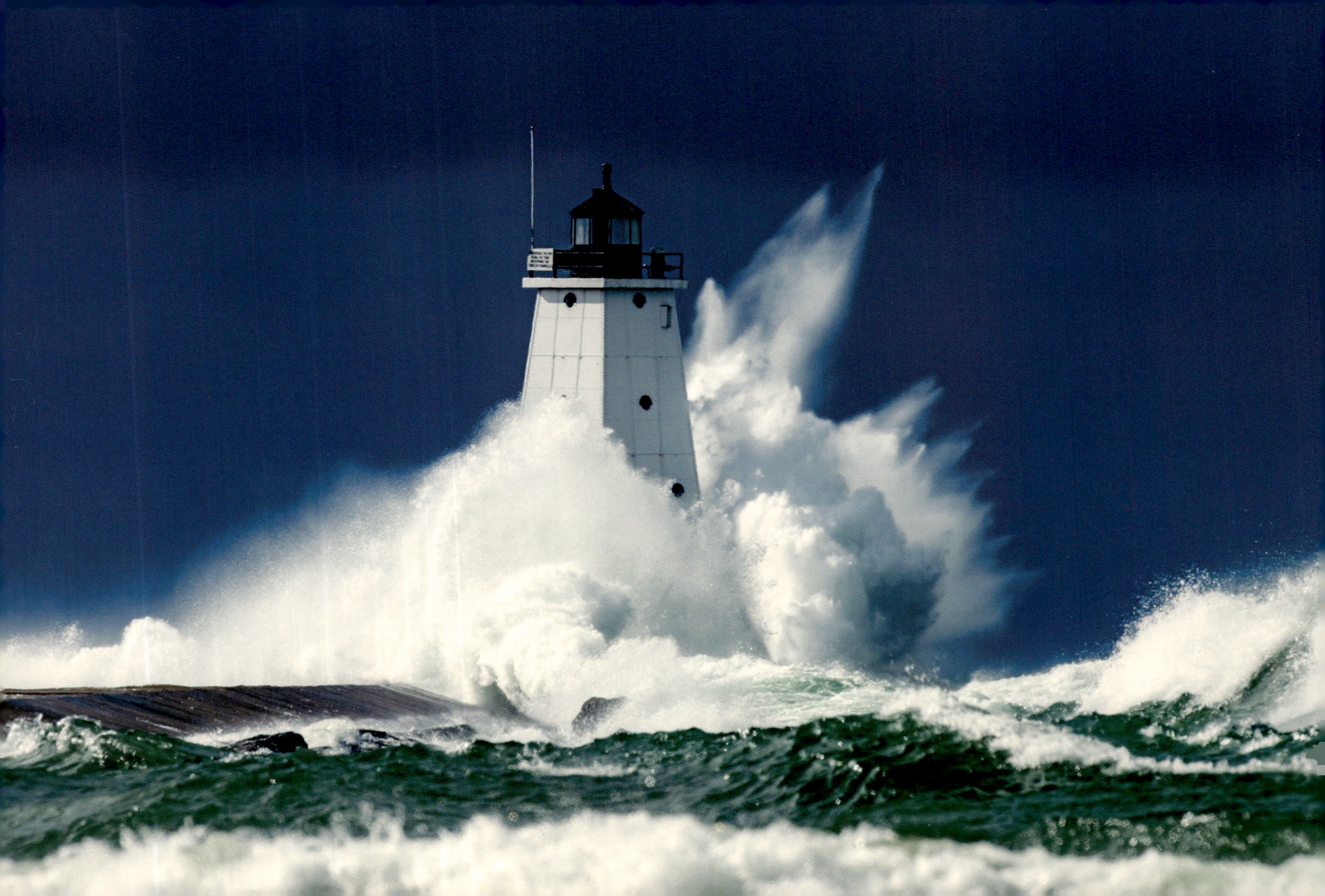

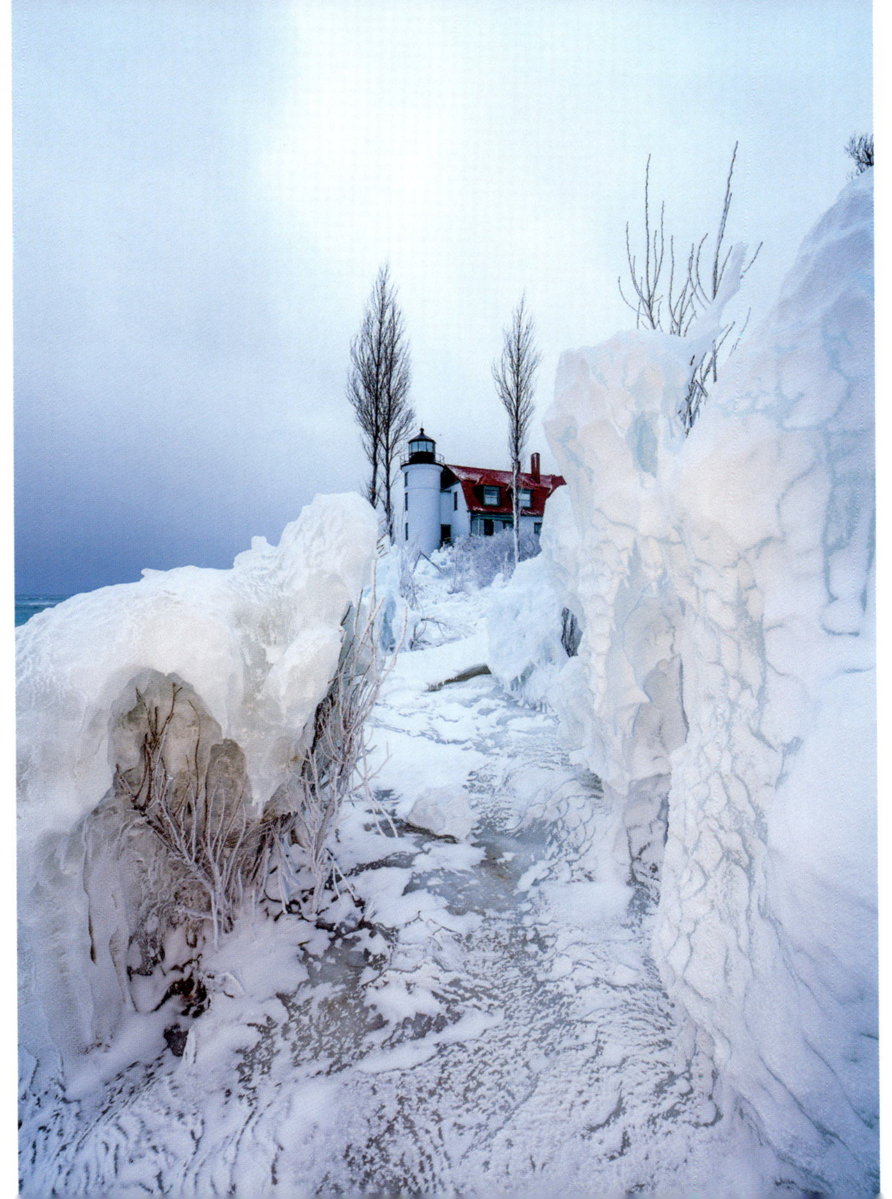

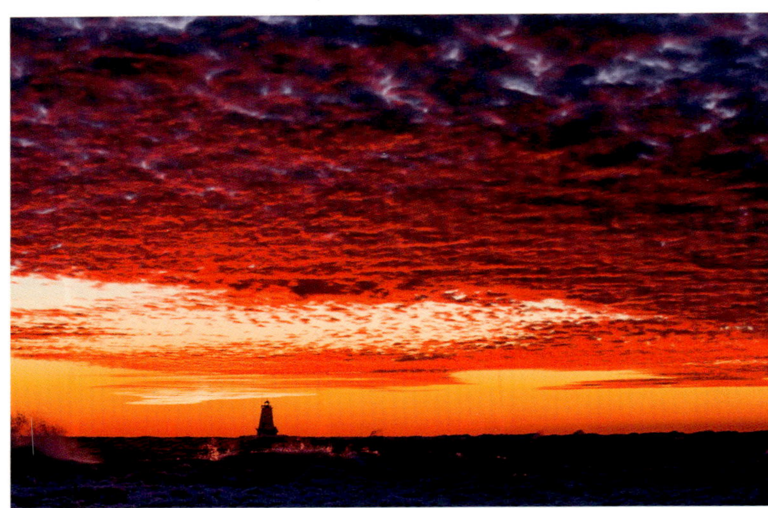

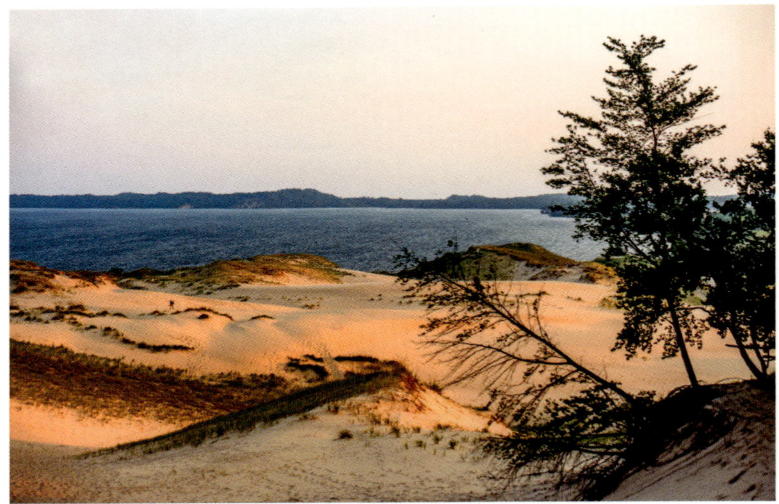

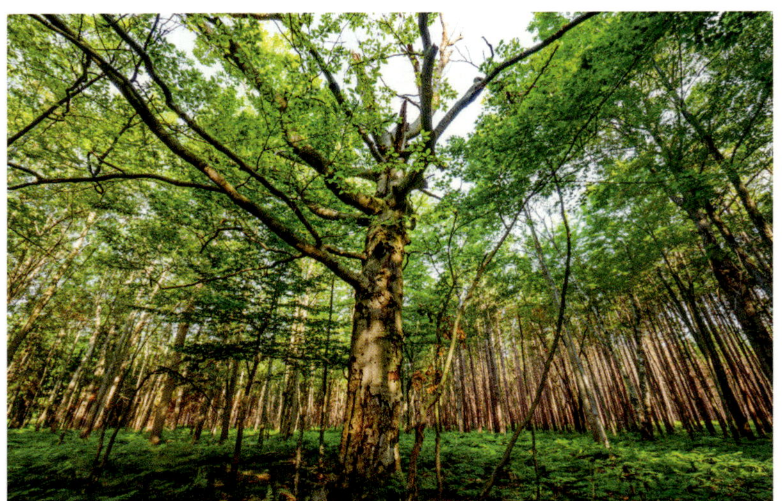

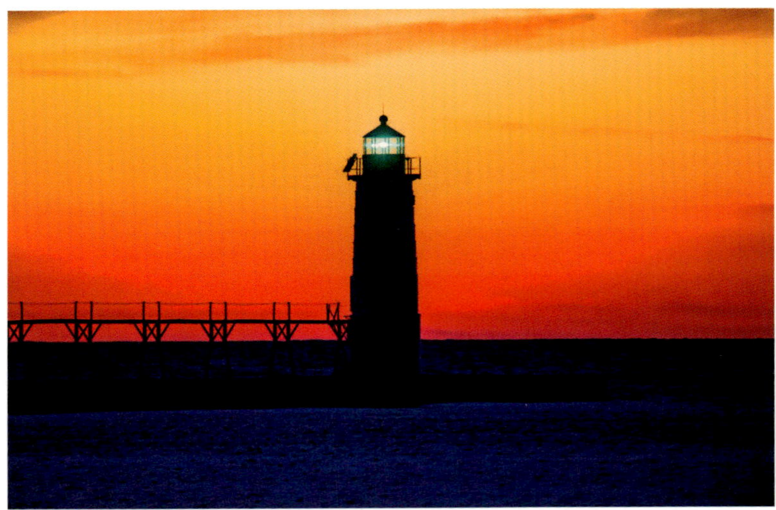

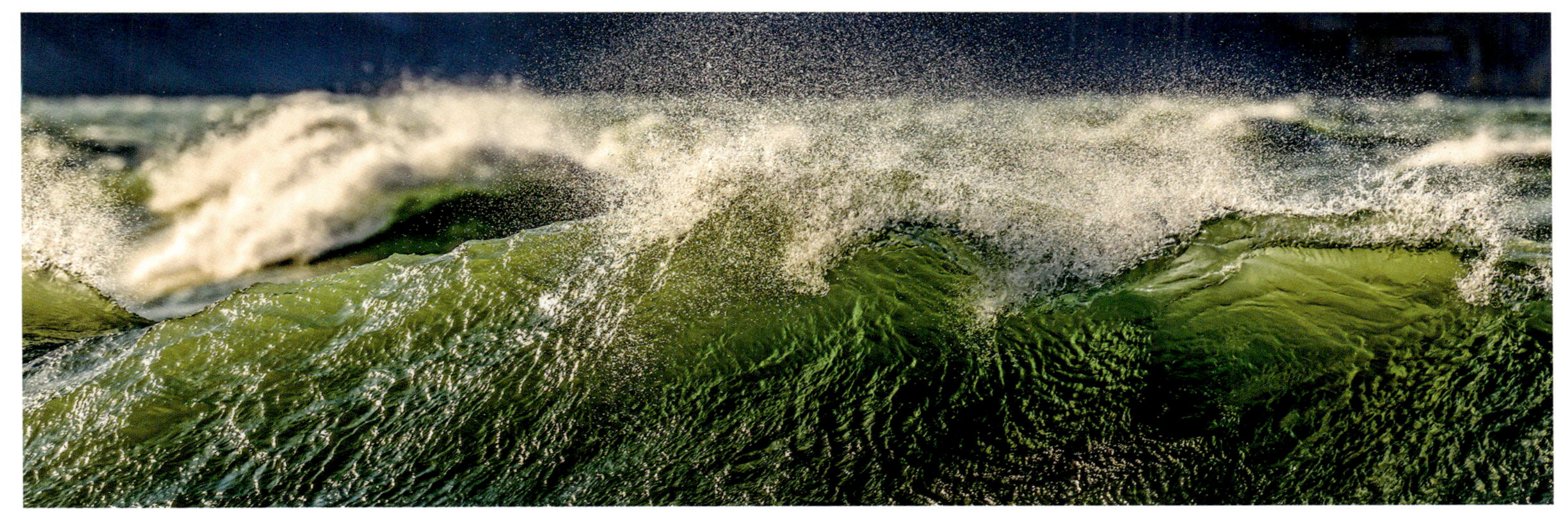

The Titles

Every image in "Wonderous West Shore" is repeated in this section as a tiny thumbnail, along with a title and the name of the photographer. If you would like to read the stories behind the images in this book and see the camera settings, please visit our website at www.ToddandBradReed.com.

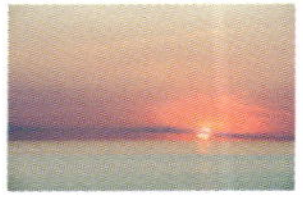

Summer Pastels - Todd

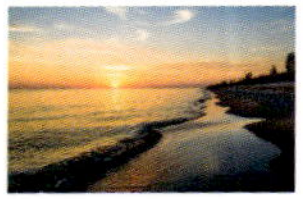

Beautiful Night - Brad

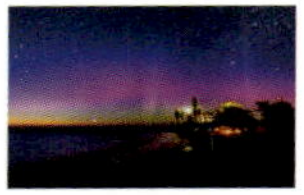

Aurora at Point Betsie - Brad

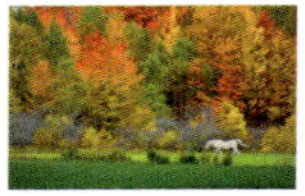

Ghost Rider - Todd

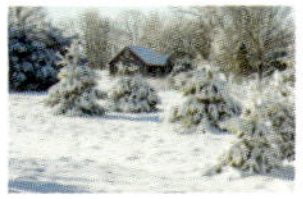

Decoration Day - Todd

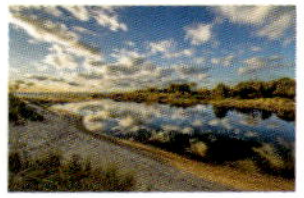

Game Time - Brad

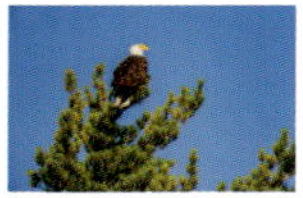

Protecting the Family - Brad

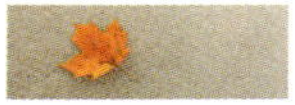

Fleeting Moment - Brad

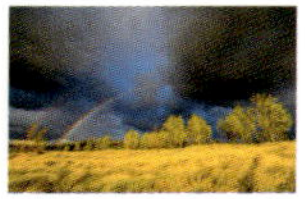

Wonderous West Shore - Brad

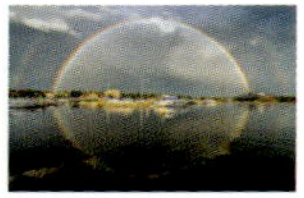

Incredible Ludington - Todd

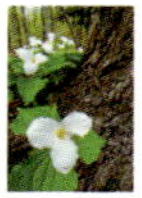

A Michigan Spring - Todd

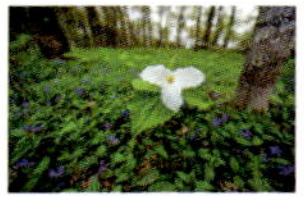

Sleepy Time - Brad

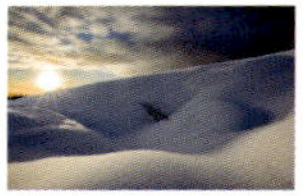

Winter Surprise - Brad

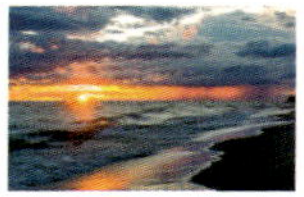

Thumbs Up - Brad

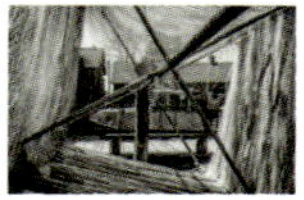

Finding Joy - Todd

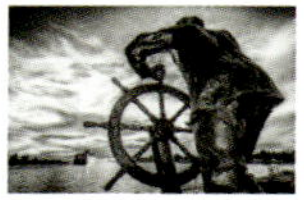

Sailor Strong - Todd

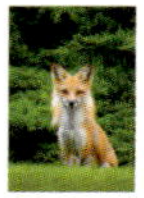

The Lion King - Todd

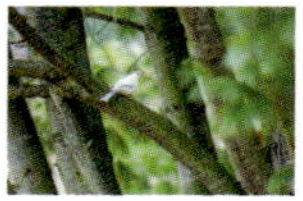

Nature Force - Brad

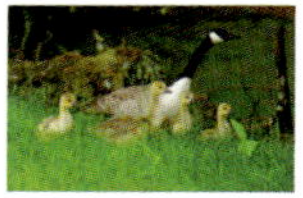

Cruising the Shoreline - Todd

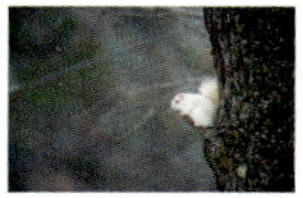

White Christmas Eve - Brad

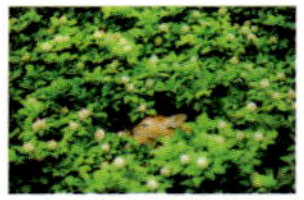

Sleeping Beauty - Brad

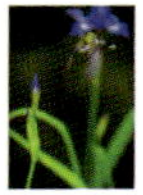

On A Mission - Todd

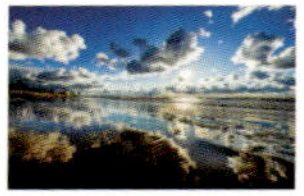

Pentwater Reflections - Brad

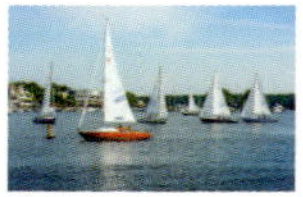

Pentwater Traditions - Todd

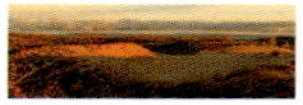

Sleeping Bear Sunrise - Todd

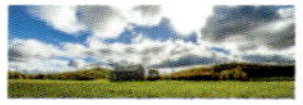

Cloud Chasers - Brad

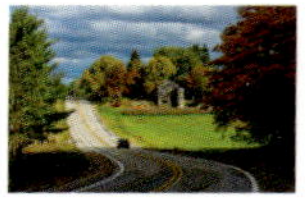

Enjoying the Drive - Todd

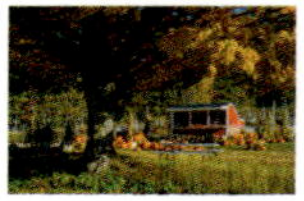

Roadside Stand - Todd

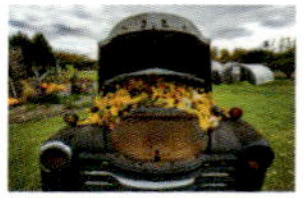

Gourdy - Todd

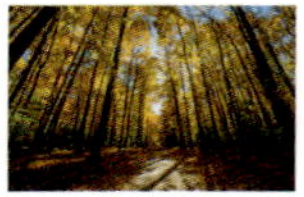

Anderson Road Fall Color - Brad

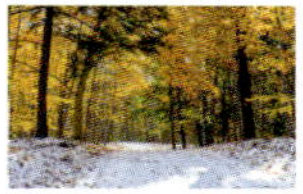

Winter is Coming - Todd

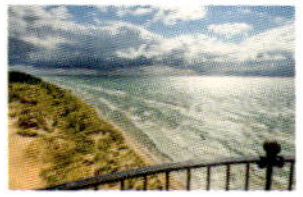

Top of Little Sable - Todd

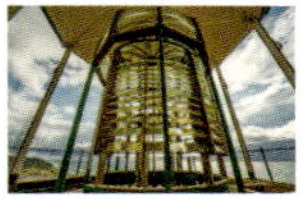

Little Sable Fresnel - Todd

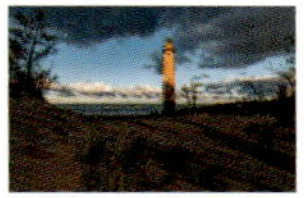

Out of the Shadows - Brad

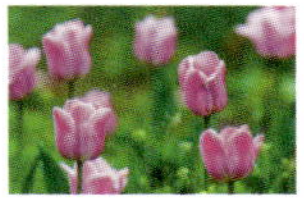

Holland Beauties - Brad

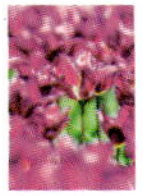

Holland Standouts - Todd

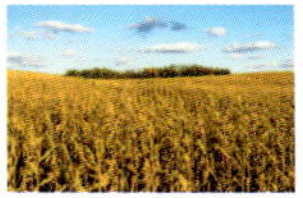

Kent County Corn - Todd

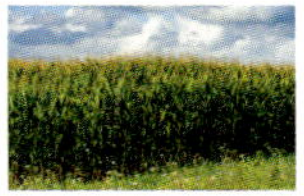

Signs - Todd

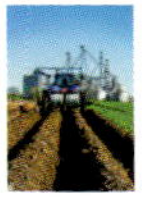

Scottville Tradition - Todd

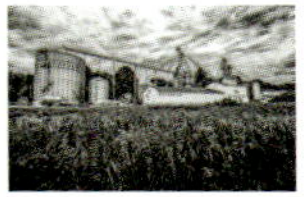

Americana - Todd

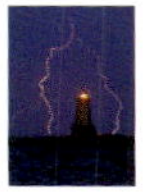

Michigan Lightning - Brad

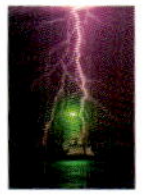

Positive Energy - Todd

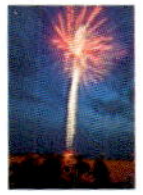

Pentwater Fireworks - Brad

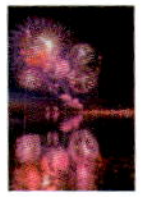

The Big Bang -Todd

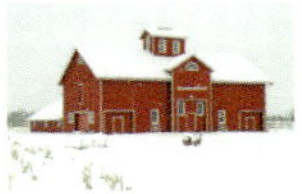

Picture Perfect Barn - Todd

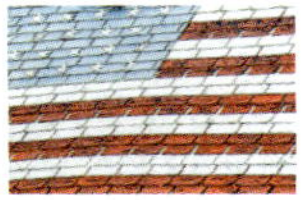

Raising the Roof - Brad

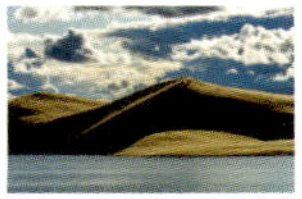

We Love Silver Lake - Todd

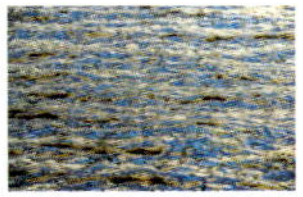

Dancing Blues - Brad

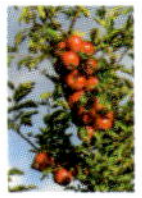

Indian Summer - Todd

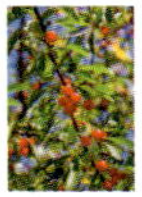

Come Alive - Todd

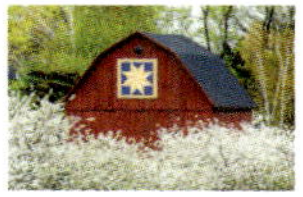

Old Mission Quilt - Todd

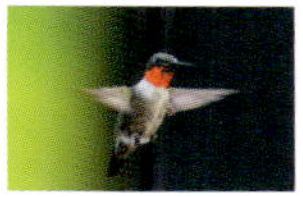

Ruby Throated Hummingbird - Brad

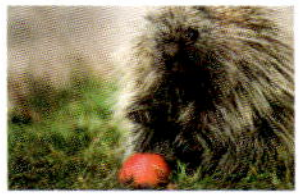

Quillis - Brad

Poetic - Brad

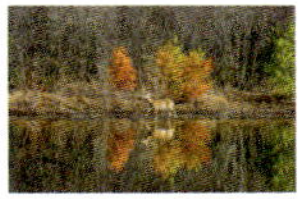

Sunday With Dottie - Todd

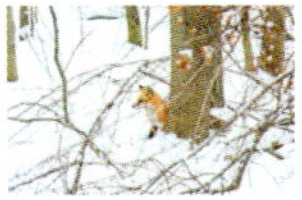

Winter Hunt - Todd

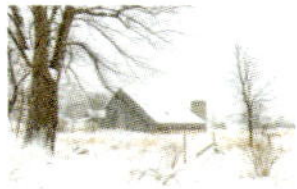

Taking Your Time - Todd

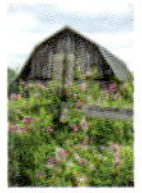

Sweet Summertime - Todd

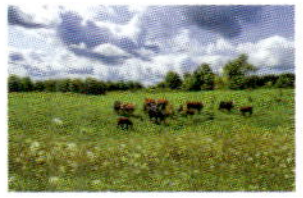

Breathtaking Moment - Todd

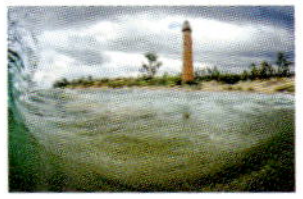

Crashing Little Sable - Brad

Enjoying the Moment - Brad

Point Betsie Reflections - Brad

Big Ice - Todd

Missing the Catwalk - Brad

Dreamy Light - Todd

White Lake Treasure - Brad

We Found Love - Todd

Storm Chaser - Brad

Making the Rounds - Todd

Pentwater On The Rocks - Todd

Old Mission Lighthouse - Brad

Family Connections - Brad

Birthday Bash - Brad

Beautiful Patterns - Todd

Dancing Sumac - Todd

Birch Gold - Todd

Cookie Cows - Todd

Ultra Vanity Fair - Brad

End of Summer Breeze - Todd

Old Fashioned - Brad

Daisies Gone Wild - Todd

Springing to Life - Todd

Window On Riverton - Todd

A Custer Morning - Brad

Outrage - Brad

Count Your Blessings - Brad

A Million Dollar View - Todd

Autumn at Portage Lake - Todd

Burning the Light - Todd

Solar Eclipse - Brad

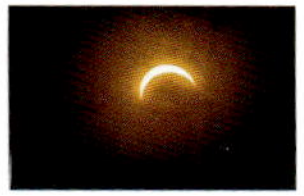

Muskegon Eclipse - Todd

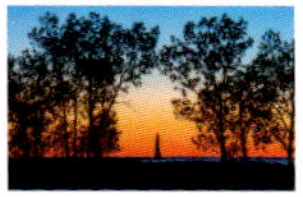

October Glow - Todd

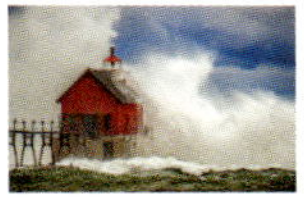

Fuel Injected - Brad

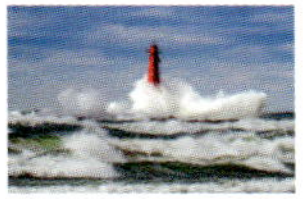

Slamming Muskegon - Todd

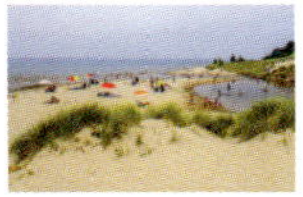

Enjoying Duck Lake Outlet - Todd

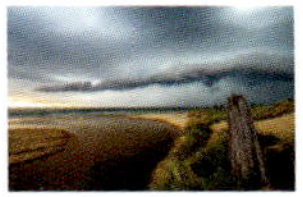

Duck Lake Outlet - Brad

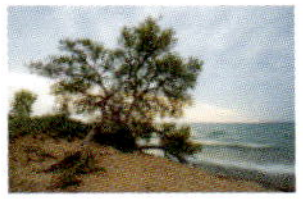

Being Alive - Brad

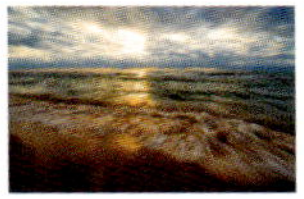

Great Memories - Brad

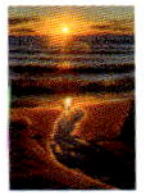

G Park - Todd

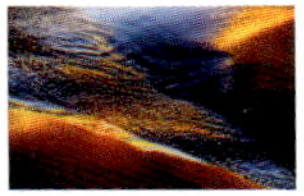

Lake Michigan Lava - Todd

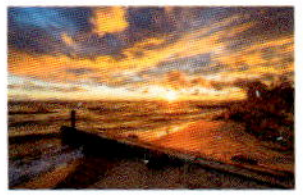

Lumiere Over Me - Brad

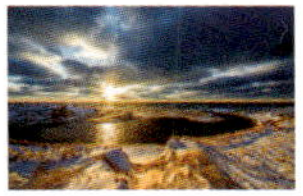

Sunshine Beauty - Brad

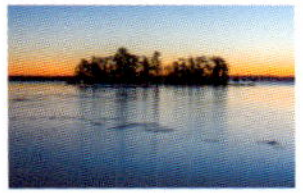

Blue Sunrise - Todd

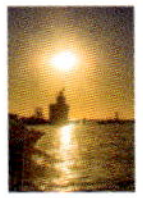

Enjoying Big Red - Brad

Life Ever After - Brad

A Great Show - Brad

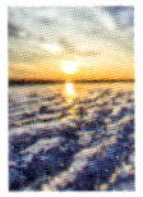

Manistee Ripples - Brad

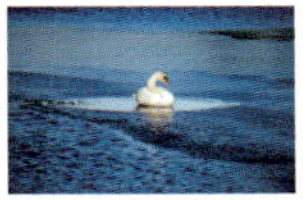

On Thin Ice - Todd

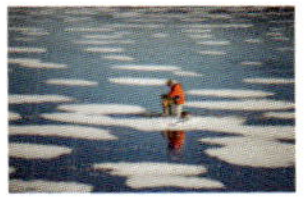

Stillness on the Lake - Brad

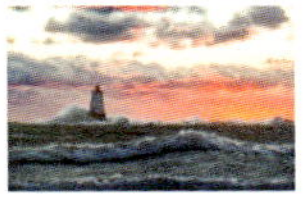

Drive - Brad

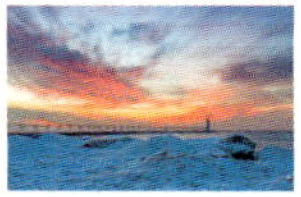

Manistee Afterglow - Brad

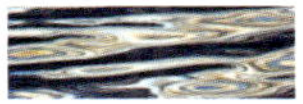

Liquidity - Brad

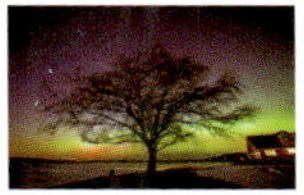

Tree of Light - Brad

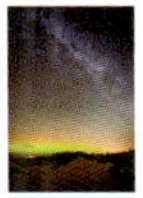

Milky Way Aurora - Todd

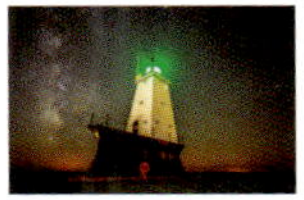

Bringing Me Home - Brad

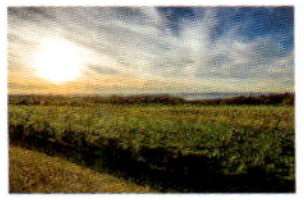

Grand Traverse Vineyard View - Todd

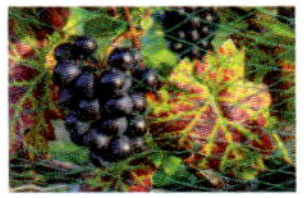

Fruit of the Vine - Todd

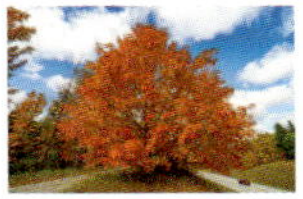

M22 Showstopper - Todd

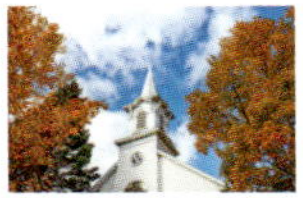

Frankfort Glory - Todd

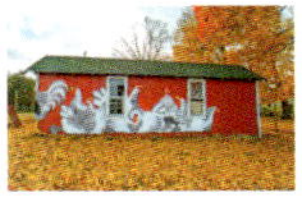

Chicken Coop - Brad

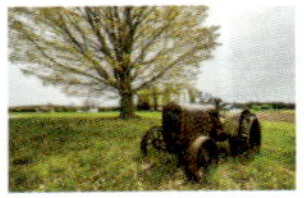

Farming History - Brad

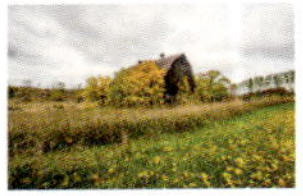

Colorful Landscape - Brad

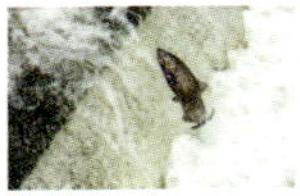

Big Fish - Todd

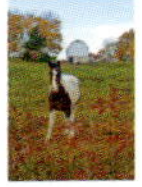

Break Free - Brad

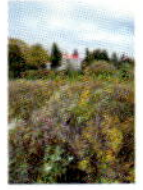

Chasing a Vision - Brad

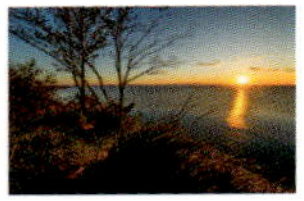

Rushing to Sleeping Bear - Brad

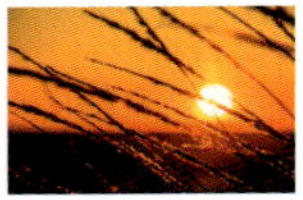

Shooting the Highlights - Brad

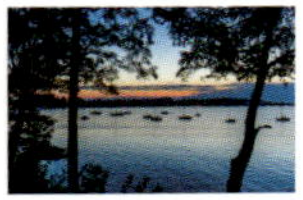

Tranquility On White Lake - Brad

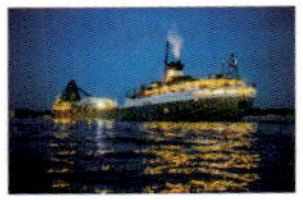

Shooting the Saginaw - Todd

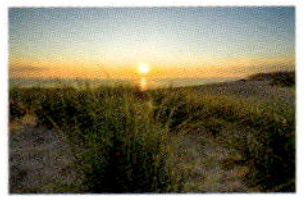

Lucky Man - Brad

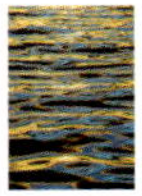

Beautiful Tones - Brad

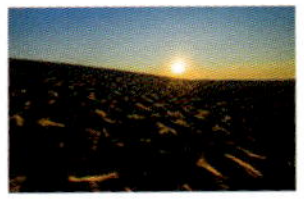

Go Muskegon - Brad

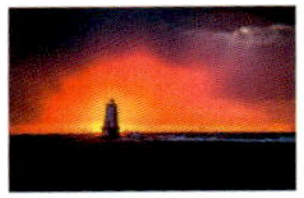

Intergalactic - Brad

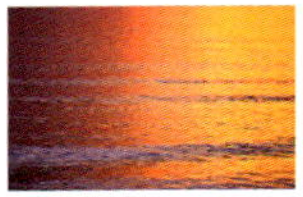

Natural Light - Brad

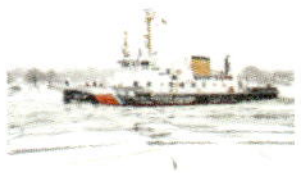

Break Time - Todd

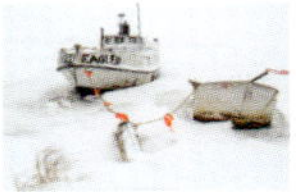

Ice-olated - Todd

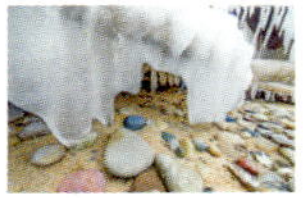

Rock Cave - Brad

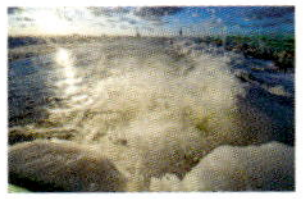

Crashing Into Pentwater - Todd

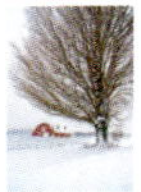

Hamlin Blizzard - Brad

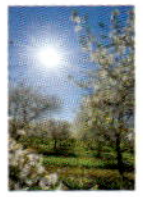

Michigan Glory - Todd

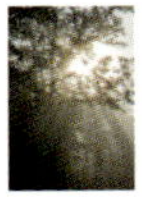

Morning Rays - Brad

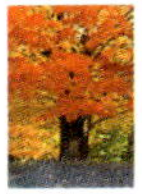

Autumn Majesty - Todd

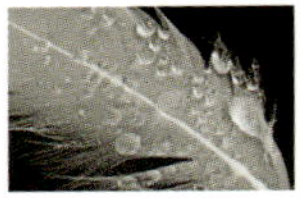

The Details - Brad

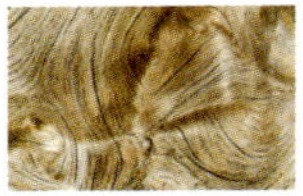

Bleach Blonde - Brad

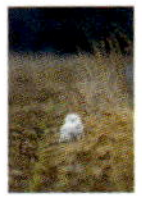

Visiting Muskegon - Brad

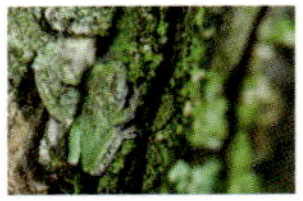

Survival Instinct - Brad

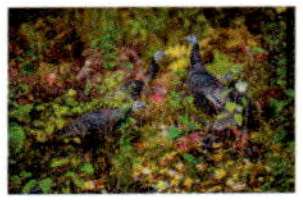

Turkey Time - Todd

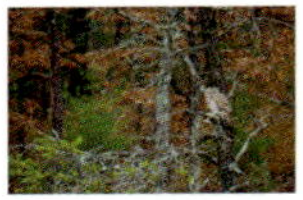

Spiritual Being - Brad

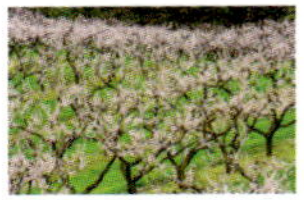

Spring Art - Todd

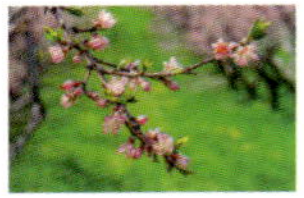

Oceana Blooms - Todd

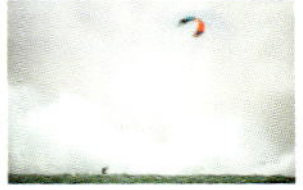

Adrenaline Junkie - Todd

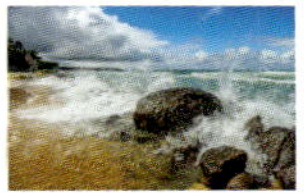

Rock Concert - Todd

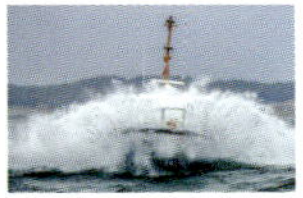

Motor Life Boat 44359 - Todd

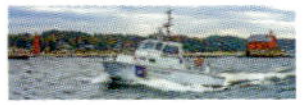

A Grand Adventure - Todd

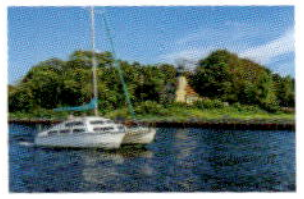

Going Sailing - Todd

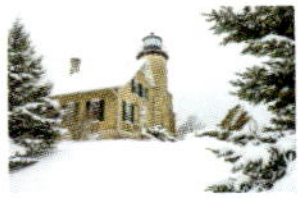

Quiet Beauty - Todd

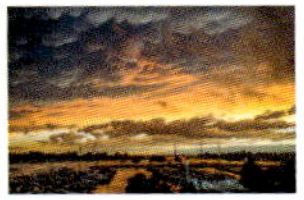

Cotton Candyland - Todd

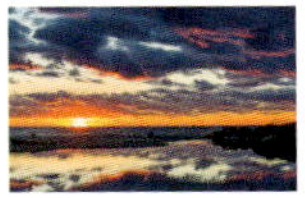

Photo Opp - Todd

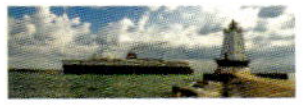

Pierly Ludington - Todd

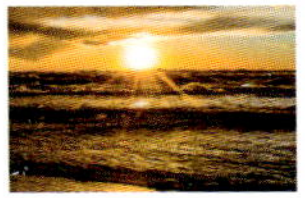

Redemption - Brad

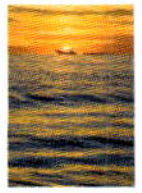

Enjoying the Big Lake - Brad

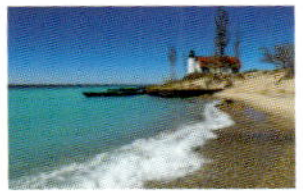

Point Betsie Splash - Todd

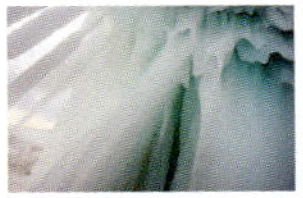

Storyteller - Brad

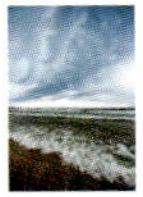

Lunchtime Rush - Todd

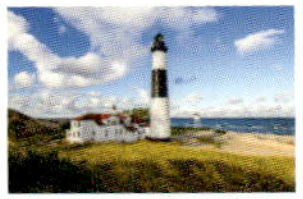

Sensational Light - Todd

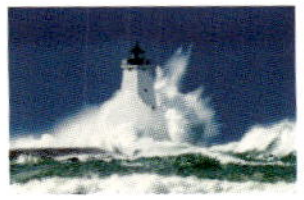

Blue Blast - Todd

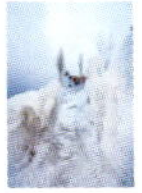

Point Betsie Blues - Todd

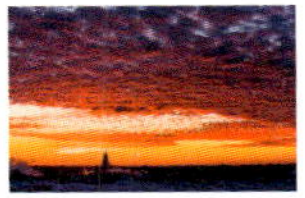

Friends Forever - Brad

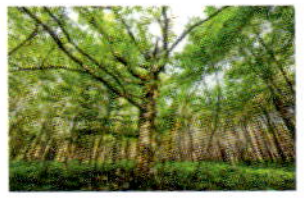

King of Nurnberg - Brad

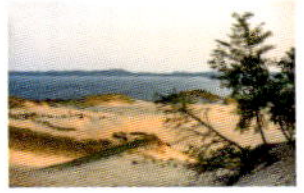

Hamlin Treasure - Todd

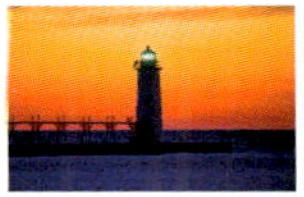

Manistee Ablaze - Todd

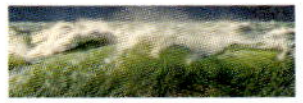

Michigan Madness - Todd

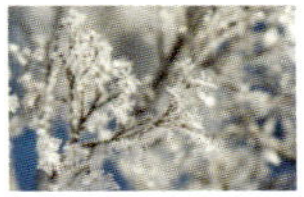

January Jewels - Todd

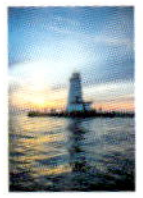

August Light - Todd

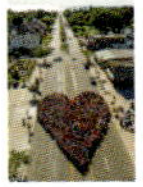

Love Ludington - Brad

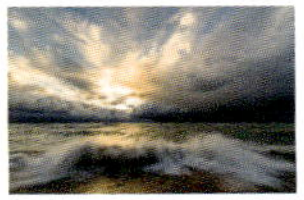

Workshop Wonder - Brad

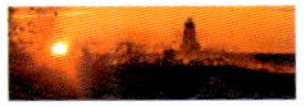

Winter Rush - Brad

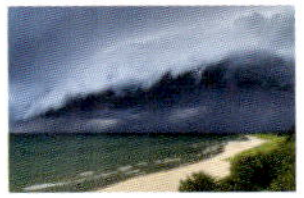

Rolling Thunder - Todd

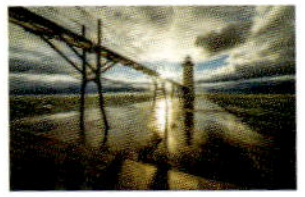

Affinity - Brad

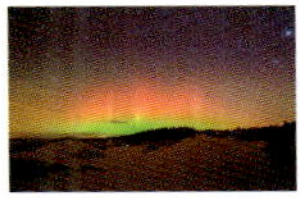

Midnight Aurora - Brad

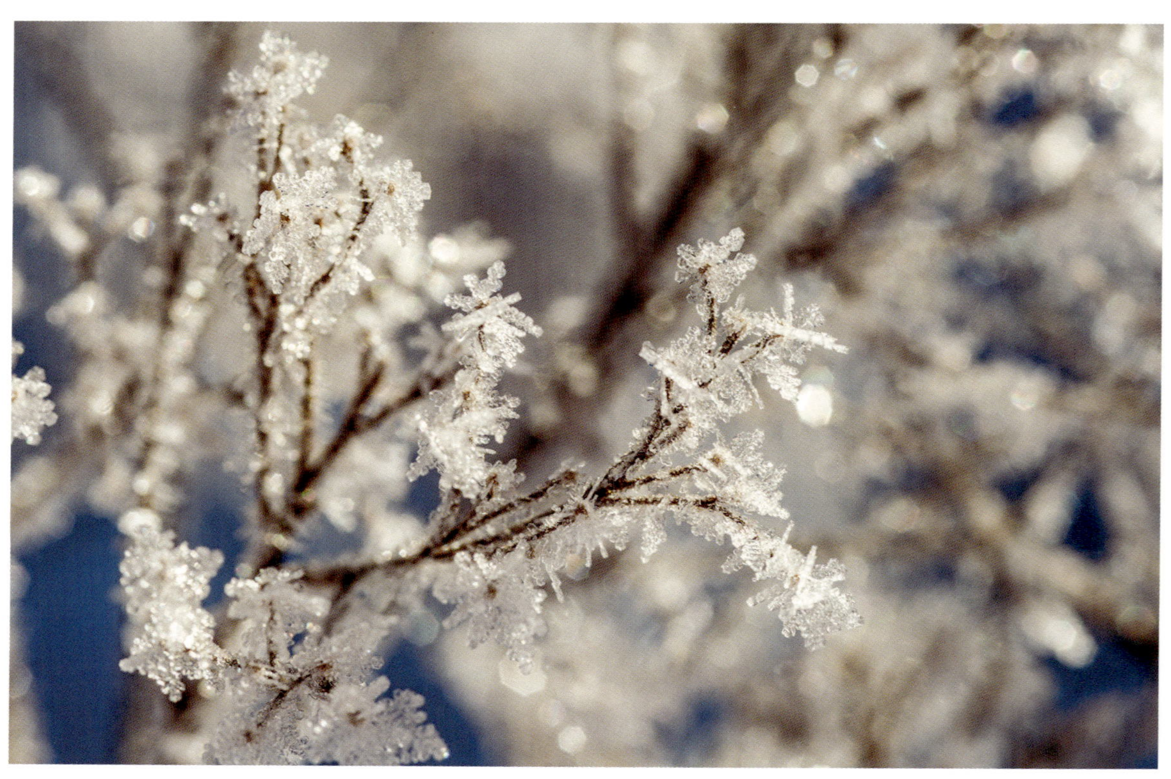

THANK YOU

We sincerely thank all the people who made Wonderous West Shore by Todd and Brad Reed and West Shore Bank possible, including:

The entire Reed and Marble families. Your continued love and support is what truly makes the Wonderous West Shore home for us.

All the members of Team Reed. You are the best employees on the planet and we love you all like family.

Rachel Gaudette for being an excellent manager for our business and for helping us design this book.

Donna Yager, Ray Biggs and everyone at West Shore Bank for working so closely with us on this entire project.

Andy Boeskool, Patrick Finn and all the employees at Foremost Graphics Group in Grand Rapids for your help and guidance with the prepress and printing of this book.

John Dekker and his staff at Dekker Bookbinding in Grand Rapids for your expertise with the binding of this book.

Betsy Reed, Kim Schneider and Susan Harrison Wolffis for their excellence in proofreading and editing.

Vanguard, Snyder's Shoes (Keen) and 108 Threads (The North Face) for sponsoring us and making our jobs easier.

Every customer we have ever had. Your support has helped us achieve great success and we can't thank you enough. We look forward to seeing all of you soon.

All Michiganders who helped us along our journeys through nine Lake Michigan shoreline and adjacent counties while shooting this project. Thank you for making West Michigan a great place to live, work, and visit.

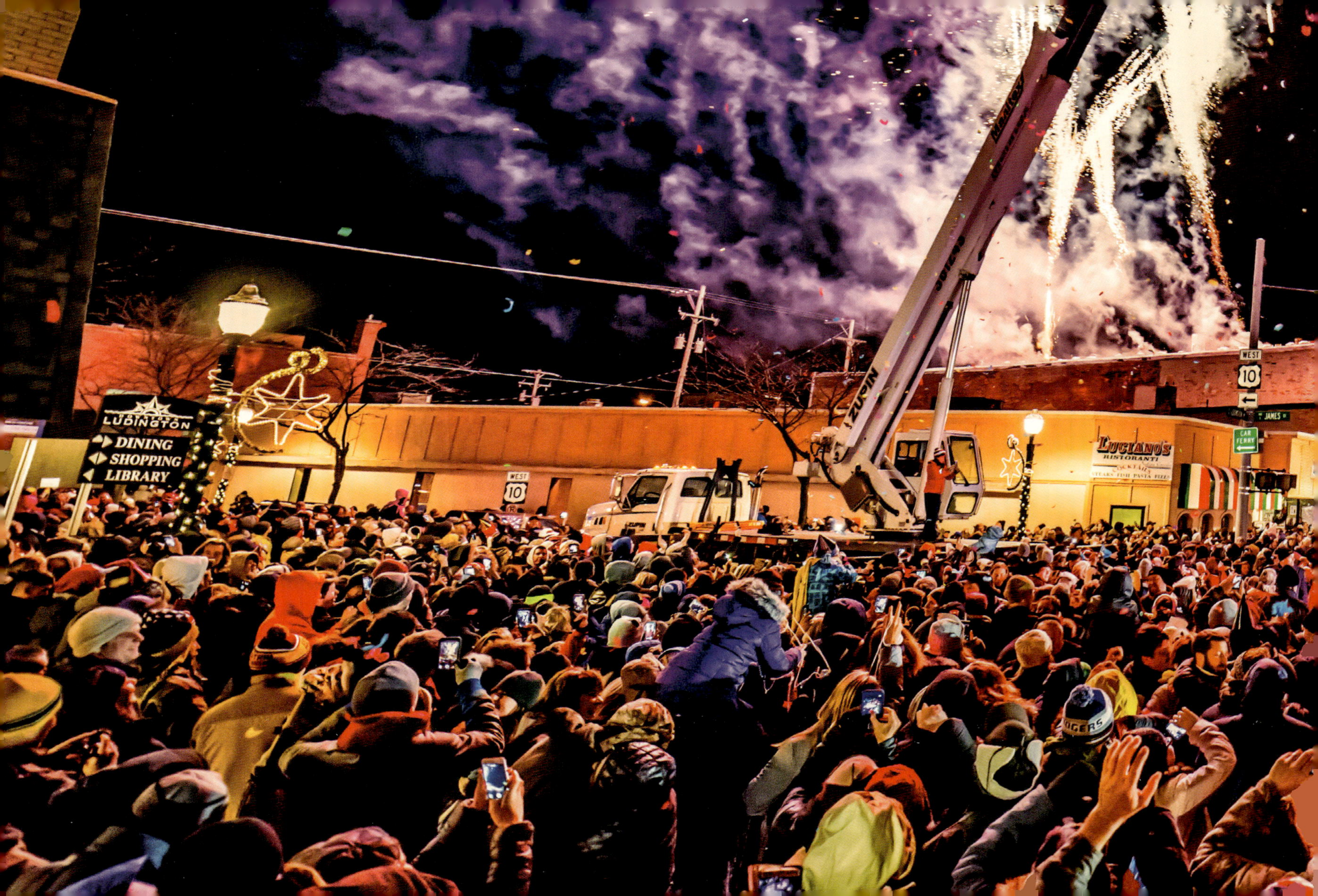
LUDINGTON
DINING
SHOPPING
LIBRARY
WEST
10
LUCIANO'S

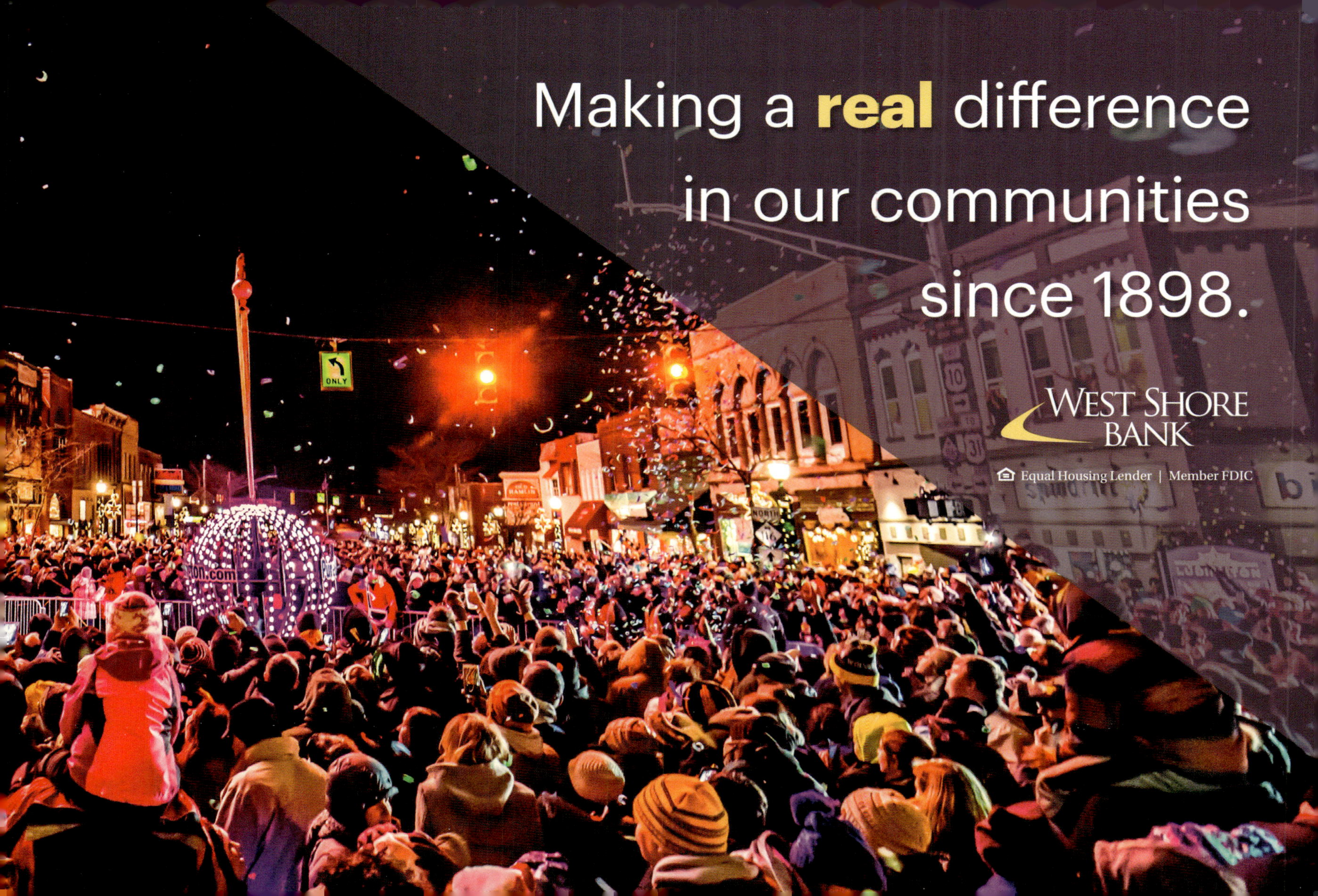
Making a real difference
in our communities
since 1898.
WEST SHORE
BANK
Equal Housing Lender | Member FDIC

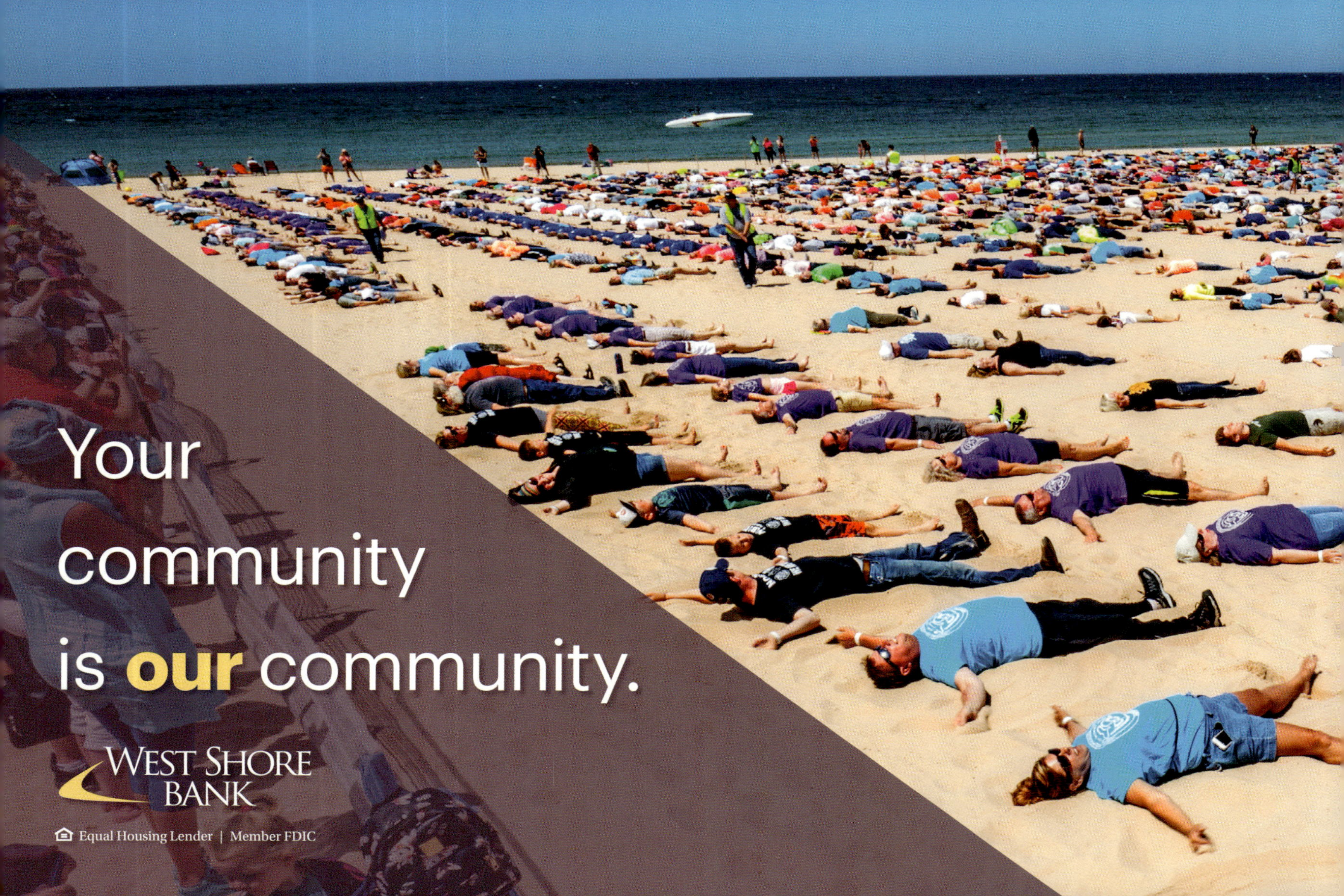
Your
community
is our community.
WEST SHORE
BANK
Equal Housing Lender | Member FDIC

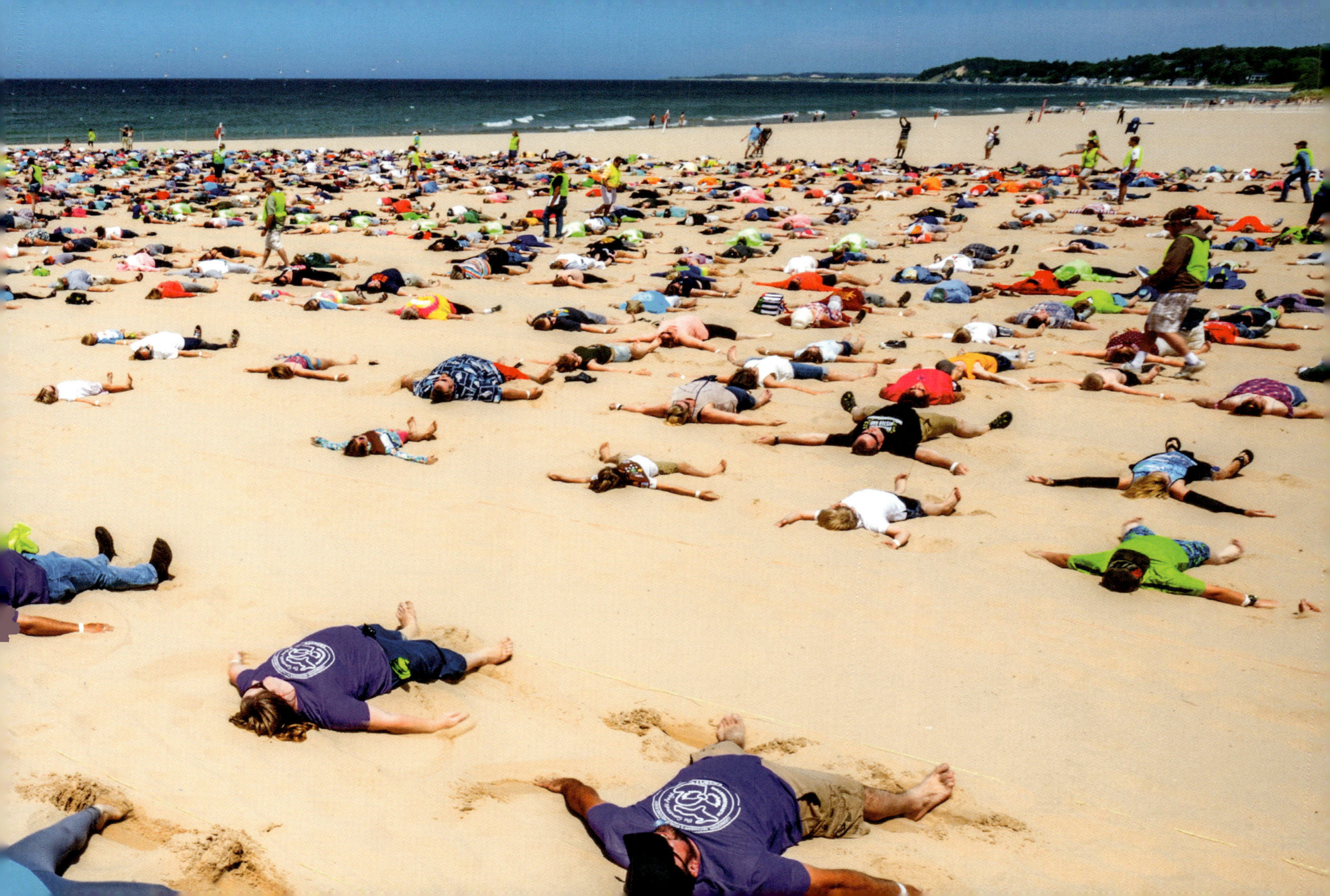

Meet Brad Reed

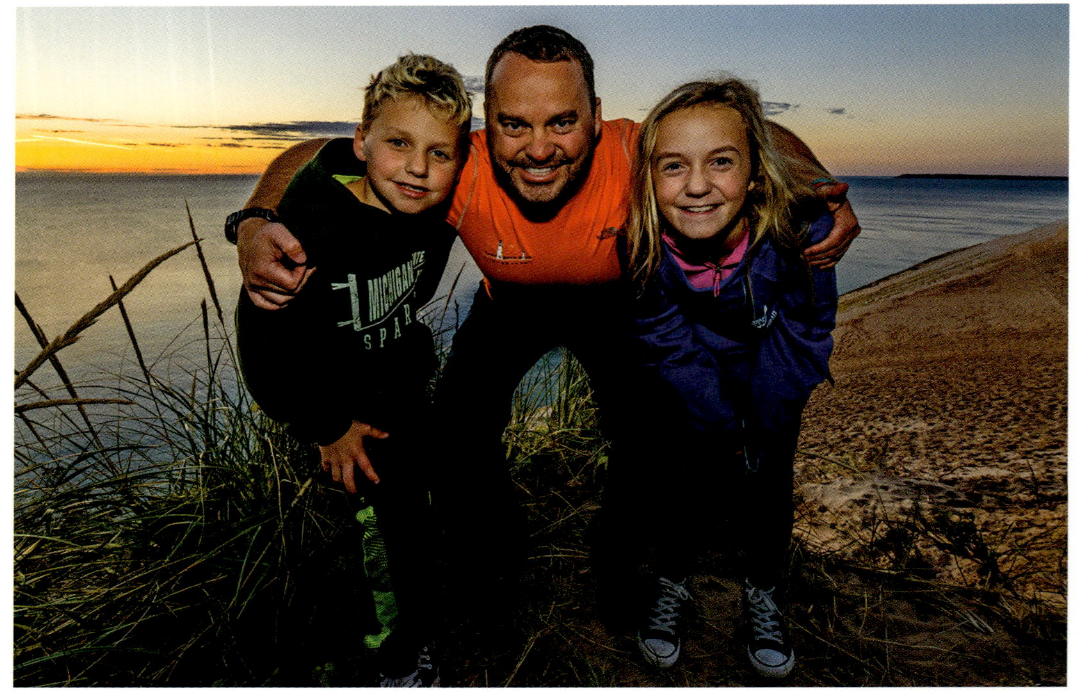

Brad Reed has been a full-time outdoor photographer for 14 years. The national and international award-winning photographer is also heavily involved in his local community of Ludington and has served on several different boards and committees. As a trained teacher, Brad enjoys meeting new photography workshop students and teaching them how to use their cameras on full manual. Brad and his two kids, Julia and Ethan, are all very adventurous. They enjoy deer hunting, hiking, working out, listening to music, watching movies, fast cars, big trucks and downhill skiing.

Meet Todd Reed

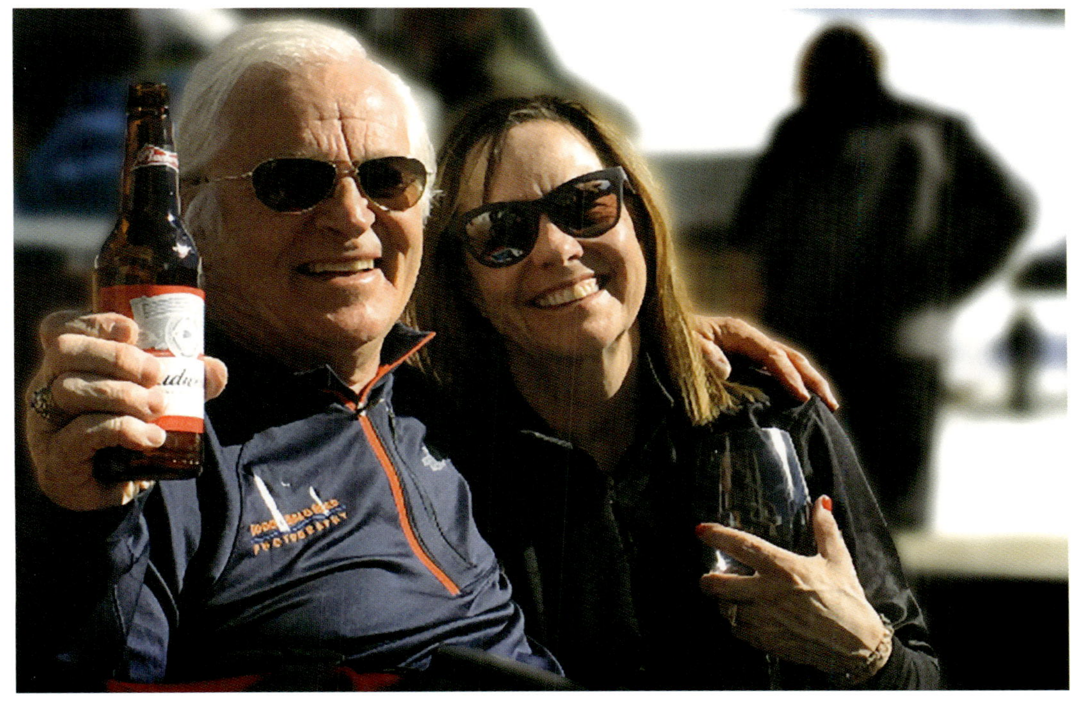

Todd Reed has passionately photographed the beauty of Michigan for nearly 50 years, first as a photojournalist for his hometown newspaper, the Ludington Daily News, then as one of Michigan's best-known outdoor photographers. Todd also served 33 years operating rescue boats in the Coast Guard Reserve and taught photography for 25 years at West Shore Community College. The national and international award-winning photographer thrives on teaching photography workshops with his son Brad and talking with visitors at their downtown Ludington gallery. Todd and his wife Debbie love exploring the Michigan outdoors, spending time with family and downhill skiing.

Meet Team Reed

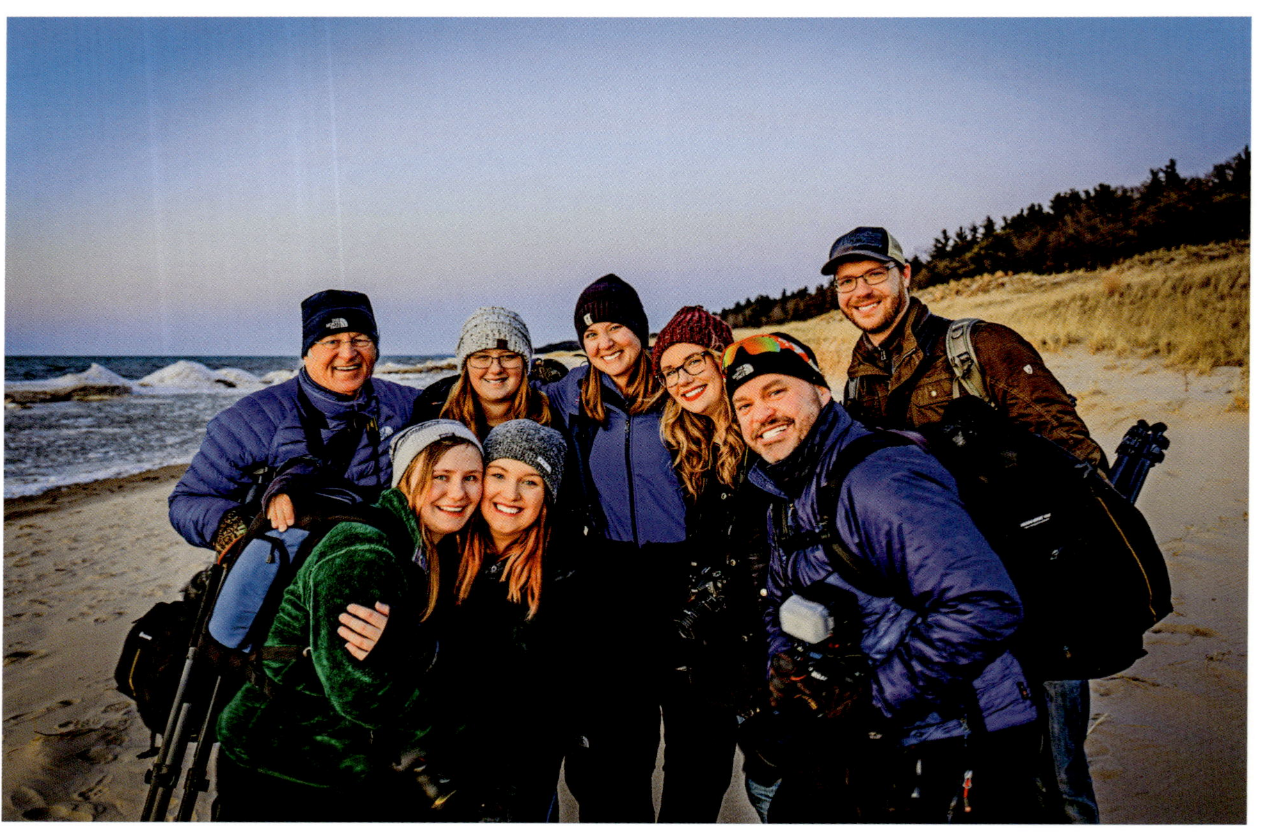

Rachel Gaudette

Rachel is the manager and oversees all aspects of the business for Todd and Brad Reed Photography. She has three amazing kids, and they all spend a lot of time working on the family farm in Custer. Rachel is a born leader and knows how to get things done. You can view and purchase her stunning photography off her website at www.RachelMPhotography.com.

Dustin Kunkel

Dustin has been working for Todd and Brad for more than five years. A Ludington High graduate, Dustin has been making photographs ever since his dad gave him his old 35mm camera and taught him how to use it 15 years ago. Not only does he love getting outside and trying to capture all the beauty nature has to offer, he lives for the technical aspect of photography as well. Dustin is meticulous in trying to bring a photo to its fullest potential. Visit Dustin's website to see his work at www.IamDKPhoto.com.

Shelby Soberalski

Since graduating from Ferris State University, Shelby worked for Pennies for Heaven before accepting her current position at FloraCraft. Shelby worked part time for the gallery during this project. She has a drive and desire inside her that helps her excel in any tasks that life may give her. She brings a positive attitude, artistic eye, and a smile to Team Reed. Shelby's website displays various art mediums, as well as her love for design at www.ShelbySoberalski.com.

Aubry Healy

After graduating from West Shore Community College, Aubry transferred to Central Michigan University. She currently is a photographer for Grand Central magazine while she finishes her Bachelor of Integrative Public Relations degree. She shares a love for photography and energy for living life. Aubry, once a high school intern, now is an important team member. Visit Aubry's website to see her beautiful work at www.Facebook.com/PhotosbyAubryHealy.

Hannah Olson

Hannah is a graduate of the New York Institute of Photography. She is currently attending West Shore Community College and will be transferring to a university to pursue a degree in graphic design. She is a very gifted, dedicated, and motivated individual. Visit Hannah's website to view her photography at www.OlsonPhotographyStudio.com.

Ashley Ingison

Ashley was recently accepted into the Ferris State University College of Pharmacy. She started working for Todd and Brad the summer of 2016 and quickly became a valued member of Team Reed. Ashley is a fun-loving and quick-witted employee and is also an excellent photographer.

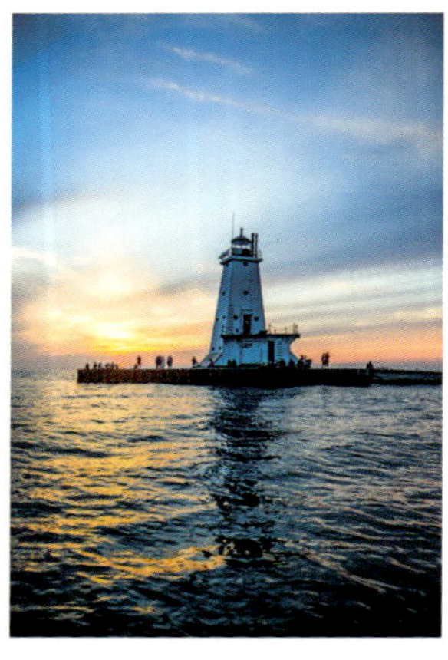

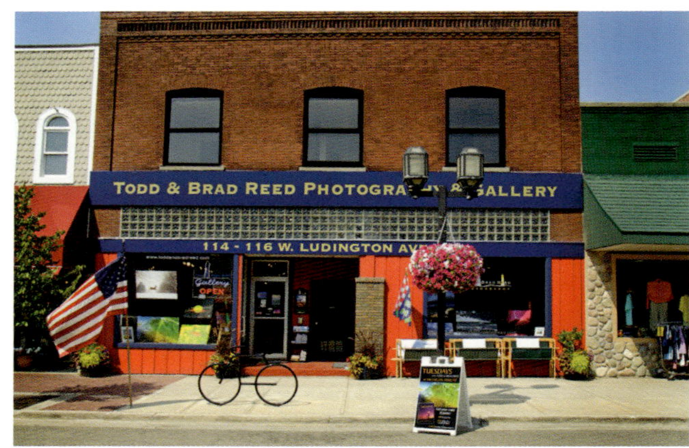

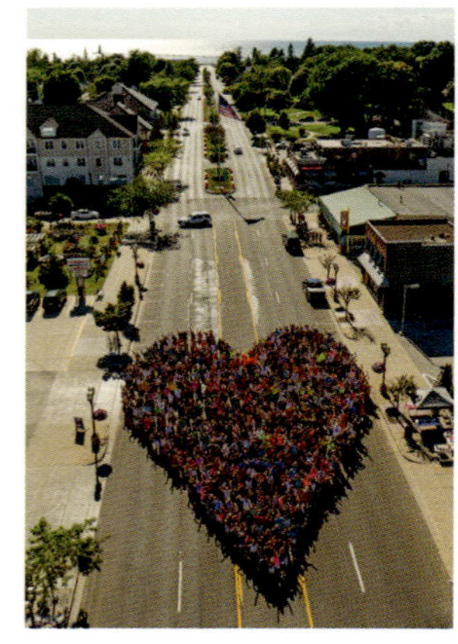

The Reeds own and operate Todd & Brad Reed Photography Gallery, 114 W. Ludington Avenue, Ludington. The gallery features Todd and Brad's work exclusively, along with custom picture framing by Timeless Picture Framing. The images take visitors on an amazing visual journey of Michigan's year-round beauty. Todd and Brad are often there to greet visitors and talk about photography.

Prints, Canvases, Books and other products

Prints and canvases from *Wonderous West Shore* are available in many sizes and prices. Todd and Brad's previous books, DVDs, and other products and images are available by calling Todd & Brad Reed Photography Gallery at 231-843-0777 or online at www.ToddandBradReed.com.

Workshops

Details about the weekend photo workshops and private photo lessons provided by the Reeds are available on their website or by calling 231-843-0777.

Newsletter

To receive free monthly photos, updates, and photo tips, register for the email newsletter online at www.ToddandBradReed.com.

Facebook

Stay current with Todd and Brad Reed by visiting their Facebook fan page online at www.Facebook.com/ToddandBradReed.

Gallery

The Reeds look forward to meeting you at their gallery in the heart of downtown Ludington, Michigan.

MADE IN WEST MICHIGAN

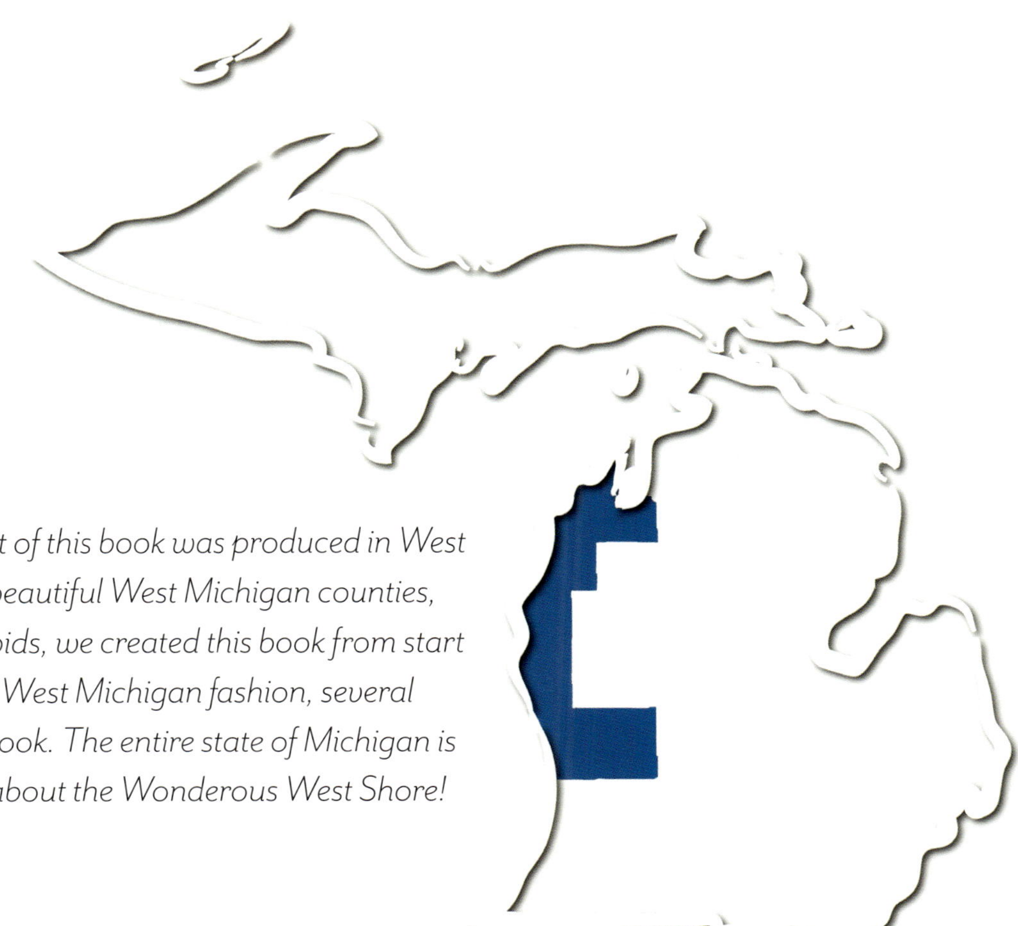

We are very proud of the fact that every aspect of this book was produced in West Michigan. From capturing the photos in nine beautiful West Michigan counties, to printing and binding the book in Grand Rapids, we created this book from start to finish in the Wonderous West Shore. In true West Michigan fashion, several small businesses came together to create this book. The entire state of Michigan is beautiful, but there is something extra special about the Wonderous West Shore!

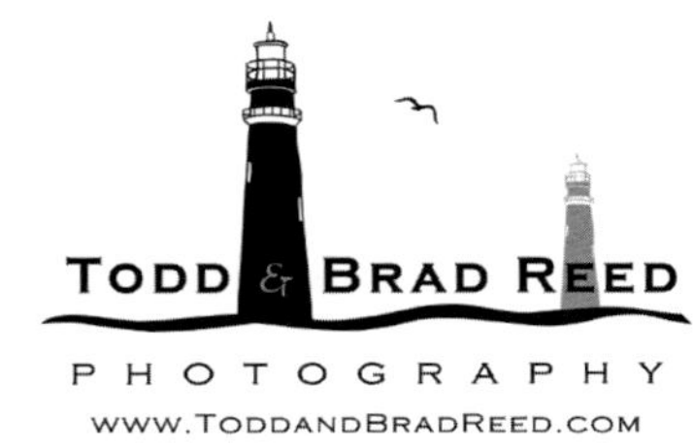

Published by Todd & Brad Reed Photography, LLC.
114 W. Ludington Avenue, Ludington, Michigan 49431
231-843-0777

Visit our website at www.ToddandBradReed.com
or call 231-843-0777.

Library of Congress Control Number: 2018903176

ISBN 978-1-5323-7048-9

10987654321

First Edition
First Printing, May 2018

Printed in Grand Rapids, Michigan by Foremost Graphics Group
Bound in Grand Rapids, Michigan by Dekker Bookbinding

Book and cover design by Todd and Brad Reed and Rachel Gaudette

Team Reed portrait and Todd and Brad Reed portrait by Aubry Healy

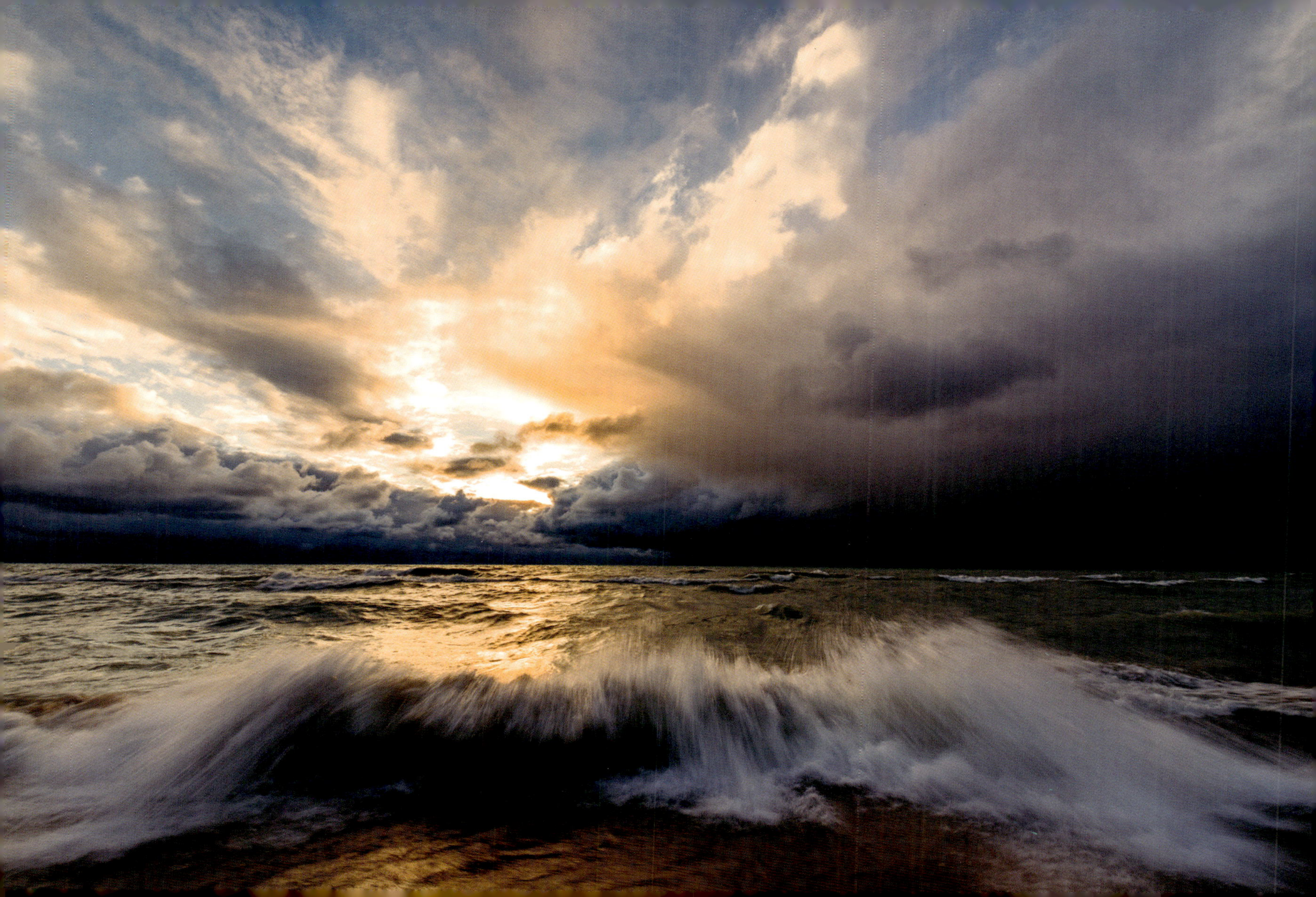

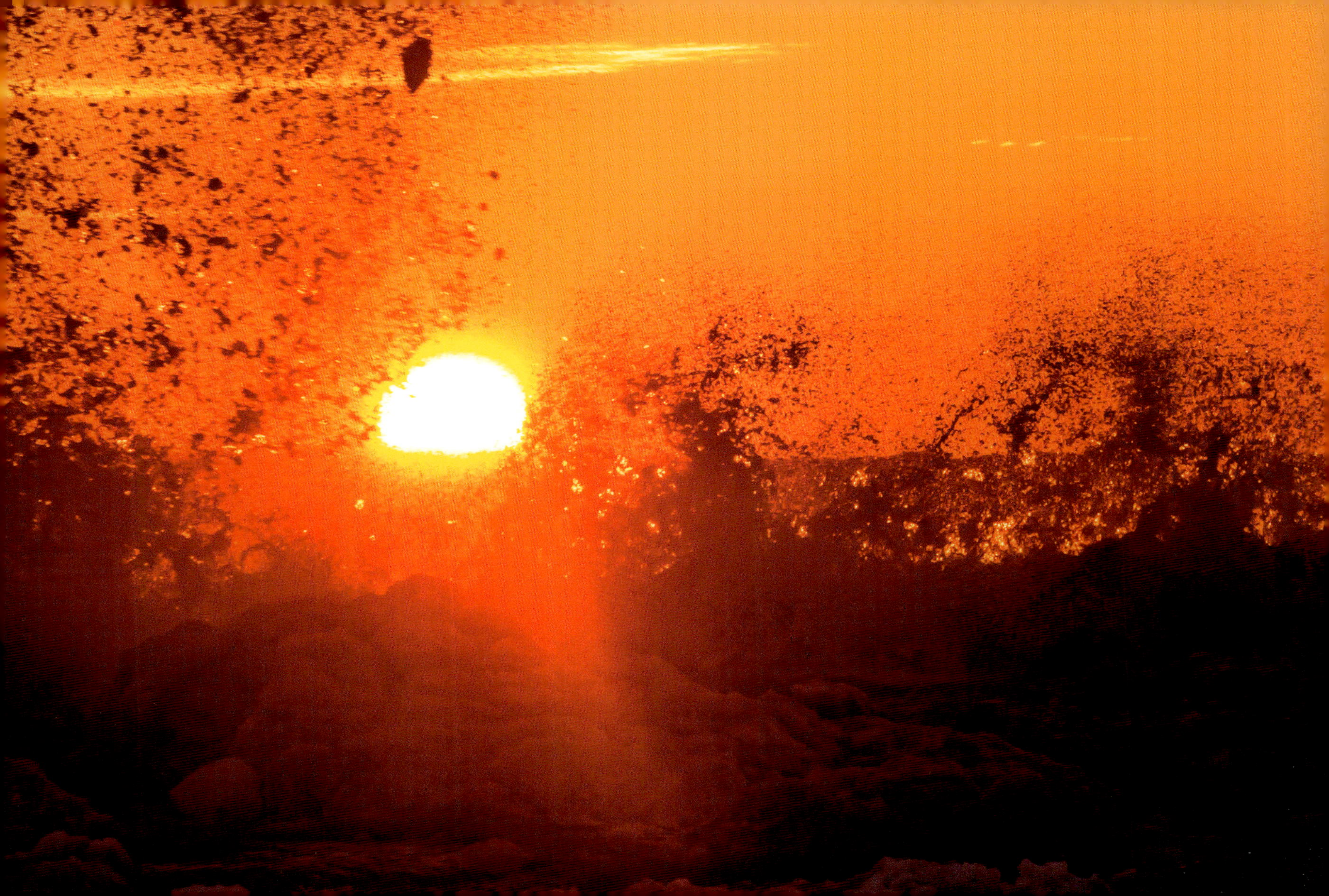

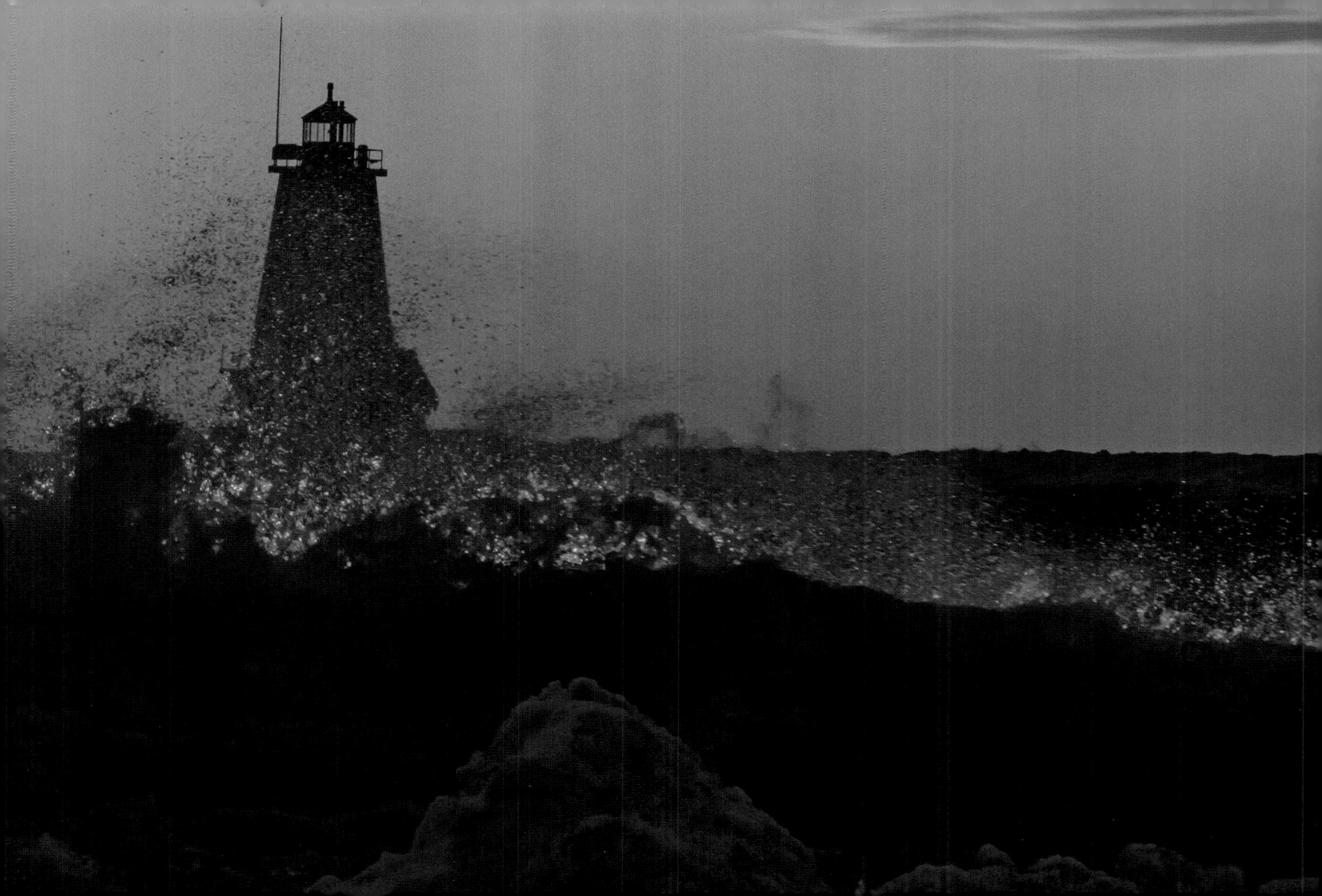

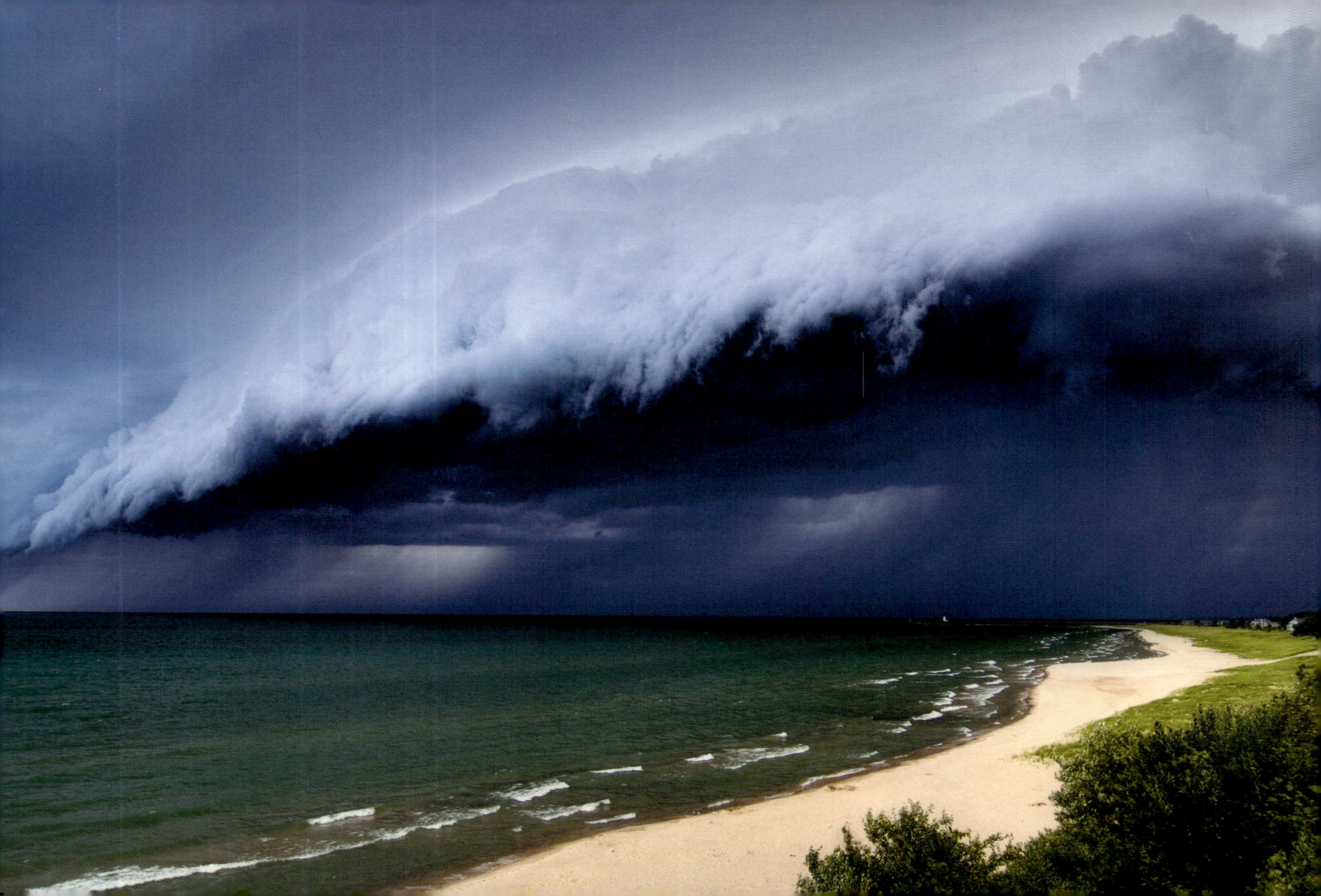

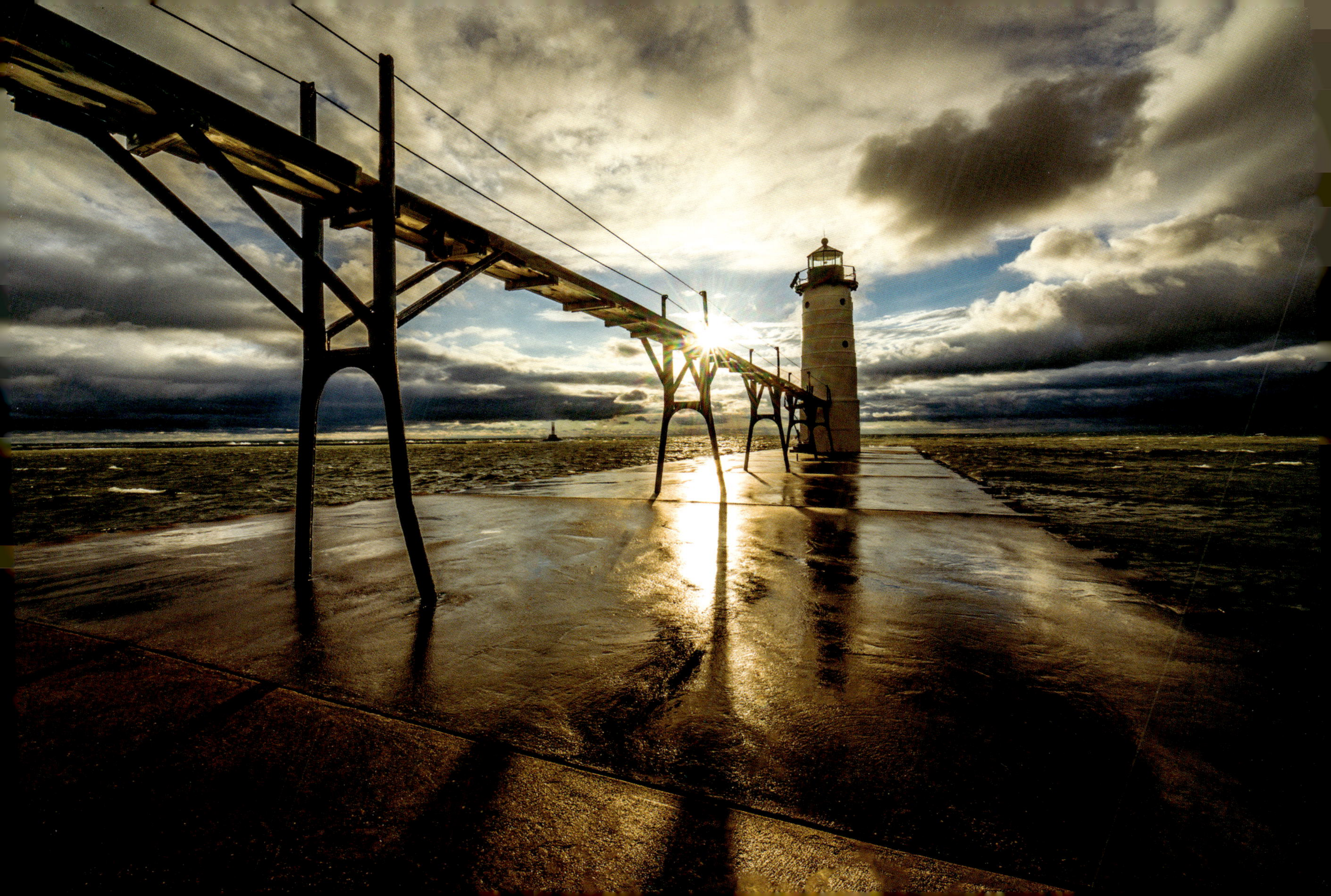

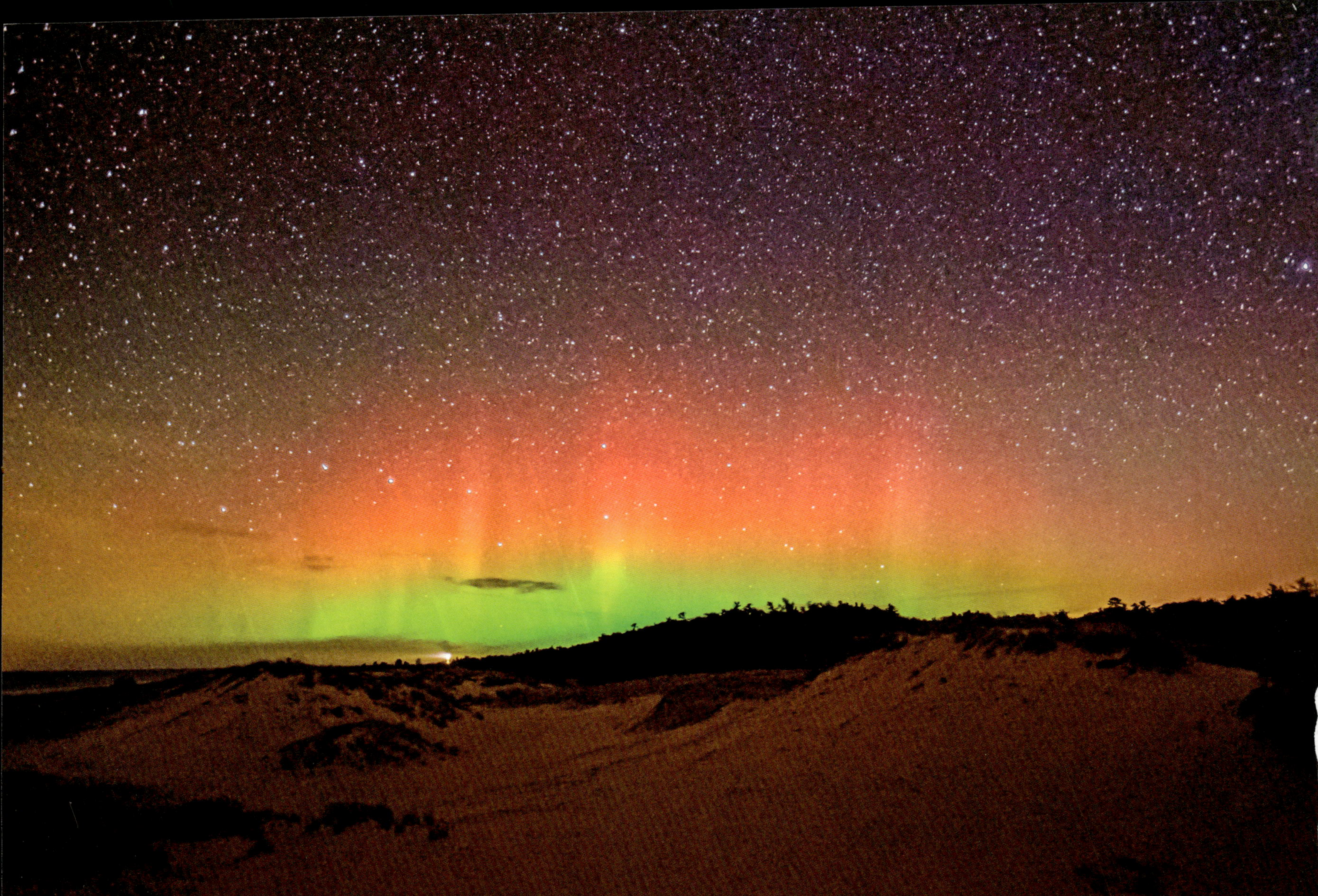

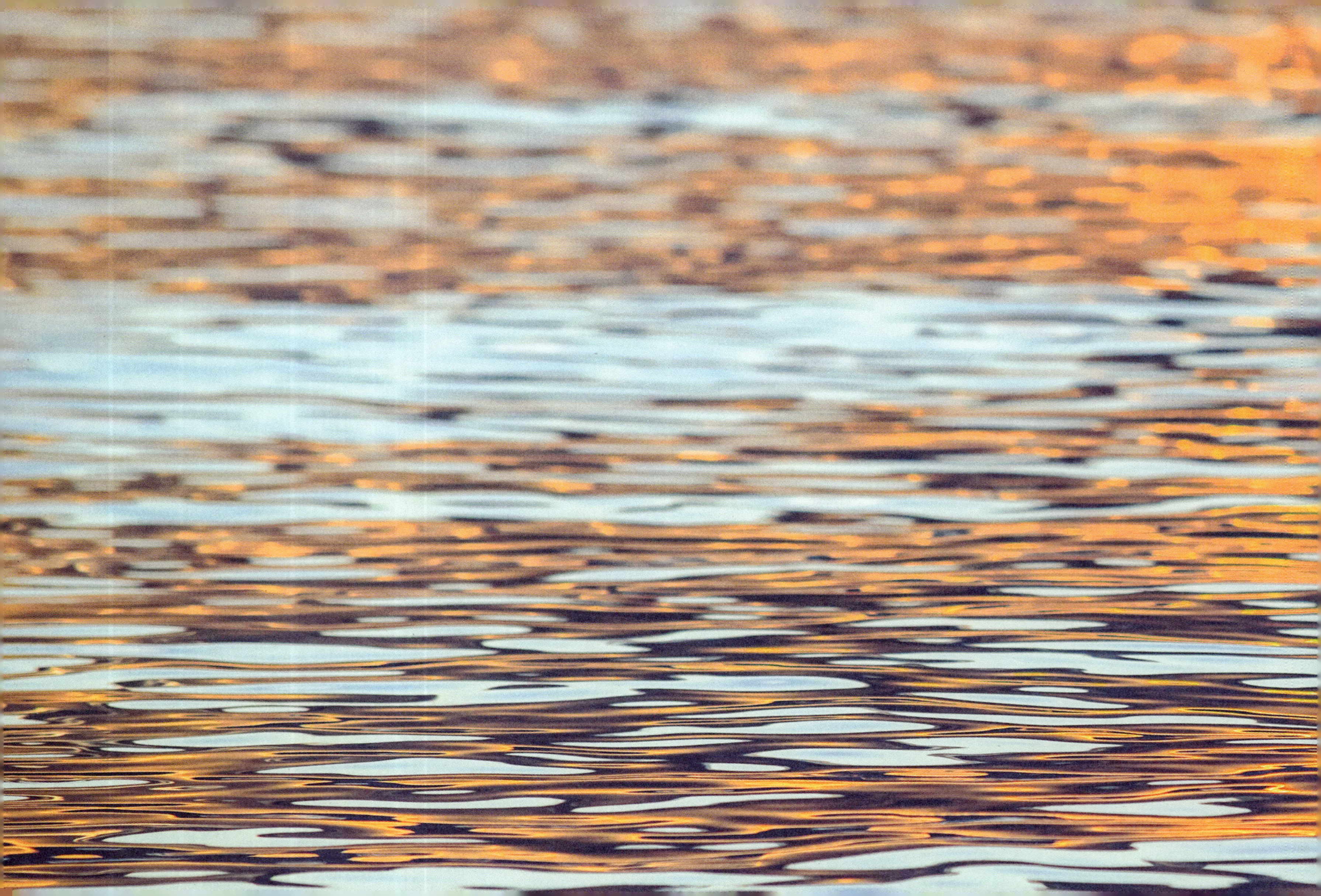